Life Lines

D1614735

New Horizons in Contemporary Writing

In the wake of unprecedented technological and social change, contemporary literature has evolved a dazzling array of new forms that traditional modes and terms of literary criticism have struggled to keep up with. *New Horizons in Contemporary Writing* presents cutting-edge scholarship that provides new insights into this unique period of creative and critical transformation.

Series Editors:
Peter Boxall and Bryan Cheyette

Volumes in the Series:
Wanderwords: Language Migration in American Literature
by Maria Lauret

Transatlantic Fictions of 9/11 and the War on Terror
by Susana Araújo

South African Literature's Russian Soul: Narrative Forms of Global Isolation
by Jeanne-Marie Jackson

Life Lines

Writing Transcultural Adoption

John McLeod

Bloomsbury Academic
An imprint of Bloomsbury Publishing Plc

B L O O M S B U R Y
LONDON · OXFORD · NEW YORK · NEW DELHI · SYDNEY

Bloomsbury Academic
An imprint of Bloomsbury Publishing Plc

50 Bedford Square	1385 Broadway
London	New York
WC1B 3DP	NY 10018
UK	USA

www.bloomsbury.com

BLOOMSBURY and the Diana logo are trademarks of Bloomsbury Publishing Plc

First published 2015
Paperback edition first published 2017

British Library Cataloguing-in-Publication Data
A catalogue record for this book is available from the British Library.

ISBN: HB: 978-1-4725-9038-1
PB: 978-1-3500-3035-0
ePDF: 978-1-4725-9040-4
ePub: 978-1-4725-9039-8

Library of Congress Cataloging-in-Publication Data
A catalog record for this book is available from the Library of Congress.

Series: New Horizons in Contemporary Writing

Typeset by Integra Software Services Pvt. Ltd.

In memory of my grandparents:
Annie and William Henderson
Rose and Archibald McLeod

Contents

Acknowledgements

This book is the product of two inseparable journeys: one scholarly, the other of a more personal nature. I am indebted to the international academic community for providing me with the opportunity to present in an early form several of the ideas which I explore in *Life Lines* at conferences and symposia and to learn from the responses and feedback of my peers. Thanks are owed to Alejandra Moreno Álvarez, Helle Schulz Bildsøe, Lorna Burns, Paloma Fresno Calleja, Alberto Fernández Carbajal, Katharine Cockin, Carmen Concilio, Ignacio Infante, Eva Rask Knudsen, Joel Kuortti, Sylvia Langwald, Conor McCarthy, Anne-Marie McManus, Belen Martin-Lucas, Stephen Morton, Annalisa Oboe, Matthew Whittle, Irene Visser and Janet Wilson. I am especially grateful to Helga Ramsey-Kurz and her colleagues at the European Association for Commonwealth Literature and Language Studies for inviting me to present my work at the 2014 EACLALS conference in Innsbruck. I thank, too, the School of English at the University of Leeds, UK, for granting me study leave to pursue my research. The staff and resources at the university's Brotherton Library have been, as ever, extraordinarily valuable.

My engagement with transcultural adoption writing was transformed when I attended the third biennial conference of the US-based Alliance for the Study of Adoption and Culture (ASAC) at MIT, Massachusetts, in 2010. At this and subsequent events at the Claremont Colleges, California (2012), and Florida State University, Tallahassee (2014), I encountered a wonderful constituency of interdisciplinary scholars and was warmly welcomed into their academic community. I cannot emphasize enough how much I have learned from my membership of ASAC. In particular, I thank Emily Hipchen, Margaret Homans, Marianne Novy and Eric Walker for their generous support and investment in my work.

Closer to home, friends and colleagues helped me pursue my research as an adopted person and supported me as this project brought together the professional and personal. I thank Sarah Arens, Ole Birk Laursen, Fiona

Becket, Shirley Chew, Geoffrey Davis, David Farrier, Denis Flannery, Paul Gilroy, Dave Gunning, Tracy Hargreaves, Caroline Herbert, Dolores Herrero, Graham Huggan, Robert Jones, Jackie Kay, Michelle Keown, Bénédicte Ledent, Dolores Mar McLoughlin, Peter Marsden, Judith Misrahi-Barak, Alex Nield, Deirdre Osborne, Matthew Pateman, Caryl Phillips, Sandra Ponzanesi, James Procter, Jay Prosser, Samantha Reive, Mark Shackleton, Eli Park Sorensen and Abigail Ward. I honour the memory of my dear friend Rick Jones.

I am indebted to Anthony Carrigan and John Whale for reading drafts of this book and providing me with rigorous and generous feedback. Professor Whale's support as I completed this book was far beyond the call of duty or friendship. I must thank, too, the Adoption and Fostering Team at Leeds City Council for guiding me through my own adoption history with such sensitivity and care.

At Bloomsbury, David Avital and Mark Richardson believed in this book from the day it was first mooted and have been a major source of encouragement. I thank them for their collegiality, patience and professionalism.

I am extraordinarily lucky to have such a wonderful family. Thanks to Margaret and Colin Adams; Jeni and Chris Gaskin; Kate Adams and Gary Stanton; Linda and Brian Joy; Madeleine Joy; Caitlin Joy and Andy Smith; and Lydia Joy and Dale Myott. I am considerably indebted to Colin for his generous help in preparing this book for publication. My parents, Veronica and James McLeod, have been steadfast in their support for this project and remain a crucial source of strength. Without them, this book could not have been written.

At every point of this journey, I have been joined by Julie Adams, who has done more than I ever thought possible to help me value the bearings of my adoption history and research. I hope she will find evidence of her wisdom, love and kindness on each page. Any flaws I claim exclusively as my own.

John McLeod
University of Leeds
@ProfJohnMcLeod

Introduction: Transcultural Adoption and Adoptive Being

In or around October 1968, a nineteen-year-old Irish migrant (let's call her Maria) living in the shadow of Victoria Station in London discovered that she was pregnant. This news was not a cause for celebration. Maria was employed as a hairdresser earning a modest salary of £9 10s per week and, as an unmarried mother-to-be, no doubt quickly realized that she could hardly afford to raise a child on a single meagre salary. Additionally, she would soon have to face the stigma of unmarried motherhood, especially daunting for someone so young and further compounded by the fact of her Catholic upbringing. Her situation would surely bring social disgrace on her family (should they ever find out), condemn herself to a life of ostracism and sentence her child to an unfortunate and prejudicial future as 'illegitimate'. Faced with prohibitions seemingly at every turn, Maria made a decision that, given these constrained economic and cultural circumstances, could hardly be called a choice. She did not inform the child's father of her pregnancy. She carried the child to term. In June 1969, a son was delivered with the aid of forceps at Westminster Hospital near St John's Gardens in London. Eight days later, Maria surrendered him into the care of a foster parent. In December, she signed a consent form agreeing to relinquish her legal right as the child's mother and to place him for adoption. An Adoption Order made in England at the time required the cancellation of the child's original birth certificate, the sealing of all records prior to the contracting of the adoption and the anonymization of birth-parents' identities. According to the report submitted to the court by the child's guardian *ad litem*, Maria asked only that her son be raised a Catholic. Suitable new parents were sourced (also Catholic and migrants: white, but Scottish, not Irish) and a 'match' agreed. An Adoption Order was granted in January 1970. The child left London. Dutifully, Maria disappeared.

This adoption tale, which left only a trace of documentary evidence, was a distinctive happening and also nothing out of the ordinary, especially in the UK of the 1960s. In general, the raising of children by those other than their biogenetic parents is by no means an unusual practice and occurs in most human societies, from the Maori of Aotearoa New Zealand to the Namibian tribes of southern Africa. Peter Conn considers it 'reasonable to speculate that adoption has been practiced from the earliest societies of modern humans' (26) and locates adoptive practices in classical antiquity and biblical times, post-classical Rome, the origins of the Muslim world and the European Middle Ages. Maria's story points specifically to the administration of adoption in First World locations in the last century or so which made adoption a legal contract with certain consequences for all those involved, frequently requiring the irreversible and willing transfer of legal responsibility for an infant from progenitors to adopters while often sealing court records so that the identities of all involved were anonymized. Barbara Yngvesson calls these 'strong' adoptions, where 'the decision of a woman to surrender her child is irrevocable, and the adoption that follows creates a permanent and exclusive relationship of adoptive kinship that cannot be "undone"' ('Placing' 231). This particular modus operandi readies new identities for all concerned – the infamous adoption 'triad' – that redesignate mother and child as 'birth-mother' and 'adoptee' and create 'adoptive parent(s)' as an acceptable substitute for consanguineous kin.

More forensically, Maria's tale also makes visible the material, social, cultural and racial circumstances of such adoption contracts. As many have noted repeatedly, adoption is fundamentally imbricated in the landscape of economic impoverishment and wealth. Usually the children of those in straitened financial and social circumstances have been surrendered via judicial procedures to the permanent care of more affluent families. As Owen Gill and Barbara Jackson record, 'adoption, at least historically, has been primarily a middle-class preserve' (3). Most adoptive parents have been middle-class professionals who adopt children from working-class or lower-middle-class women. Socially, adoption's conditions of possibility are firmly linked to prevailing mores and values, often to the particular detriment of women. Certain kinds of gendered behaviours – sex out of wedlock, or with someone deemed ethnically different; the transgression of caste or scriptural precepts concerning legitimate reproduction – place the participants and their offspring in highly vulnerable, often isolated and loathed, positions (as 'sinful', 'shameful', 'illegitimate') and devoid of filial, communal, emotional or state support. In turning to the contracting of adoption arrangements as a 'solution' to the social problems which normative pedagogies produce in the first place, matters of race and culture are always involved because the ideal adoption, as Cynthia Callahan has observed, is one which does not overtly threaten 'the fundamental rule of blood kinship' (17). The divisive and prejudicial discourse of race has often worked to entangle and mystify biogenetic and cultural attachments. In adoption, racial matching usually functions to approximate cultural similarity between adoptees and adoptive parents, despite the highly complex and sometimes radically different provenances of race and culture. As Mark C. Jerng has argued, adoption actually exposes the complex processes of projection and introjection which *produce* race through attempts at 'matching' and uncovers the ultimate precariousness of race as a reliable category of social collectivity in general: 'Race is not so much a given as it is something that gets materialized through the uncertainty of relating the individual to the social contexts that precede and condition it. [...] Adoption reminds us that racial identification is located in that space of anxiety and insecurity between world and self in which social norms are continually in flux' (121–2). In the example with which we began, the matching of the adoptee with white parents endorses a racializing belief in biogenetic inclination that circumscribes differences of nation and culture – Ireland, Scotland – that are themselves tidily aligned by the problematic perception that birth- and adoptive parents are broadly from the 'Celtic fringe' and not too culturally remote to begin with. 'Whiteness' can only ever be approximate here. Race compensates for a lack of biogenetic attachment by proffering the reassurance of racial and cultural consanguinity as an equivalent, but always imperfectly coincident, 'match'. These converging conditions of material constraint, social stigmatization and racialization are several of the key reasons why only some children are deemed adoptable, particular mothers surrender them and certain families receive them.

Life Lines is concerned with the creative and cultural consequences of adoption's complex and problematic materiality, with particular reference to literary responses to transcultural adoption in British, Irish and American contexts. In selecting and exploring the work primarily of twelve creative figures across a range of genres – screenplay, fiction, memoir, travelogue – I seek to place centre stage the fact that transcultural adoption is far from an exceptional historical phenomenon. Research into such adoptions in recent decades has predominantly preoccupied scholars in the social sciences whose important empiricist work and engagement with case studies only occasionally considered creative representations and the formative role of narrative. An exceptional example is Amal Treacher and Ilan Katz's edited collection *The Dynamics of Adoption: Social and Personal Perspectives* (2000), which intercalates essays based upon social work and adoption practice with poetry by Margot Henderson. In literary studies, critical discussions of adoption representations were until very recently extraordinarily rare and have only just begun to appear, as we will witness presently. And in the domain of postcolonial studies, the absence of an attention to transcultural adoption lives, histories and texts is almost total – a surprising omission, given that transcultural adoption is central virtually to all incidences of modern transcultural contact and shaped by the advent and legacies of imperialism, colonialism, migration and global conflict. *Life Lines* responds to this deficiency across postcolonial, literary and cultural studies, while opening an opportunity to explore in depth the cultural consequences of transcultural adoption which work in the social sciences has touched upon rather than pursued. The imagining of transcultural adoption shapes ways of seeing not readily found elsewhere and constitutes an archive vital to our understanding of and responses to adoption phenomenology. As I shall discuss presently, I fashion the term 'adoptive being' to capture the distinct and transfigurative rendition of transcultural adoption's possibilities as it emerges across a range of creative texts.

Many popular and prevailing representations of transcultural adoption generally want to tell a pious story of the global North as involved in humanitarian acts of rescue, saving anguished children from a future of impoverishment overseas; or for facilitating transcultural families that offer a palatable, saccharine vision of post-racial human relations, intimate or otherwise, so that 'colour-blind' filiation or 'rainbow' families are applauded for challenging racism (rather than criticized for evading it). Cynthia Callahan is one of several scholars to note that the 'rescue narrative is magnified by the current prominence of transnational adoption among celebrities, as the move from abject "orphan" to privileged child of celebrity parents enacts a kind of rags-to-riches narrative of salvation that obscures the more complex politics of adoption' (36). As we shall see, the literary narration of transcultural adoption in First World locations often reveals an everyday condition of neocolonial agency and postcolonial betrayal, of racist profiling and misogynistic authoritarianism.

At the same time, *Life Lines* is fundamentally interested in the unguessed, generative and creative possibilities which transcultural adoption has been imagined as making possible, and not simply for those inward of adoptive relations. To be sure, the administration of adoption in general, as we shall see, has frequently sought to confirm normative models of filial relations exemplified by the heterosexual, patrician and nuclear family, or has used middle-class white families as a private realm of assimilation for so-called cultural others into the wider cultural and national milieu. Yet transcultural adoption has also made possible firm grounds for the critique of such filial norms and opened up alternative ways of imagining families in transcultural, non-biocentric, post-racial and queer terms, amongst others. 'Adoption is an effect of the hegemonic position of the biological family', argues Sally Sales, 'but also a potential resistance to its particular ways of inscribing belonging' (20). Many of the writers I explore in *Life Lines* are interested in *what transcultural adoption makes possible*, socially and imaginatively. In an essay on the relational self shaped in memoir writing, Nancy K. Miller has fashioned the concept of the 'transpersonal' as naming the process 'through which the self moves into and out of the social, psychic, and material spaces of relation' (168). What new ways of thinking and enacting intimate transpersonal relations have been materialized by transcultural adoption? How might the prevailing understanding of racial, cultural, national and biogenetic attachments be progressively revised in the light of transcultural adoption stories? What new modes of being – singular and interdependent – might be figured for all through the recounting of transcultural adoption? Which new narrative forms does transcultural adoption require and create? If some transcultural adoption writing is concerned with the materiality and phenomenology of adoptive life for the adoption triad, then other texts are keen to engage with adoption at the same time as a site of figurative possibility – as bearing emergent ways of thinking innovatively and transformatively, not only about the immediate concerns of filial relations but also regarding the wider contexts of race, culture and belonging in which transcultural adoption is situated. As we shall see, the relationship in some texts between the phenomenological and the figurative can soon become problematic especially if the latter is pursued in ignorance of adoption's affective and material particulars. But it is the capacity to think through transcultural adoption as a mode of possibility and not as ever complicit with the dominant mode – as an opportunity for dissident production not normative reproduction, if you like – that is the core concern of this book. In writing transcultural adoption, what emergent ways of thinking and being might be struck for all?

In rendering transcultural adoption as fertile ground of enquiry, I am not seeking thoughtlessly to claim some kind of political or ethical justification for adoption, not least because of transcultural adoption's entanglement in and complicity with the highly complex cultural inequalities which obtain globally and function locally. Maria's sombre act of surrender should not be quickly forgotten. A great deal of valuable scholarship has recently emerged in the humanities and social sciences which attend in fine detail to the complicity of transcultural adoption in the neocolonial fortunes of national polycultures and globalized international relations. In Toby Alice Volkman's words, 'all adoption that crosses borders – of culture, race, ethnicity, nation, or class – is shaped by profound inequities in power, by contradictions and ambivalence' ('New Geographies' 3). Wherever there has been intercultural subjugation in the world, either internecine or between nations, adoptable children have been produced, as well as the narratives which legitimate their adoption transculturally – suspect narratives of rescue and utilitarian selflessness, of a child's 'best interests' and the virtues of 'colour-blindness' pitted against the vices of race thinking. The entanglement of gendered precepts, economic disenfranchisement, cultural subjugation and discursive justification has shaped the particular conditions which favour and broker the contracting of transcultural adoptions, so that the transcultural adoptive families which result are ever marked by these complex histories no matter how hard they may or may not try to ignore them. That said, to regard transcultural adoption as entirely constrained by these unhappy circumstances is to miss the transfigurative agency it may also engender. I shall have more to say about this assertion in due course. For now, let us prepare to accept that there is an important interplay between textual representations of transcultural adoptions and the contexts from whence they spring; between the phenomenon of transcultural adoption and its creative figuration across a range of cultural media. These lines of connection are unbreakable but also unpredictable. Our task in *Life Lines* is to assess a range of texts' transfigurative possibilities in relation to the vexed circumstances which have shaped and suggested both their problems and possibilities.

Before we proceed further, some justification is required for my choice of 'transcultural' in the subtitle to this book. There are particular conceptual and strategic reasons that motivate my choice of this term. Transcultural studies tends to value the untidy and variable consequences actively created when a range of cultural inventories come into contact, often as a way of challenging the imperious, monocultural and exclusionary protocols of illiberal manifestations of race or nation. As Frank Schulze-Engler puts it, 'it is precisely the practice of thinking of "cultures" in terms of "national cultures" as well as the assumption that transcultural phenomena occur in "peripheral" rather than "central" constellations that have been called into question in recent transcultural debates' (xi). Rather than imagine cultural transactions and encounters as always happening at the margins, safely minoritized as the local consequences of (and for) diasporic peoples who live precariously in-between homelands old and new, transcultural thought requires us to approach everyday life at all points as shot through with the experiences and inventories of manifold cultures, so that it becomes impossible to lay claim to any kind of authentic or unsullied cultural purity beyond the reach of outside influence. In an influential essay, Wolfgang Welsch has argued in favour of transculturality as especially appropriate to the migratory and globalized conditions of recent history which have made cultures 'extremely interconnected and entangled with each other' (197). These '[m]acro-level' matters are matched by the micro-level reformulation of individuated lives in transcultural terms which has now become an ordinary rather than exceptional mode of existence: 'Work on one's identity is becoming more and more work on the integration of components of differing cultural origin' (199). Lest we glibly enthuse about this state of affairs, Welsch warns that transculturality is both progressive and precarious. It empowers a way of thinking outside the borderlines of race, nation and monoculture, but also fuels a recalcitrant reaction to the loss of identitarian distinctiveness and particularity: a 'return to tribes' (204) and an ongoing 'demand for specificity'

(204). The transcultural does not classify an inherently progressive new world order but instead points to the terms of engagement that help to shape a distinctly contemporary but by no means unique predicament. As Mary Louise Pratt has famously explored, transcultural contact has a long global history and was central to the European expansionism of modernity. Pratt's work is worth recalling, too, not least because of its attention, first, to the fact that transcultural contact is always structured by 'highly asymmetrical relations of domination and subordination' (7), and, second, to the agency which transculturation enables within constrained circumstances: 'While subjugated peoples cannot readily control what the dominant culture visits upon them, they do determine to varying extents what they absorb into their own, how they use it, and what they make it mean' (7).

For these reasons, in this book I do not take the term 'transcultural adoption' to signify either a finite legal act or a single event of mobility in which an adoptee is appropriated from one culture and situated in another. Rather, the term identifies an ongoing aggregation of cultural conditions, transactions and negotiations which *perpetually* designate an adoptee or their family as transcultural and in which they can intervene. Transcultural personhood is performatively constructed in real time, not a fact of natal or legal arrangements. Adoptees, especially the very youngest, do *not* mystically or reliably bring with them the inventories of one culture into another. They do not carry natal culture innately nor act as infant ambassadors for remotely headquartered cultural domains. As many adoption scholars have pointed out, the idea of 'birth culture' is an oxymoronic one which assumes the cultural provenance of one's birth constitutes an ever-present authentic origin of personhood. This assumption is usually imposed upon adoptees and activated to compensate for the lack of knowledge of their biogenetic origins. For Volkman, 'the paradoxical formulation: *birth culture*' signifies both lack and the response to it: 'In the absence of the mother's body, the longing for origins may be displaced onto the body of the nation and its imagined culture. The genetic lineage of the child is unknown, but the cultural heritage can be studied, celebrated, performed and embodied' ('Embodying' 97). Margaret Homans has also described 'birth culture' as a simulacrum that traffics in 'role models of a child's race or ethnicity' (112) and which uses 'cultural fragments (holidays, food, clothing) that are meant to be authentic but that are, inevitably, translated and hybridized' (112–13). An adoptee's transcultural disposition as such is provided for them in normatively biocentric environments which declare, for example, that a Caribbean-born UK-raised adoptee must think of the Caribbean as a source of identitarian cultural origin, as 'birth culture'. *How* those inward of the adoption triad might respond actively to the predicament of being told that their cultural origins are always a matter of biogenetic primacy – challenging assumptions about biocentric origins or mobilizing their manifold cultural heredities transfiguratively and dissidently – is one of the central concerns of *Life Lines*.

The adoption contexts we consider in *Life Lines* collectively constitute one particular, little-discussed example of transcultural border-crossing where the creative kinesis of transcultural entanglement encounters, through family-making, the normative protocols of race, nation, monoculture and identity formation that attempt to persist while under pressure. Transcultural adoption reminds us that transcultural encounters are not always matters of civic, public or societal engagement, but obtain in intimate contexts and animate the ways in which human lives are authenticated through the biocentric vocabularies of birth, blood and natal origins. In so doing, it suggests that the alignment between macro- and micro-transculturality may not be as co-ordinated as Welsch assumes. Particular occasions of transcultural adoption may intervene in the wider political management of transcultural admixture. Pratt's attention to transculturation as a dynamic, interventionist activity by subordinated people is vital to maintain: as Mark Stein has argued, in Welsch's model 'the relationship between transculture and the individual agent or individual cultural product is not interrogated' (254). Transcultural adoptions offer, then, particularly telling examples of how transcultural personhood might be formulated, experienced and legitimated *agentially*, for the attention of those within the adoption triad and for others too: as Callahan argues, adoption texts 'access issues of authenticity and belonging that resonate far beyond an individual family' (3). Such adoptions remind us of the deeply uneven terrain of transcultural contact that structures local and global relations, as well as of the stubbornly insoluble discourses of filial nativism to which transcultural adoption is often made secondary, as a substitute or next best thing. Using Pratt's terminology, let us think of the transcultural adoption contract as a distinct materialization of a transcultural 'contact zone', in which the threshold of transpersonal encounter – between birth-parents, adoptees and adoptive parents, between natal and adopting cultures – is never a meeting of equals but always structured by a wider domain of inequities: as a place where 'subjects get constituted in and by their relations to each other' (8) in very particular ways.

In proceeding with the adjective 'transcultural' as opposed to 'transracial' or 'transnational', I do not intend the former term to substitute for the latter two, or for it to be considered their precise equivalent. That said, arguably 'transcultural' carries with it an horizon of flexibility which facilitates the strategically comparative critique I seek to open in *Life Lines*. Not all transcultural adoption is overtly transracial, as we shall notice in my discussion of Sebastian Barry's writing. Nor is transcultural adoption necessarily transnational, as evidenced in Catherine McKinley's life-writing or E. R. Braithwaite's work. For the purposes of this book, 'transcultural adoption' enables us to think tactically across the diverse array of adoption texts and contexts where appropriate while keeping in play the transitive entanglements of culture, race and nation. In what follows, I will inevitably need to reach for these analogous but not identical terms, especially when used by fellow scholars or when they are particularly appropriate to the critical task in hand. But as often as possible, I will speak of 'transcultural adoption' in order to keep the discussion tidy as well as conceptually fluent.

*

As Barbara Yngvesson describes it, 'always there is a combination of conditions that are simultaneously local and global and have the effect of placing certain categories of children at risk of becoming a liability in one location, even as they become objects of desire in another' (*Belonging* 29). Even a brief account of a handful of examples bears out the historical recurrence of such conditions of risk that produce 'adoptability' and convert mothers into birth-mothers. Let us note just a few for the purposes of illustration. In 1975, as US forces withdrew from Vietnam, 'Operation Babylift' transported 2,000 supposedly orphaned children to the United States for adoption. Laura Briggs records that the operation 'was warmly embraced by liberals and conservatives alike as an opportunity to salvage something from the horror of the war' (156). Many of the children 'were of mixed ancestry, literally embodying the U.S. (and French) war', but investigations into their biogenetic parentage were not especially rigorous: 'Some witnesses expressed uneasiness, suggesting that children were being hurriedly picked off the streets of Saigon and packed into airplanes, without any effort to find their parents, as the city fell to advancing North Vietnamese troops' (156). To take another example, the increasing rates of adoption of Chinese-born children by American families at the end of the twentieth century owe something to China's one-child policy and gendered positioning of boys as of higher cultural value, as gender and material contexts conspire to produce new adoptees. Sara Dorow explains that today's 'Chinese adoptees quite literally embody the history of China's bid to develop and succeed as a nation on the global stage by reducing the size and increasing the quality of its population [...]. In all cases, social policies that limit family size and undermine social support services (including medical coverage) interact with individual circumstances so that certain families feel they must give up their children, even after trying to keep them' (20). In the UK, new shifts in patterns of migration after the Second World War saw the advent of a new black British population as many travelled from the colonies to the metropolis to find work, often in blue-collar or service industries, amidst an increasingly racist atmosphere. The social and cultural constraints that soon obtained contributed to the appearance of a distinct constituency of adoptees by the 1960s, black or (more often) of mixed race, that welfare officers found hard to place with adoptive parents due to racist attitudes both at large and in the welfare services themselves. The situation prompted a London-based initiative known as the British Adoption Project in 1965, which attempted to place approximately sixty British-born adoptees of black, Asian or mixed-race ancestry with adoptive parents, the vast majority of whom were white. In Lois Raynor's words, British adoption agencies 'accustomed to placing English babies with English adopters [...] found it difficult, if not impossible, to meet the requests to arrange for the adoption of these babies' (24). The project was an attempt to solve this issue and consequently aid 'the development of adoption services generally' (23). Around the same time in Canada and the United States, state-sanctioned endeavours upheld structures of disenfranchisement via transcultural adoption practices, such as the 'sixties scoop', where First Nations children were taken from their parents and adopted by settler-descended Canadian families (a practice which extended into the 1980s), and the United States' Indian Adoption Project, begun in 1958, which sought to relocate Native children in white families and was part of a wider attempt to remove children involuntarily from reservations and place them in boarding schools, away from their primary cultural and filial networks. And as has recently been brought to widespread attention by Martin Sixsmith's book *The Lost Child of Philomena Lee* (2009) and Stephen Frears's film adaptation, *Philomena* (2013), postcolonial Ireland's Catholic hierarchy used the country's church-run mother and baby homes – where unwed women, some as young as fourteen, were banished to have their children and then work for at least two years after to pay for their keep – to construct a source of adoptable children, many of whom were adopted by Catholic families overseas in return for a suitable financial donation.

Such examples point to a wider range of transcultural adoption contexts that also circumscribe South America, sub-Saharan Africa and Australia, amongst others. They require us to acknowledge, in the words of transcultural adoptees Julia Chinyere Oparah, Sun Yung Shin and Jane Jeong Trenka, that transcultural adoptions are 'the intimate face of colonization, racism, militarism, imperialism, and globalization' (7). No wonder, then, that transcultural adoption emerged at the end of twentieth century as a key political battleground, often for those living in minoritized or subjugated communities in the West. The passing of the Indian Child Welfare Act (ICWA) in the United States in 1978 after a long legal campaign brought the matter of Native adoptions within the jurisdiction of tribal courts and set clear parameters for future transcultural adoptions. A little earlier, in 1972, the famous 'Position Statement on Trans-Racial Adoption', published by the United States' National Association of Black Social Workers (NABSW), opposed the placing of black children with white families as an assimilative practice of ethnic deculturation – although Briggs has argued that the NABSW statement only 'slow[ed] down the rate of interracial placements' (56) and more black children had entered the welfare system by the 1990s. Influenced by these activities, in Britain during the 1980s, the Association of Black Social Workers and Allied Professionals (ABSWAP) began to advocate a similar politics. In the words of John Small, one of its key activists, transracial adoption was a strategy that threatened the future of black British peoples, 'by definition a weakening of the process whereby the black community will be able to withstand the pressures on it' (133). Small saw the black family and by extension the black community as an essential 'survival mechanism' (133) in a racist country without which inequality would triumph. Black adoptees in white families would be culturally and emotionally impoverished, subjected to an 'assimilative process that functions within the substitute family [that will] inculcate the dominant attitudes and values of white society at large' and leave the adoptee unable to cope with exposure to the racist realities of 'the real world, to the aggression and hostilities of society at large' (135). Such arguments influenced the 1989 Children Act which, in Derek Kirton's summary, gave 'the first formal recognition to issues of "race" and ethnicity in [British] statute child care law' (26), in that it required local authorities to be much more mindful of religious, racial, cultural and linguistic background when organizing the provision of care. In late twentieth-century Australia, the political claims of Aborigines and Torres Strait Islanders were furthered at one level through their protests against the involuntary removal of indigenous children by the state – the so-called 'Stolen Generations' – resulting in the issue of a formal apology by the then prime minister Kevin Rudd on 13 February 2008.

This wider terrain of transcultural adoption and organized resistance to it in recent decades opens up two issues. First, in recognizing the multiple axes of transcultural adoption – colonial migrant, African American, Irish Catholic, South-east Asian, etc. – we might discern how the desirability of adoptees is constructed comparatively due to the different values attached to particular constituencies. As Sara Dorow points out in her study of Chinese American transcultural adoptions, South-east Asian adoptees are often considered more attractive to white adoptive parents in the United States when set against 'the construction of black difference as less assimilable difference' (42). Chinese-born children may be assumed to emerge from a context where unenlightened gendered prejudice has meant that many girls have been surrendered, whereas African American children are perceived to be mired in contexts of delinquency, impoverishment and the long history of racial conflict indebted to slavery. '[M]otifs of model Asian America play off the construction of abject black America and failed black-white relations', writes Dorow, 'allegedly manifest in welfare dependence, criminality, and ingratitude' (42). Indeed, the construction of Chinese-born adoptees as part of a 'virtuous model minority' (41) helps keep in place the denigration of other adoptee constituencies as part of a wider childcare economy. Transcultural adoptions are not strictly bidirectional or involve only the cultural provenance of surrendering birth-parents and adopting families but are inflected by a wider and untidier cultural complex where 'adoptability' is transacted.

Second, and of particular importance for *Life Lines*, we need to confront thinking about adoption as an often paradoxical affair, critical of and complicit with normative discourses in turn. 'How', asks Dorow, 'do we account for the divergent but simultaneous meanings of transracial adoption migration – for instance, the joyful intimacy of making family next to the unjust history that it might recall?' (3). This predicament, if not responded to imaginatively, can complicate quite severely the ability to make confident declarations about adoption's radical or reactionary political propensity, or to decide upon its ethical justification or erroneousness. As we have just seen, while the administration of transcultural adoption has been clearly complicit in unacceptable acts of disenfranchisement, the voicing of opposition to transcultural adoption has often ended up paradoxically supporting the very conceptual vocabulary upon which the enforcing of transcultural adoptions has relied. Race thinking, fictions of national distinctiveness, notions of cultural purity – the intellectual components that have structured modern and colonial modes of thought remain live in much political objection to transcultural adoption. Small's line of thought received stern criticism in 1994 from Paul Gilroy who noted its complicity in race thinking, argued stringently that '[c]ultural sameness and common bodily characteristics do not, by themselves, promote good parenting' (x), and challenged the assumption that '"race" *is* culture and identity rather than profane politics and complex history' (xii). Opponents of transcultural adoption have sometimes pursued an anti-racist politics by using the very notions which transcultural adoptions may put on the move: racial distinctiveness, consanguineous kinship, cultural heredity, the assumptions that race carries culture or that culture is a matter of racial ancestry. So we need to dwell for a while upon the paradoxes which often arise when adoption is discussed, not least because an understanding of adoption in terms of paradox constitutes one of the most important drawbacks that works against us thinking more progressively about transcultural adoption's transfigurative possibilities.

Adoption is not a paradoxical affair as such. It is made to seem so in a discursive milieu fixated on biogenetic primacy and normative modes of identity, where consanguineous confluence and the place of one's birth are

regarded as constituting the true origins of self, anchor points of family
and proper cultural and national identity. In this zone of family-making,
adoptive relations are both legitimate and fraudulent: sanctioned in law but
seen at large as synthetic or second-hand. As Barbara Yngvesson puts it, 'the
difference of the adopted child takes shape against a backdrop of assumption
that "blood", "genes" or "descent" constitute "natural" identity in an Anglo-
European cultural and legal universe' (*Belonging* 25). With normative models
of self, family and community confected biocentrically, matters of biogenetic
descent clinch the cult of authenticity beloved of modernity. The prizing
of blood-lines, birthrights and national and cultural 'roots' has become the
modern norm, regardless of how arbitrary it may be firmly to establish these
things extra-discursively. This imaginative synchronizing of the birth of the
body with the origins of identity is both disrupted and confirmed by adoption,
because the meaning and experience of adoption is always circumvented by
the norms it seems to dispense with. For example, in his spirited discussion
of transcultural adoption and inauthenticity, Vincent Cheng notes that
arguments over whether or not adoptees should have access to birth records,
often sealed as part of 'strong' adoptions, 'repeatedly buy into the notion that
your birth certificate and your birth records constitute "your identity"' (66)
and fuel assumptions that 'the adopted baby's cultural roots and heritage – as
manifest by the racial, ethnic, or national background of the birth mother – are
a vital and functional key to the child's innate identity' (66). The primacy of
biogenetic filiation constrains adoption within a paradoxical position because
its undertaking actually upholds models of 'natural' kinship that have been
secreted not expunged.

Adoption arrangements in the West have frequently sought to mirror
normative consanguineous families by re-rooting adoptees in exclusive rather
than transitive terms, concealing biogenetic origins and minimizing disruption
to blood-lines through attempts at cultural and racial matching (as we have
noted). Consequently, paradoxes have proliferated. As Sales argues, Britain's
1949 Adoption of Children Act sought to make blood relations less significant
in adoptive families (previously adoptees did not enjoy transfer of inheritance
rights) by establishing 'a framework through which the adoptive family is more
exactly modelled on the pattern of the post-war biological family. […] In this new
post-war formulation, the "otherness" of the adopted child would be completely

assimilated within a new adoptive family who would mimic in every possible respect the biological tie between parents and children in "natural" families' (64). But if normative family relations turn on the privileging of the biocentric filiation as 'natural' or 'real', the forging of adoptive families interrupts this ideological manoeuvre at the very moment it seeks to be compliant: 'The "real" model of family life is clearly unsettled when "real" mothers give their children away. These mothers, then, must be re-categorised as unreal, in spite of their biological connection to the child, and situated as either unnatural or pathological' (70). Adoption practices are caught up in seeking to uphold the normalization of biological ties through forging 'mimic' families at the very moment when biocentric notions of 'natural' mothering are disarticulated and demythologized. In Yngvesson's study of transcultural adoption in Sweden, such paradoxes characterize adoption's mechanics and consequences as it engages with the central 'tension inherent in adoptive kinship – that it simultaneously constitutes and disrupts a genealogical imaginary of what a "real" family looks like' (*Belonging* 15). For Yngvesson, consanguineous families are legitimated and realized ironically through the adoption arrangements that mimic them, so that 'adoption becomes a site for the reenactment of identity thinking and a "crossroads of ambiguity" […] at which identity seems to break apart' (37). These are two examples of how adoption gets caught in a repeated cycle of compliance and critique: opening up possibilities for challenging received notions of identity and attachment that are not permitted to be taken, ultimately remaining constrained by normative models of self and family.

This paradoxical predicament is not enough to broker transgressive or transformative changes to the ways we have been schooled to think about core categories of self, identity, culture, community, race and nation. Yngvesson concludes, a little glumly, that the 'disruptive and confirming' agency of transcultural adoption ultimately 'moves us away from familiar trajectories but provides no models' (176). Upholding biocentric norms of kinship in adoptive arrangements produces often vexed and anxious lives for those inward of the adoption triad. The pathologization of birth-mothers as 'unnatural' rather than as oppressed by unkind social circumstances has sentenced many to a deeply traumatizing experience of pernicious stigmatization, in Ann Fessler's words 'burdened with feelings of low self-esteem and unworthiness, and laden with secrets, shame, loss, and grief' (152). One of the birth-mothers whom she interviewed, Karen, puts it thus: 'You are never whole. Never. [...] I was not an *authenticated* mother. I was an illegal mother. I was a denied mother. [...] It's as if I was an unwilling accomplice to the kidnapping of my own child. So you have to live with the trauma of losing your child and then you have to live with the trauma of knowing you didn't stop it. How do you do that?' (163). With cultural identity regarded as essentially consanguineous, the quandaries for adoptive parents also become emotionally freighted. Cheng writes sensitively of the 'guilt' (66) of parents of transcultural adoptees keen not to withhold from them the cultural and national particulars they believe have been 'handed down by one's cultural, racial, ethnic, or national "heritage"' (67). Although such acts of retrieving 'birth culture' may pander to clichéd notions of cultural flavour and confections of national custom – Chinese dragon-boat races, Irish country dancing, Indian cuisine – Cheng reminds us of 'the basically ethical impulse behind this urge for authenticity on the part of adoptive parents and adoption experts: the attempt to be sensitive to the issues of difference is an important, responsible, and honest response to the challenges of raising a foreign child' (79).

For adoptees, growing up in a realm where consanguineous relations are the guarantors of racial and cultural identity and stabilizers of self has compelled many to think of themselves as incomplete, because they lack knowledge of their 'natural' beginnings and heritage from which they have been damagingly sundered. This predicament has been calcified by clinical discourses which maintain biocentric thinking and construct the reality of 'being adopted' as a sundered, serrated self torn from its definitive origins. One thinks of Nancy Verrier's popular 'primal wound' thesis which pathologizes adoptee selfhood as emotionally scarred by the adoptee's separation from their birth-mother because their 'psychobiological continuum is interrupted' (29). This line of thinking locates adoptee trauma and behavioural difficulties in a primal experience rather than as discursively produced or the consequence of adoptees' post-adoption fortunes of having to move in a world that perpetually declares them as inauthentic. Pushed to extremes, in a biocentric discursive context, adoptees and birth-mothers appear to form part of a delinquent circle, entirely responsible for their problems due to poor genes. In their book *Being Adopted: The Lifelong Search for Self* (1992), the adoption experts David M. Brodzinsky, Marshall D. Schechter and Robin Marantz Henig – respectively a psychologist, a psychiatrist and a medical writer – suggested that adoptees were at increased risk of learning disabilities because 'many of the personality traits that go along with learning disabilities – impulsiveness, poor judgement, immaturity – also go along with unplanned and unwanted pregnancy. Young women who give up their babies for adoption, therefore, may be more likely to be learning disabled themselves – and to pass on a genetic predisposition for this problem to their babies' (88). In the light of Fessler's work on birth-mother testimony, these sentences are hard to read today. But even adoption activists have become problematically complicit with biocentric models of transpersonal attachment. Adoptee and adoption rights campaigner Betty Jean Lifton, who did much to break the silence surrounding adoption in the late twentieth century, argued that adoptees could not consider themselves whole until they searched for their biogenetic relations. Those who did not were essentially living a narcoleptic life, yet to awaken from their 'Great Sleep' (*Lost and Found* 71).

Ensnared by adoption's paradoxes born from the ascendency of biocentric norms, little appears productive. Birth-mothers are scripted as unnatural delinquents and not oppressed women failed by families, communities or the state. Adoptive parents wrestle ethically to raise their children who allegedly belong to an elsewhere often kept secret or appearing as inscrutable. Adoptees attempt to grow while ever conscious of their life as a puzzle in two senses: as an enigma, with secrecy sitting where the reassurances of roots should be found; or as a jigsaw puzzle with missing pieces, incomplete and lacking its full dimensions. Margaret Homans has pointed out the preponderance of puzzle, collage and jigsaw images in adoptee texts (224). If identity must be a matter of biogenetic attachment to people, place, race, culture or nation, then each identity position in the transcultural adoption triad is inevitably characterized by broken lines of connection. Administered thus, adoption's paradoxical condition ultimately marks not its transformative agency but its constraining propensity, the neutering of its transgressive capacity that is glimpsed but rarely gained.

*

How might we release from the problems of paradox the critical opportunities which adoption promises and begin to realize responsibly the transgressive agency it bears? One of the central arguments I propose in *Life Lines* is the need to recognize and reject a fixation with identity as normatively conceived because it perpetuates the paradoxical predicament of adoption's stalled agency. While identity in its prevailing mode remains primary, adoption will ever be a conundrum for those it involves who seek to assemble their lives in pursuit of those core attachments prized at large – origins, resemblance, belonging – that have been lost. It is a predicament captured in the words of mixed-race adoptee Catherine McKinley, whose trace memoir *The Book of Sarahs: A Family in Parts* (2002) I explore in Chapter 3: 'I sit down in someone else's paradigms and try to figure myself out' (287).

In turning now to think about adoption beyond identity and paradox, I do not wish to forget the ways in which a great deal of significant adoptee activism has been pursued precisely in terms of identity politics and rights. Demands for unsealing adoption records and breaking the legally endorsed secrecy that keeps biogenetic relations ignorant of each other have been powerfully advocated by key figures such as Jean Paton and Betty Jean Lifton in the United States who refused to accept the history and practice of keeping adoption hidden from view. But we must recognize, too, as we did with the example of John Small and ABSWAP, that always working within the prevailing norms of identity may perpetuate the primacy of roots, race and natal origins as the essentials of self – the very ideas which have helped create neocolonial conditions of adoptability in the first place. While this primacy remains, those inward of the adoption triad will continue to prioritize consanguineous attachments and 'birth culture' as a panacea to the alleged incompleteness of self. In an essay on transcultural adoptive families' 'roots return' trips, Toby Alice Volkman records the practices of white US mothers of Chinese-born children who take their families to China in search of what she calls 'some tangible connection to their daughters' past' ('Embodying' 101). In one case that she mentions, two mothers discovered the derelict orphanage from where their children had been adopted and 'managed to retrieve, and carry home to Massachusetts, a single brick' (101). Another mother and daughter 'dug up some rich, brown, moist and fragrant earth from Sierra Song E's beloved China' (101). These examples index the prevalence, amongst some transcultural relations, of turning natal environments into rarefied landscapes of origin, with bricks and soil possessing a mystical propensity to materialize a tryst with missing roots and origins. Instead, we might follow Kimberly Leighton's lead and insist upon biogenetic identity and its concomitant conundrums for adoptees as by no means innate, natural or primary. As Leighton proposes, the 'genealogical bewilderment' from which adoptees perennially are deemed to suffer, harmed by not knowing their biogenetic ancestry, is the product of the identitarian terrain in which they move, rather than an inevitable or inherent consequence of surrender. It is an effect of power formulated in and imposed by a discursive dispensation menaced by alternative filial attachments which challenge, amongst others, the metaphysics of race. The diagnosis of this condition, she argues, 'reflects the anxieties of those who view forms of family-making as dangerous when they are outside of purportedly natural sexual production through which genetic ties can be traced with (imagined) certainty' (69). The pathologization of adoption through such diagnoses serves 'the maintenance of family as a means for reproducing bodies according to norms of gender, sexuality, and race' (92). If we want adoption to facilitate things other than pathology and paradox, I would hazard, we need to treat identity mistrustfully, putting the assumptions upon which it rests under pressure.

Conceptually speaking, identity is fundamentally transpersonal rather than the discrete possession of a singular self. Identities are always negotiated at large. They align individuals with wider collectivities that are sought out or imposed; and these collectivities themselves gauge the predominant ways in which human lives are categorized, divided and hierarchized. As Kwame Anthony Appiah summarizes, identity 'is always articulated through concepts (and practices) made available to you by religion, society, school, and state, mediated by family, peers, friends' (20). Like others, Appiah perceives identity in terms of narrative. The norms and models of identity create 'scripts: narratives that people can use in shaping their projects and telling their life stories' (23). It is worth reminding ourselves of the role of narrative in synchronizing individual and collective identities, not least because of its consequences for transcultural adoption writing:

> It is not just that, say, gender identities, give shape to one's life; it is also that ethnic and national identities fit a personal narrative into a larger narrative. For modern people, the narrative form entails seeing one's life as having a certain arc, as making sense through a life story that expresses who one is through one's own project of self-making. That narrative arc is yet another way in which an individual's life depends deeply on something socially created and transmitted. (23)

We have seen how in a biocentric environment the absence of biogenetic attachments is read in terms of severance, so that the lines of connection between 'one's life' and the 'larger narrative' of identity norms are considered broken. If crises must follow adoption's sundering of blood-lines (genealogical bewilderment, etc.), then Appiah's words help sensitize us to a concomitant crisis of narrative for those inward of the adoption triad. The impossibility of situating oneself in relation to the prevailing scripts of identity confounds narrative-making in the dominant mode, the capacity for 'seeing one's life as having a certain arc'. If adoptees feel that their selves suffer from missing pieces, it is because they cannot happily make themselves up using the prevailing narrative which renders the self, via the scripts of identity, reassuringly tidy. These feelings may be intensified in the context of transcultural adoption. 'One thing that matters to people across many societies', argues Appiah, 'is a certain narrative unity, the ability to tell a story of one's life that hangs together' (23). When it comes to adoption, the quest for securing identity is fundamentally precarious because it is extremely difficult for those inward of the adoption triad to secure selfhood using identity's prevailing narrative resources.

As Marianne Novy has pointed out, the preponderance of adoption stories in European and American literature over many centuries tends ultimately to support normative biocentric models of family-making and uphold 'the assumption that [an adopted] child has, in effect, one set of parents' (*Reading* 7), although such paradigms can be complicated considerably (her examples include the works of William Shakespeare, Henry Fielding, Charlotte Brontë, Charles Dickens and others). She identifies 'three mythic stories' (7) – the disastrous adoption, the search for biogenetic parents and the happy adoption – which never adequately capture the complexities, entanglements and possibilities encountered by those with an experience of adoption: 'for me, and for many others, all three narratives are inadequate' (7). This insufficiency of received narratives of adoption has consequences for literary form. Mark C. Jerng notes that the appearance of adoptees in literary and cultural history often manifests itself as 'a problem of narrative form in which the capacity of narrative to "take in" the adoptee opens up issues central to the political and social conditions of personhood' (xxviii). Unsurprisingly, prevailing attempts narratively to accommodate those in the triad and secure normative positioning are at best precarious and often produce a (self-)perception of incompleteness and fraudulence: the 'unnatural' birth-mother, the 'unfinished' adoptee-puzzle, the 'proxy' parent.

Appiah's work helps us understand that many of the perplexing problems and constraining paradoxes of adoption are products of the prevailing dispensation of identities – its assumptions, standpoints and scripts – and *not* a natural consequence of the act of adoption itself. As Dorow claims, adoption results in the rupture of those narratives which 'are meant to bring coherence and unity to identity, telling us who we are', so that 'the various narratives used by parents, social workers, facilitators, and officials to "fix" [narratives]' constitute 'the identificatory work between individual and collective, local and transnational, past and present' (27). Rather than propel adoptees towards narrative forms in which they can fit only paradoxically, representations of transcultural adoption suggest that a reconditioning and resequencing of narrative is required. They often point us towards the significance of narrative in forging new ways of rendering adoption productively and help us wonder how adoptive lives might 'hang together' through different narrative designs.

But let us remember, too, that narratives of identity have ontological as well as social consequences. They fashion perceptions of existence and modalities of being. This situation makes the matter of narrative particularly pressing, especially given Jerng's observation cited earlier. If one's life cannot 'hang together' with recourse to the sanctioned scripts of identity, how can one's being otherwise be struck? Are there alternative *ontologies* which adoption narratives materialize? How might transcultural adoption prompt us not simply to revise the prevailing norms of identity but more radically transfigure a conception of being?

In making transcultural adoption an ontological rather than a strictly identitarian concern in *Life Lines*, I am not seeking to disinvest the significance of identity politics nor sideline the achievements and ongoing necessity of those political manoeuvres that demand visibility, legitimacy and support for the standpoints of birth-mothers, adoptees and adoptive parents. I, too, work within the cross-currents that characterize adoption scholarship as Homans describes them: 'thinking about adoption requires simultaneously questioning assumptions about essential – biogenetic, innate – identity and at the same time honoring the urgent social and political claims of those who find their lives' meaning in such forms of identity' (18). Nevertheless, while prevailing notions of identity remain firmly fixated upon biocentric norms when adoption is considered, I find the nomenclature of 'identity' unhelpfully toxified and its utility curtailed. Installing and advocating a new collective identity of 'adoptees' in the current milieu, while politically gainful in some very important respects, does not fully empower or release adoption's transfigurative potential.

I would respectfully take issue with Barbara Yngvesson's conclusion, cited earlier, that transcultural adoption ultimately 'moves us away from familiar trajectories but provides no models'. In looking closely in this book at a selection of transcultural adoption texts, we might discern, contrariwise, how writers are formulating alternative ontologies of self that record but also push beyond the paradoxical and approximate identities that result from 'being adopted' towards what I shall term 'adoptive being'.

*

According to Jean-Luc Nancy, Being (in the capitalized philosophical sense) is ever singular and plural. It is singular because each instance of Being is never entirely coincident with another, just like each day is different to the next: 'A "day" is not simply a unit for counting; it is the turning of the world – each time singular' (9). But Being can never be in itself or for itself, alone. We cannot designate a singular Being as a 'one', *sui generis*, unique, wholly originary or original, because to count to one is already to acknowledge the presence of others that gives meaning to the one: '"one" cannot be counted without counting more than one' (39). Being is plural because meaning always happens amongst and across, passing between and over beings rather than springing from them. 'That which exists', Nancy notes, 'whatever this might be, coexists because it exists' (29). While everything 'passes *between* us' (5), the between

> does not lead from one to the other; it constitutes no connective tissue, no cement, no bridge [...]; it is neither connected nor unconnected; it falls short of both; even better, it is that which is at the heart of a connection, the *inter*lacing [*l'entrecroisment*] of strands whose extremities remain separate even at the very center of the knot. (5)

Just as the existence of meaning emerges from coexistence, necessitated by the interplay of a heterogeneous 'us' that transacts and negotiates meaning, so too is being formulated interconnectedly, shaped from the inevitability that being is always 'being-with' (27). Nancy insists upon the concept of 'being-with' in recognition of the irrefutable sociability of human life, the fact that it does not exist for itself and cannot be meaningful purely on its own terms. Replete with the umbilical hyphen that marks both attachment and separation, being-with 'as it relates to meaning [...] is never for just one, but always for one another, always between one another' (27). Crucially, being-with does not signal a relation or rapport between one and the other (or, philosophically speaking, between I and the Other), but rather witnesses the presence of the other within the one, at the origin, just as connective strands formulate a solid knot. The 'with' is not a bridge between imminent selves, as we have noted; it is not anterior to Being nor its postscript. It is neither secondary nor supplementary. If 'Being is being-with' (30), writes Nancy, 'then it is, in its being-with, the "with" that constitutes Being; the with is not simply an addition [...]; the with is at the heart of Being' (30).

In sum, because the meaning of Being is always resulting at large from interaction, attachment, coexistence and association, there can be no unique, immanent meaning or being at source, without reference to anything outside of itself; in other words, there is no pure origin. The 'spacing of meaning' (5) that necessitates its circulation betwixt and between always happens right at the source, at the point of origin, so that origins are never total or unique: 'The origin is together with other origins, originally divided' (13). With Being reconceived as 'being-with', the singular life is inevitably polyform, a distinct plurality that neither replicates the lives of others nor enjoys totality or immanence. Nancy sees the desire for origins as an attempt to secure Being in place and deny the associative disposition of being-with: a 'desire to fix the origin, or *to give the origin to itself*, once and for all, and in one place for all, that is, always outside the world' (20). (As he points out, the quest to fix Being in place, as one or the Other, has been darkly complicit with modernity's technologies of horror.) Instead, he counsels the necessity to embrace the 'plural singularity of the Being of being' (13), to recognize that we acquire meaning by taking our turn in a wider transpersonal horizon of interaction which is neither fully determining of nor indifferent towards us. 'People are strange' (8), we often think, says Nancy, because they appear unlike us. The strange singularity of being-with is enacted each time we happen, which constitutes an origin as such, but never an original or Adamic origin: 'What occurs there, what bends, leans, twists, addresses, denies – from the newborn to the corpse – is neither primarily "someone close", nor an "other", nor a "stranger", nor "someone similar". It is an origin; it is an affirmation of the world, and we know that the world has no other origin than this singular multiplicity of origins' (9). Our singularity – the fact that 'the world begins *its turn with you*' (6) – can never be an essence, just as plurality is never a collective totality, 'neither the sum, nor the incorporation' (33) of singularities into a regimented, regulated whole. Plurality carries with it the associative challenge of 'being-with', the recognition that 'the essence of Being is only as co-essence' (30). To put things succinctly, our personhood is always in concert, because what constitutes each of us 'at heart' is fundamentally correlative, like the interlacing strands that fashion the singular knot.

The value of Nancy's notion of 'being singular plural' for adoption studies, I think, is at least twofold. First, let us recognize the critique of origins it enables. Biocentric models of identity and personhood rest upon some key manoeuvres. They invest in the idea of origin as possessing exclusive explanatory power, and they identify certain particulars of personhood as commensurate with one's origins that hold their significance indefinitely: place of birth, consanguineous kin, the racialized identity of biogenetic parents, national culture that happens to obtain at the location of nativity, etc. Nancy's 'being-with' makes no distinction between consanguineous association and affiliative rapport, and derealizes blood-lines as possessing particular kinds of transpersonal immanence or forging elevated occasions of 'with-ness', if you will. If 'being-with' can be thought as *textile*, like a firm knot made from many strands, then these threads and lines of connection are sourced severally, not exclusively or only biogenetically. Second, let us note that Nancy does not do away with origins per se but recognizes instead their proliferation and abundant manifestation in his conception of the singular plural: '"Origin" does not signify that from which the world comes, but rather the coming of each presence of the world, each time singular' (15). It is not that origins do not matter; it is that they matter differently to the ways we are often schooled to think they matter. This point is crucial not least because, and as much adoption writing in general articulates, the issue of origins remains of enormous significance especially to adoptees. Dismissing or deconstructing origins as bogus or of no meaningful significance is a theoretical nicety that misses the ways in which adoption writing invites us, prompted by Nancy, to think about how the cult of consanguineous origins *might be made to mean differently.*

Let me put things this way. What might happen if we were to think about blood-lines *in another mode*: as vital life lines of connectivity to a circulating complex of material histories and cultural traces, and not as the primary substance of inherent cultural identity and personhood biocentrically conceived? Could we think of blood-lines more like the life line that creases the palm of a hand: the lined epidermis, biogenetic creation of our birth-parents, that tells our fortunes, not necessarily theirs? How might we handle the hidden historical and cultural legacies we have been handed from our biogenetic relations, to deal (with) as we please, not as we must?

More so than others, those impacted by adoption are acutely, sometimes obsessively concerned with matters of origins, blood-lines and natal culture – unsurprisingly, I have argued, in a milieu where the biocentric is rendered essential to self-knowledge and the body's biogenetic heredity is conceived as the *ur*-text of identity. We must take care, then, to avoid being quaintly counterintuitive and set against consanguineous models of origins a cheerful advocacy of nurture over nature by presuming that transpersonal relations are exclusively virtual rather than meaningfully bound by the realities of the visceral, even in small measure. Adoptees and their families are not freed to move nomadically through infinite cultural inventories rendered laissez-faire. To say that biogenetic heredity cannot mean anything essential or self-stabilizing is not the same as thinking that it cannot mean anything at all. Consanguineous kinship needs demythologizing, to be sure, but not simply deleting. It requires rethinking rather than rejecting out of hand, I want to suggest, if we are to grasp fully the possibilities that arise when we think of adoptive being in terms of multifarious strands, as a firm yet fraying knot that takes its place *in turn*, as non-originary origin.

Rather than liquidate the consanguineous through deconstructing the origin as immanence, transcultural adoption stubbornly *puts back in play* theoretically thorny and discomfiting discussions of roots, race and natalism – of the body cleaved from the native or transplanted from the geneticist blood-lines of cultural ancestry. Homans importantly reminds us that 'biogenetic identity remains forcefully real for a large constituency' (15) of adoptees.

At times this desire for biogenetic origins can lead to the perpetuation of identitarian paradoxes or a complicity in a biocentric rendering of cultural contracts, as captured in transcultural adoptee Jane Jeong Trenka's worrying phrase 'the language of blood' and in her advocacy of 'racial memory' (208) unsundered by adoption's broken lines which denigrates adopted life as perpetual 'inadequacy' or 'incompleteness' (180). But on other occasions, as we shall see severally in *Life Lines*, blood-lines can be rethought in much more imaginative and non-essentialized ways, as one filament of the polyform personhood that adoptive being proposes. Devoid of explanatory mysticism, consanguineous genealogies may lead us to the oft-hidden concrete conditions and hidden histories which speak of the neocolonial global relations that constrain and produce adoption, as well as offer important lines of material legacy for writers to *make something from agentially*. It requires us to treat biogenetic and adoptive models of kinship as concomitant instances of 'being-with', as ontologically commensurate and frictionally co-operative rather than fated to be forever counterpointed as nature or nurture, roots or routes, science or culture. 'Adoptive being' does not prioritize nurture over nature in the old style, nor is it a simple commingling of filial and affiliative modes. It reconceives biogenetic relations beyond the biocentric, just as it refuses to recognize adoptive relations as synthetic, substitute or disembodied.

Here, and finally, I want to underline the crucial materiality of my notion of adoptive being, inspired by Nancy, by turning to Michael Rothberg's work on the 'multidirectional'. Rothberg's argument in *Multidirectional Memory* (2009) concerns the necessity in acts of public remembrance to think comparatively and not competitively. Acts of memory are productive because they are always 'subject to ongoing negotiation, cross-referencing, and borrowing' (3). They assist in the formulation of identity which consequently can never be 'pure and authentic' (4) due to the multifarious resources upon which both memory and identity draw. Rothberg rejects the view 'that a straight line runs from memory to identity and that the only kinds of memories and identities that are therefore possible are ones that exclude elements of alterity and forms of commonality with others' (5–6). Instead, the relations we strike with the past to constitute our present happen 'never straightforwardly and directly, and never without unexpected or even unwanted consequences that bind us to those whom we consider other' (5). This commitment to a certain multidirectionality when we remember the past resonates powerfully with those inward of the adoption triad, positioned at the cusp of material histories and intimate transpersonal relations. Adoptive family-making affords an opportunity to expose the diverse unequal entanglements of (already untidy) cultural inventories drawn from biogenetic and adopted genealogies – China and the United States; Eritrea and the UK, say – that blur the lines and combine unpredictably, productively and intimately in adoptive personhood. Just as multidirectional memory draws attention 'to the dynamic transfers that take place between diverse places and times during the act of remembrance' (11), so might adoptive being expose something of the polyform cultural transactionality upon which creating personhood depends – something which is perceivably true, but not exclusively so, for those inward of transcultural adoption. Brought into the context of transcultural adoption, multidirectionality allows us to register the network of associations that proliferate within and beyond distinct forms of attachments – the manifold cultural capillaries that nourish adoption's creativity by calling up and coalescing the material and historical contexts of one's biogenetic *as well as* adoptive filial attachments. Using the example of the Chinese-born transcultural adoptee in the United States, we might put things this way: 'Chinese blood' does not define or exhaust the cultural personhood or identity of the adoptee, but rather is one unsteady line of attachment that involves the adoptee in the unequal material conditions that produced them. It presents to them one important creative resource amongst others which *might or might not* prove useful in helping the adoptee and their family to act transculturally. We cannot choose these resources any more than we can choose our parents (biogenetic or adoptive). They *confront* us, as well as offering possibilities for productive creativity. Each multidirectional manifestation of adoptive being takes its singular turn always as a plural, taking 'dissimilarity for granted' (18) when striking up progressive forms of intimate and political relations amidst or against the wider landscape of inequality and constraint that conditioned each originary instance of adoptability.

By renting Rothburg's notion of multidirectionality for a discussion of transcultural adoption writing and adoptive being, I am seeking to keep my approach to the progressive possibilities of transcultural adoption firmly grounded in the materiality of those transcultural adoption histories, central but not often remarked upon, that we considered earlier. But I also want to protect the progressive possibilities of representing transcultural adoption from being written out, so that the textual opportunities they fashion are *not* encased within the unhappy contexts which have made transcultural adoptions happen. I am in firm agreement with Sara Dorow that we need to get past politically polarized approaches to transcultural adoption that quickly condemn or applaud it and think more judiciously and daringly about what might also be made out of, or made from, its painful predicament. 'We need to move', writes Dorow, 'from asking whether we are "for or against" transnational or transracial adoption to asking what adoption, *as practiced*, is for and against. And this entails understanding how adoption is practiced *in situ*' (279). The psychosocial scholar Barry Richards articulated a similar position over twenty years ago when he insisted that, like it or not, we must recognize 'the whole history of racial oppression, of colonialism and racism, is relevant to our experience of race issues in adoption today' (102). But as he warns, the oppressions of the past must not overshadow the practices of the present. If they do, then the 'evocation of colonialism is mistaken for its enactment; the pain of historical relationships evoked is so intense that thinking becomes simplistic and concrete. [...] The social task we all face, of creating new forms of relationship while living under the shadow of old ones, is thus abandoned' (103). There is a postcoloniality of transcultural adoption which representations of its practices, past and present, invite us to read and realize.

*

The texts which I explore in *Life Lines* offer a range of transcultural adoption representations. Some take us towards adoptive being in the formulation of their narratives. Others fall short, sometimes unexpectedly so. As these texts are engaged in the task of exploring 'new forms of relationship', in Richards's phrase, matters of narrative form are a central concern when it comes to capturing the particularities and possibilities of transcultural adoption's experiences. If, following Appiah and Jerng, the phenomenon of adoption poses problems for the predominant scripts of identity and accepted narrative arcs, then we should not be surprised if many of those who write about transcultural adoption search for reconditioned narrative structures that bear better witness to the multidirectional cultural inventories that plait biogenetic with adoptive legacies and pluralize origins across seemingly diverse places and temporalities.

As Nancy claims, as being-with deals 'a blow to ontology' (37) it also challenges the very grammar of thinking being: 'Being singular plural: in a single stroke, without punctuation, without a mark of equivalence, implication, or sequence' (37). In his study of transnational fiction, *The Grammar of Identity* (2009), Stephen Clingman argues in a Nancyian vein that 'what makes fiction transnational are questions of *form*. [...] At this level form becomes content – a mode of being and seeing. Novels working in this manner become not only a way of exploring the world but also a *kind* of world to be explored' (10–11). Clingman's sensitive attention to the navigational mode of much transnational fiction attends to its ontological productivity: how the 'syntax of the self – its combinatory, unfolding possibilities – is a transitive syntax' (16) commensurate with the navigational itinerancy of spatial motion. In other words, transnational writing does not passively reflect an experience of passage but formulates a fresh image of being from the exploration of transitivities rather than the endorsement of boundaries, even if one is 'a writer who never leaves home' (10). Such texts enact in their very unfolding this new syntax, these new conceptualizations of worldly being which express formally 'the protocols of *encounter*, where touch, contiguity, gap, transitivity, become an essential part of [...] a different kind of story' (31, 32). As we shall see in *Life Lines*, several transcultural adoption narratives also seek to phrase such encounters by striking through narrative, often knotting together several strands of selfhood none of which is complete in itself or sufficiently explanatory. I want to consider if the possibilities brokered in transcultural adoption writing emerge most fruitfully when writers push against the tidiness of normative narrative forms. If the notion of 'life lines' materializes differently *biogenetic* lines of connection, as I proposed, then this term also bears us multidirectionally towards the commensurate realm of *discursive* creativity: the lines on a page or a screen that you are currently reading, an actor's lines, narrative lines refashioned and reformulated, the lined hand that holds a pen or hovers above a keyboard.

Clingman's argument is also useful in its suggestion that a writer of transnational fiction need not have left home; that a textual exploration of navigation and transitivity need not necessarily rest upon an experience of passage. One of the aims of *Life Lines* is to bring to critical attention the phenomenon and figuration of transcultural adoption and, concomitantly, shine a light on its little-considered histories and texts. But I do not ground adoptive being exclusively within adoption phenomenology or suggest that its narration is only within the gift of adoption's participants. In the following pages, I shall argue that *My Fathers' Daughter* (2005), the trace memoir of Hannah Pool, an Eritrean-born British adoptee, struggles to free itself from the overriding arcs of identity against which Pool's experiences strain, whereas the Caribbean-born British-raised novelist Caryl Phillips, who is not an adoptee, offers an inspired representation of adoptive being in his novel *Crossing the River* (1993). To be sure, it is fair to argue that those inward of the adoption triad are quite precisely positioned to broker transgressive ways of seeing as part of a wider political response. The transcultural adoptees Oparah, Shin and Trenka have written readily of their determination not to be 'trapped' by proscriptive thinking: 'Instead, we bring forth our unique creativity and spirituality as adoptees of color, to reinvent ourselves and our world' (14). The preponderance of texts produced by adoptees – Mei-Ling Hopgood, Hannah Pool, Catherine McKinley, Jackie Kay – which I explore in this book, and the many others I mention, maintains a focus in particular on transcultural adoptee experience as potentially productive and transformative. But we must also consider film and fiction by the non-adopted: Mike Leigh, Andrea Levy, E. R. Braithwaite, Toni Morrison, Sebastian Barry, Buchi Emecheta, Barbara Kingsolver and Caryl Phillips. Theirs are not tales of personal experience. Each has sought to find in transcultural adoption histories profound possibilities for political and ethical transformation.

If transcultural adoption puts proscriptive thinking under pressure, then we should not be too surprised that it has become an attractive theme for transcultural writers in general seeking to tackle widespread forms of marginalization and silencing on the grounds of ethnicity, race, cultural prejudice, economic disenfranchisement, gender and sexuality. We should value, too, the work of those *not* inward of the adoption triad who are seeking to respond to the challenges which transcultural adoption presents generally, especially if we agree with Homans that 'adoption raises the most vital questions about human identity and the value and meaning of individual human lives' (1). In her study of American adoption writing, *Kin of Another*

Kind (2011), Cynthia Callahan has argued that if adoptees have 'to find other ways to locate a stable self; in contrast, the nonadopted must relinquish the fantasy that origins can be completely knowable' (139). If the non-adopted are engaged with adoption's many challenges, then this welcome state of affairs should remind us that the meaning and consequences of adoption are not exclusively the business of those within the triad but impact upon the non-adopted too.

The situating of representations of transcultural adoption and adoptive being in relation to *both* the concrete and the imagined requires a further word of warning. As we will see, the possibilities of adoptive being are often most effectively realized via formal inventiveness and figurative innovation. Yet the tendency to metaphorize the transcultural adoptive family as a ready sign of dissident or transgressive transpersonal relations carries its own risks, not least the freighting of adoptive units in symbolic terms with little sustained engagement with the painful histories and experiences which underscore their materialization. Such thinking is in danger of freighting adoptees in particular with an iconic potentiality which can metaphorize them at the expense of their experiential materiality in situ. For many adoptees, we have to remember that adoption names an ongoing and deeply painful predicament, and so any enthusiastic rendering of transcultural adoption's possibilities or cheerful advocacy of 'adoptive being' must not belittle nor forget the challenges of 'being adopted', what Lifton has called 'the hidden phenomenology of the adoptee' (64). That said, let us accept, too, that the writing of some adoptees in particular may often fall back on consanguineous conceptions of identity and take comfort in discovering and securing those narrative arcs of identity otherwise put under pressure, understandably so perhaps. Being adopted is a not a prerequisite for adoptive being. In some texts we will consider, the former may inhibit rather than enhance the latter.

For these reasons, in this book I resolutely resist drawing a clear line that connects the provenance of transcultural adoption experience to the proprietorship of its representation, one that would automatically exclude the work of those outside of the adoption triad. As Callahan intimated, adoption may offer the non-adopted an extremely important vehicle in which to think about self and with which to free themselves from their own adherence to the protocols and prohibitions of consanguineous and biocentric models of originary identity. The histories and possibilities of transcultural adoption are there to be written about by all. But due to the unequal political and cultural landscape within which such adoptions are always contracted, these histories and possibilities are not to be trifled with nor appropriated without attentiveness to the political and ethical concerns which obtain. Writers outside of the triad who approach transcultural adoption imaginatively are often at their most productive when they have pursued some research and seek to engage informatively and sensitively with transcultural adoption's vexed materiality. We shall see, too, that those inward of adoption's tender actualities often engender highly powerful ways of rethinking being when they work experimentally as well as experientially with the formal and figurative consequences of adoption experience.

My choice of the writers and texts which preoccupy *Life Lines* is purposefully selective. Due to the ubiquity of transcultural adoption across the globe, I have selected transcultural adoption texts in English set in Britain, Ireland and the United States to keep the range of materials delimited and relatively coherent. In addition, discussions of transcultural, transnational or transracial adoption have tended to stay interrogatively within a primary national formation, usually the United States – one thinks of groundbreaking and inspiring studies such as Cynthia Callahan's *Kin of Another Kind: Transracial Adoption in American Literature* (2011) or Mark C. Jerng's *Claiming Others: Transracial Adoption and National Belonging* (2010). Scholarly works which indeed range internationally and historically do not necessarily prioritize the specifics of transcultural adoption in bringing to attention the long tradition of adoption writing. Marianne Novy's *Reading Adoption: Family and Difference in Fiction and Drama* (2005), to which so much adoption-writing scholarship is indebted (including my own), artfully explores a wealth of adoption texts from Sophocles's play *Oedipus the King* (?429 BC) to the fiction of George Eliot and Barbara Kingsolver; Margaret Homans's rigorous and exhaustively imaginative book *The Imprint of Another Life: Adoption Narratives and Human Possibility* (2013) deliberately chooses not to distinguish between conspicuously transcultural texts and others because, as she states, 'the questions and controversies that interest me cross these lines' (5). *Life Lines* supports these recent scholarly endeavours and responds to their wisdom, as well as takes things forward through my strategically comparative approach which puts transcultural adoption texts from Britain, Ireland and the United States in close critical contact with each other for the first time in a book-length study – so that Catherine McKinley's work can be thought of in relation to Jackie Kay's, or Toni Morrison's writing can share the same analytical provenance as Sebastian Barry's. I focus, too, on texts not always subject to sustained analysis as transcultural adoption writing, such as Andrea Levy's and Caryl Phillips's fiction, alongside works which have featured prominently in adoption criticism, such as Mike Leigh's cinematography and Barbara Kingsolver's early novels. In so doing, I seek to establish a centre-point for adoption literary and cultural studies happening outside of the United States where most research monographs thus far have been produced.

My focus on British and Irish texts also makes an intervention more locally. While there is a fine scholarly tradition of studying matters of race, culture and nation in the British Isles, much of this valuable work has been pursued by scholars working in the disciplines of social policy, sociology and history, often as a consequence of their work as adoption workers and practitioners, based upon case studies – one thinks immediately of the achievements of John Triseliotis in the UK and the many colleagues he inspired. Much less has been achieved as regards the cultural representation of adoption matters in Britain and Ireland, or how the wisdom of textual creativity might be brought productively into dialogue with existing empirical research. In Ireland, recent revelations and representations of the so-called Magdalene Laundries and mother and baby homes has prompted the emergence of some important new work, while the writing of British figures such as Jackie Kay and Lemn Sissay has attracted a growing number of essays and readings that deal with the theme of transcultural adoption in contemporary literary studies. *Life Lines* looks to open wider the space for discussing the aesthetic consequences of transcultural adoption in Britain and Ireland, and to empower scholars to take the opportunity of bringing the wider histories of transcultural adoption into literary studies more centrally (indeed, representations of black British transcultural adoption would merit a book-length study of their own).

Inevitably, my delimiting of context means that other highly important transcultural adoption contexts, such as those found in Australia, Canada and South Africa, are not covered in the following chapters. I have elected to put a select archive of chosen texts under sustained critique and pursue the comparative consequences of thinking analytically about some of the recurring themes they raise rather than describing the field more generally. While I would not want to claim friction-free portability for some of the ideas I fashion in *Life Lines* to other contexts, I hope that much of the ensuing discussion will resonate productively beyond the particular horizon of this book's concerns.

The following chapters are organized around four recurring issues in the representation of transcultural adoption: secrets, histories, traces and bearings. In Chapter 1, I explore the centrality of the notion of secrecy to the administration of adoption contracts seemingly violated in conspicuous transcultural adoptive families, and the troubling ethical and political consequences when adoption is maintained as a matter of secrecy. I look at two texts – Mike Leigh's film *Secrets and Lies* (1996) and Andrea Levy's novel *Small Island* (2004) – which at first sight seem to expose the UK's secret history of transcultural adoption and the damage done by keeping adoption secrets, but ultimately are surprisingly complicit in exactly the practices of secrecy they ostensibly critique. I contrast these with Mei-Ling Hopgood's trace memoir *Lucky Girl* (2009), which positions an ethical commitment to breaking both birth- and adoptive-family secrets as an important lineament of adoptive being.

In Chapter 2, I consider examples of some of the seemingly private histories which are excavated in transcultural adoption writing and read the ways in which texts uncover the prejudicial public milieus that transcultural adoptions index and critique. I claim that E. R. Braithwaite's account of his life as a 1960s Welfare Officer in London in *Paid Servant* (1962) presents transcultural adoption as a highly valuable opportunity to subvert British racism that ultimately falls foul of Braithwaite's Anglophilic and solipsistic concerns. My reading of Toni Morrison's *Jazz* (1992) acknowledges the novel's intra-racial adoption stories as sculpted by early twentieth-century transcultural asymmetries of power and reads its critique of biocentric origins as central to a racially progressive future. My encounter with Sebastian Barry's novel *The Secret Scripture* (2008) attends to the long-suppressed history of single motherhood and illegitimacy in Ireland while prizing Barry's attempt to use that history to move beyond biocentric and nationalist modes of identitarianism. Especially in these latter two novels, we see how an attention to the often silenced material histories of transcultural adoption is crucial to the figurative rendering of adoptive being against public constraints.

In Chapter 3, I attend to the recurring trope of the adoptee tracing their biogenetic ancestry and think about how search and reunion narratives empower new possibilities of adoptive being through reconditioning narrative and figurative modes. My reading of Hannah Pool's memoir *My Fathers' Daughter* (2005) looks at the dangers of persisting with the assumption that reconnecting with biogenetic relations delivers completed personhood, as well as how difficult it is to pursue the unguessed and alternative possibilities which tracing relations engenders. When looking at Buchi Emecheta's *The New Tribe* (2000), I note how this novel seeks sensitively to acknowledge the compulsion towards biogenetic ancestry and also exposes the fraudulence and endangerment of being which tracing risks. In reading Catherine McKinley's trace narrative *The Book of Sarahs* and, briefly, her memoir *Indigo* (2011), I show how the deeply painful emotional journey she depicts leads ultimately to a remarkable realization of adoptive being, which resequences biogenetic and adoptive relations and captures these through enriching figurative tropes of the photomontage and textile.

Finally, in Chapter 4, I look at the new bearings of adoptive being which transcultural adoption texts chart in orienting readers beyond the constraints of normative identity. I critique Barbara Kingsolver's attempts to fashion post-anthropocentric models of kinship which turn problematically to Native American adoption contexts in her novels *The Bean Trees* (1988) and *Pigs in Heaven* (1993). In looking at Caryl Phillips's engagement in his novel *Crossing the River* (1993) with one of transcultural adoption's least-remarked histories, I prize his profoundly moving depiction of a white British birth-mother of a so-called 'brown baby' in 1940s England. Lastly, I explore the sophisticated and endearing rendition of adoptive being found in Jackie Kay's astonishing memoir of her Scottish upbringing and her quest to meet her birth-parents, *Red Dust Road* (2010).

It is not unusual for scholars of adoption writing to be inward of the adoption triad themselves, and several intertwine their responses to textual materials with their evolving sense of themselves as (most commonly) an adoptee or adoptive parent. Marianne Novy's salutary work demonstrates in a particularly compelling fashion how her academic pursuits are bound up with her reflections concerning 'where I now am as an adoptee' and how 'some of the ways being adopted has affected my current close family relationships, and the way they, in turn, relate to the ways I think about being adopted' (*Reading* 223). Most of the critics I have mentioned in this introduction – Margaret Homans, Barbara Yngvesson, Vincent Cheng, amongst others – are adoptive parents, and they bring this standpoint to bear on their critical insights without claiming special justification for their points of view. Theirs is an ethical as much as an experiential or intellectual declaration, and one which I must also make too. So let me confirm here, for better or worse, my own standpoint as an adoptee. I was just over nine weeks old when my parents and I met for the first time. I am not sure if my adoption history empowers more than it delimits my critical engagement with the texts I have chosen, but it is threaded through the scholarly endeavour of *Life Lines*. I bring to this study a particular but not privileged investment in the problems and possibilities of adopted life. I have found that researching and writing this book has often unexpectedly enabled me to think about my own multidirectional personhood as it shifts precariously but productively between the vectors of 'being adopted' and 'adoptive being'. I will have a little more to say about this in the short coda which concludes *Life Lines*. There I shall plait my scholarly, adoptive, biogenetic and biographical lines of thought in response to the enriching insights that many adoption texts gift their readers, adopted or not, and to which we now turn.

1

Secrets: Mike Leigh, Andrea Levy, Mei-Ling Hopgood

For many years, on each side of the Atlantic, a successful adoption was something which you could not tell – in both senses of the phrase. The commitment to racial and cultural matching in the administration of adoption contracts serviced the assumption that an adoptive family ideally should be inconspicuous, with parents and children sharing perceived common bodily and behavioural characteristics. Adoptees were meant to look the part, not stand apart from their new parents. As Sally Sales summarizes, the UK's 1949 Adoption of Children Act installed the principle that 'the "otherness" of the adopted child would be completely assimilated within a new adoptive family who would mimic in every possible respect the biological tie between parents and children in "natural" families. This was reflected in new practices for the recruitment of adopters, who had to "pass" as biological parents' (64). The necessity of resemblance encapsulated not only bodily features but also cultural and personal behaviours. In terms of the United States, Mark C. Jerng has written of 'the supposedly empirical traits such as racial and religious background to less definable traits such as temperament, intelligence and personality' that were 'supposed to add up to some kind of identification between parent and child', despite the fact that similarity is no guarantee of connection but rather the product of 'narrative imagination' (95). The focus especially on racial and cultural resemblance in adoption matches should alert us to the centrality of biocentric attitudes towards the craft of family-making, where physical similarity is taken to signify and secure appropriate filial attachments. Ideally, it seemed, the adoptive status of a family should be unremarkable, not noticeable at large.

At the same time, the administration of adoption functioned to keep quiet the predicaments and circumstances of its key participants. As John Triseliotis, Julia Feast and Fiona Kyle write, while adoption 'is a crucial long-term institution in virtually all societies [...] in Western societies it has also come to be closely associated with secrecy' (1). Keeping adoption a secret has often had an important societal function. According to Sally Sales, in post-war Britain adoption 'emerged as a response to both the infertile parent, incapable of contributing to the pronatalism campaign [of the time], and the unmarried mother, producing children but under the wrong moral conditions' (63). Through adoption, infertile women could keep to themselves their medical circumstances, while women deemed immoral need not have to live with the consequences and the stigma of unwed single parenthood. Adoption often meant that few, if any, others need know about such private circumstances – sometimes even the adoptees themselves – and that the normative values of the day remained undisturbed. Once the adoption had been finalized, nothing need be said.

Secrecy has been built into both the culture and legislation of adoption arrangements. Several of the US birth-mothers whom Ann Fessler interviewed spoke of being sent away as soon as their pregnancies began to show or being made 'to hide in the house so their pregnancy wouldn't be seen, drawing the drapes and making them duck down when they were in the car' (72). Even after surrendering their children, the matter remained firmly silenced. One interviewee, Marge, reported that '[i]t's still not talked about in my family, still not mentioned. If I bring it up, people will say, "Oh, that was so long ago, why are you thinking about it now?"' (83). Most adoption contracts, until only relatively recently (and even then only in a few places), required the sealing of the birth-mother's identity so that adoptees would have no right to this information and be unable easily to trace their whereabouts in later years. In England and Wales, it took the Children Act of 1975 to grant adoptees access to birth records, although all those whose adoptions were contracted before 1975 must attend a compulsory meeting with a social worker before they can apply for their initial birth certificate (as I experienced when I requested my documents in January 2014). In a similar vein, the names of the adopting parents were rarely conveyed to birth-mothers who today often still have no legal right of access to their children's whereabouts. Some adoptees do not necessarily know of their adopted status. Triseliotis, Feast and Kyle record – most worryingly, to my mind – that 'the secrecy encouraged by the legislation also influenced a significant number of adoptive parents not to disclose the adoption to the child and may also have contributed to the perceptions of the birth family as potentially intrusive, both emotionally and physically' (16). As is explored in *So Many Ways to Begin* (2006) – Jon McGregor's novel of a British man born to an Irish birth-mother in London – the discovery later in life that one is adopted can have profound emotional consequences.

It might be presumed that transcultural adoptions conspicuously interrupt the machinations of adoption from functioning secretly and transgressively break the silent trysts often struck to uphold societal standards. Especially in transracial families, where bodily resemblance is perceived as remote rather than intimate, the perception of non-consanguineous family attachments has the capacity to lay bare the presence of adoption contracts in daily life and to challenge normative modes of family-making which require evidence of biogenetic ancestry. But things are not so predictable. Actually, transcultural adoption has been often mobilized precisely to keep in place, rather than disrupt, normative social and cultural attitudes.

In his memoir *Where Are You Really From?* (2010), the Belfast-born mixed-race adoptee Tim Brannigan memorably tells of his conception in the mid-1960s by his Catholic white birth-mother, Peggy, and a black junior doctor, Michael (both were married to other people at the time). The scandal of Peggy's pregnancy would have brought 'disgrace upon her family' (14). By chance, Peggy was a volunteer at the St Joseph's Foundling Home in Belfast run by the Nazareth Sisters, which housed 'the children of young women who had become pregnant out of wedlock, sometimes as a result of rape and incest. Those keen to adopt were spoiled for choice and the number of children available meant that checks for parental suitability were often perfunctory' (9). When Peggy delivered her son, she lied to her family that he had been stillborn and had Tim secretly housed at the Foundling Home. After a year of bringing him to visit her family home each week, Peggy was encouraged by her family formally to adopt Tim due to the emotional attachment she seemed to have struck with him:

> She was able to claim, plausibly, that I was another of the black kids she always brought home, randomly chosen by her from those in care. 'I just told everyone I felt sorry for you in that home', she told me years later.

'Everyone knew black children didn't get picked for adoption, so people were sympathetic and didn't think to question anything.' (18)

In this example, Peggy's highly gendered act of perceived sexual and moral transgression is accommodated through a secret act of transracial adoption which permits normative attitudes towards race and sexuality to continue undisturbed. It is intolerable for Peggy genetically to produce a mixed-race son as this violates the performative scripts of female and racial propriety that demonize the consanguineous consequences of interracial sexual intercourse through vile notions such as miscegenation. But Peggy *can* be an adoptive mother to a mixed-race child, because an adoptive family contract evidences the compassionate face of an otherwise prejudicial culture that does not permit racialized blood-lines to be transfused. In adopting her own biogenetic child, then, Peggy secured her future as a legitimate mother.

Brannigan's is an extraordinary but also indicative incidence of how transracial and transcultural adoptions are able to stabilize rather than unseat biocentric norms. Peggy's manipulation of the racist culture she inhabits marks both her determined ingenuity and the constraints with which the administration of adoption is often complicit. In her study of the adoption of predominantly Indian-born children by Swedish families in recent years, Barbara Yngvesson discusses how transcultural adoption enables the nation to perform a version of itself as a tolerant, compassionate and multicultural society, receptive to the needy and untroubled by accommodating difference. Through the creation of transcultural families, 'the adoptee came to emblematize Sweden's vision (and its hope) to become a multicultural nation' (*Belonging* 97). The appearance of such families as transcultural becomes something of a ruse. Rather than form a culturally pluralized unit that facilitates a greater literacy of contact between diversified cultural inventories, such families act as conduits for cultural assimilation where the adoptee is inducted into the cultural and national protocols of Sweden, tolerated as a consequence of their compliance but ever marked by their perceived difference. Such adoptees, then, are particular kinds of privileged and idealized immigrants, conveniently decultured, brought not just to Sweden but into Swedishness without the disruptive traces of Indian cultural activity (language, costume, faith, behaviour), and meant to be willingly and gratefully assimilative of the dominant mode. Their presence in Swedish families confirms the romantic notion of adoptive parenting as 'a form of love that exceeded the boundaries of nations and the ethnicized and racialized exclusions through which national identities are constructed' (99). In other words, the celebration of the Swedish transcultural family as transcending race and ethnicity kept secret the continuing agency of race and nation in national discourses, so that 'the racialized world order that produced transnational adoption could be made invisible' (104). While Yngvesson also records the capacity of transcultural adoption to exceed this modus operandi and menace normativity – she points to 'the struggles of the adopted to change the meaning of "belonging"' (104) – her research suggests that, in turning now to representations of transcultural adoption, we must not mistake the occurrence of transcultural families as evidence of transfigurative agency at large. Transcultural adoptions can be complicit in keeping secrets despite the often conspicuous adoptive make-up of the family unit.

As Triseliotis, Feast and Kyle rightly remind us, the issue of secrecy in adoption is not only a legal or political concern, 'not an empirical but an ethical issue' (16). At the level of intimate transpersonal relations, keeping secret the particulars of those who constitute an adoption triad and the reasons why children have been surrendered in many ways supports a deeply problematic status quo. Secrecy holds in place biocentric norms by stimulating a sense of lost origins and broken lines of primary attachment which, as I argued in the previous chapter, broker troubled selves. It maintains the suppression of the realities of cultural inequality and disenfranchisement, so that the material conditions which produce adoptability are cloaked by sob stories of foreign neglect and domestic rescue. Secrecy keeps one in the dark about consanguineous lines of connection and limits the knowledge of an adoptee's embedding within biogenetic and adoptive life lines. It amplifies feelings of fraudulence, powerlessness and insubstantiality – all inimical to adoptive being – because keeping secrets usually means telling lies. And it renders subservient the rights of adoptees in relation to other people's circumstances, with emotional and psychological consequences. In the words of adoptee novelist A. M. Homes, the bureaucratic cloistering of adoption can make adoptees feel that they 'don't really have rights, [that] their lives are about supporting the secrets, the needs and desires of others' (20).

How, therefore, does transcultural adoption writing seek ethically to challenge not just the incidence but the principle of secrecy? And what do we do with those transcultural adoption texts which, despite seeming otherwise, perpetuate rather than terminate transcultural adoption's complicity with secrecy?

In pursuing this latter question first, let us turn to Mike Leigh's celebrated film, *Secrets and Lies* (1996). This film was important for calling widespread public attention in the 1990s to the little-discussed matter of transcultural adoption in the UK, while it also resonated with audiences overseas. The success of *Secrets and Lies* at the 1996 Cannes Film Festival (where it received the Palme d'Or), along with the Oscar nominations gained by several of its cast, secured its visibility in the UK, Europe and North America. Its popularity led several adoption scholars and activists to appropriate the film as underlining the need to open up the secret histories and sealed records of adoption. In the new Afterword to the 2006 edition of her 1975 memoir of adoption, *Twice Born*, activist Betty Jean Lifton mentions *Secrets and Lies* as disclosing 'a positive attitude toward reunion in the imagination of the culture' despite the 'lobbyists'' prediction of doom and gloom should adoptees search' (269). As Marianne Novy writes in her introduction to the edited collection *Imagining Adoption* (2001) – the paperback edition of which features a still from the film on its cover – the film joins several other contemporaneous texts which help fashion a 'new world of adoption' where matters of nativity, genealogy and adoptees' subjectivity have become 'much more visible' (6). Paris De Soto's essay in Novy's collection captures the tenor of many early responses to the film in her emphasis on its seemingly productive, upbeat and appealing message. The film, she claims, eschews 'uncritical claims of authenticity and wholeness' and productively proposes that the biogenetic relation between birth-mother and adoptee 'is not a stronger or more stable bond' (204) than other kinds.

My response to the film is much less satisfied with its representation of transcultural adoption, and for several reasons, the most pressing of which is the secrecy that *persists* in its representation of race and its history in post-war Britain. Contrary to appearances, *Secrets and Lies* suffers from damaging problems of memory regarding adoption and race. Indeed, its dearth of engagement with the cultural and social particulars of the adoption contexts it evokes (Caribbean and black British) is a major reason why no meaningfully transfigurative vision of adoptive being appears. Instead, the family unit which results from *Secrets and Lies* is assimilative rather than transgressive. It is distinctly *not* transcultural in any dynamic or active way, but one where the mixed-race adoptee is accommodated snugly within a normative filial unit, the lineaments of which she refreshes rather than reshapes.

Writing in the *Hudson Review*, Bert Cardullo argues that Leigh's film 'is not about race in the way it would be had it been made in America. Race is a factor in *Secrets and Lies*, yes, but not a hateful, divisive, deeply ingrained one. Class is more of a factor here, as it is in all English films' (484). This remark may well turn on some well-worn assumptions about the differing visibility of race in public discourse on either side of the Atlantic, as well as on the cliché of English culture as essentially class-obsessed. Yet the film's relaxed engagement with matters of race in Britain is not so easily explicable. *Secrets and Lies* appeared only a few years after the fierce debates in the 1980s about race and adoption pursued by ABSWAP and others, as well as after a decade in which matters of racial minoritarization and discrimination more generally were confronted by the so-called 'second generation' of British-born black Britons. Given its historical moment and its subject matter, the minimal and problematic role which race plays in the film today looks rather astonishing. Leigh's attitude to race in a film of transracial adoption seems worryingly unconcerned with exploring in meaningful depth both the materiality and the complexity of the issues it inevitably raises, and so misses – by quite some distance – an opportunity to attend to the lives of black Britons and mixed-race adoptees with his much-lauded naturalism. If, as Tony Whitehead argues, Leigh works closely with his actors to 'create fully rounded characters whose lives and personalities are too complex to be shoe-horned into the tidy conventions of "realist" drama' (9), then *Secrets and Lies* falls short of this mark when it tries to deal with those impacted by adoption. Rather than take us into the interpersonal minutiae of those caught up in adoptive relations, Leigh at best offers an approximate rendering of adoption, and especially the adoptee, primarily as metaphor. This approach dispiritingly dissolves the materiality of adoptive experiences rather than negotiates between adoption as formative and figurative. Rather than read *Secrets and Lies* in terms of Leigh's much-vaunted cinematic naturalism, I suggest that the film presents an imperfectly imagined fantasy of adoptive attachments which struggles to connect with adoption's racial materiality and, most damagingly, is complicit in the ethically problematic practice of keeping adoption secrets. *Secrets and Lies* ends up keeping secret the particulars of its primary historical context upon which the film's cheerful message of filial openness ultimately rests. As such, Leigh's film cannot articulate a transfigurative envisioning of adoptive being because it cannot materialize the multidirectional lines of connection that are knotted in the figure of the transracial adoptee.

Secrets and Lies concerns the decision of a 27-year-old Londoner Hortense Cumberbatch (Marianne Jean-Baptiste), raised as the black daughter of migrant parents from the Caribbean, to trace her birth-parents following the death of her widowed mother. Her search leads her to Cynthia Purley (Brenda Blethyn), a 42-year-old working-class factory worker who lives alone with her temperamental daughter Roxanne (Claire Rushbrook), and to the discovery that her birth-mother is white. This news means that Hortense is actually genetically mixed race, something of which she had not been aware. Cynthia is the sister of Maurice (Timothy Spall), whose successful career as a photographer has enabled him and his upwardly mobile wife, Monica (Phyllis Logan), to buy a large house in a middle-class suburban environment. Monica is proud of her new home but seems emotionally tense and imperious at times in her dealings with Maurice, and she clearly has little time for Cynthia. As Hortense and Cynthia's relationship grows after an initially precarious and emotionally taxing search and reunion, Cynthia's unhappy life seems to revive, although she keeps Hortense's identity a secret from her family not least because Roxanne was never told that she had a biogenetic sibling who was surrendered for adoption.

Matters come to a head at a birthday-party barbeque held by Monica and Maurice to celebrate Roxanne's twenty-first birthday, where a number of family secrets are at last laid bare. Fuelled by drink, Cynthia reveals that Hortense, who has attended the party under the guise of Cynthia's 'friend', is actually her daughter. During the emotional scene that follows, Cynthia tells Roxanne at long last of the identity of her father (who is American, and whom she met on holiday in Spain's Benidorm resort). Maurice chooses this same moment to reveal that Monica cannot bear children, which prompts the release of years of pent-up emotion and the beginnings of a rapprochement between Monica and Cynthia, of whom Monica admits she has been jealous. 'Secrets and lies', laments Maurice at the film's emotional climax. 'We're all in pain. Why can't we share our pain? I've spent my entire life trying to make people happy, and the three people I love the most in the world hate each other's guts, I'm in the middle and [shouting] *I can't take it any more*.' The birthday party marks the reconciliation and rebirth of consanguineous relations triggered by Hortense's arrival into the Purleys' lives and her public acknowledgement by Cynthia. The film ends on an optimistic note in Cynthia's back garden as she enjoys a cup of tea with Hortense and Roxanne that signals the women's refreshed relationships and the blending of a new family unit from these biogenetic attachments.

As this short plot summary may suggest, throughout *Secrets and Lies* Leigh's attention is primarily focused on the fortunes of the Purleys and their many tense and often uncomfortable family relationships. These are by no means loveless, but they are corrupted by feelings of pain, fear, loss and jealousy. Important elements of the Purleys' various back-stories are provided so each character can be located in a wider familial and emotional matrix. Cynthia and Maurice's mother died when they were young, which left Cynthia to fill the void in the family from a young age; the disappearance of Roxanne's father prior to her birth meant that Maurice at the age of seventeen took on a fatherly role as regards his niece. Monica also lost her father as younger girl and has not seen her brother in years. Yet while some information is provided about Hortense, we are given very little detail of her background. Many vital questions are left unanswered or unexplored. The film's opening scene, which depicts the burial of her mother, shows that Hortense has been raised in a large black British family and community. She tells Cynthia that she has two brothers, although their names are never given. It is hinted that her parents were from Barbados and her mother was a midwife, but any further information about their lives is not disclosed. In a conversation with her friend Dionne a single reference is made to a mysterious Bernard (a friend? a lover?) who has sent a sympathy card after her mother's funeral, but for the bulk of the film Hortense lives alone and does not have a partner. Indeed, in a scene set on her birthday she sits alone contentedly reading a copy of Jung Chang's *Wild Swans: Three Daughters of China* (1991) with only the birthday cards sat on the shelf behind her reminding us that she has unseen attachments. Her distinctly solitary life means that at the film's climax she can join the Purley family without bringing with her the complications of children, or a partner, or siblings or surviving adoptive parents. She becomes the catalyst for the Purleys' communal confession. But of her own life, little is revealed: Leigh repeatedly uncouples Hortense from the inconveniences of pre-existing relations. We see her two brothers minimally, squabbling over her deceased mother's property rather than talking to their sister, while her friendship with Dionne preoccupies only one scene.

In tandem with Stephen Bourne's conclusion that Hortense is merely a 'white liberal's creation' (62), we might think of Hortense as much more cipher than character, denied a distinct disposition and saved from flatness and anonymity only by a spirited performance by Marianne Jean-Baptiste. Even Tony Whitehead concedes that Leigh 'does play down "the black experience", in the sense that we see little of Hortense's personal life apart from that brief glimpse of her family' and her exchange with Dionne, although he tries to minimize its significance with unconvincing words about Leigh nobly choosing *not* to make a film in which black characters' 'ethnic background is specifically relevant' (127). The film's wilful inability to know or say much about the politics and practices of adoption and race severely contradicts its feel-good message of openness, acknowledgement and forgiveness when it comes to family affairs.

The elision of black family or community attachments in Leigh's film is part of a wider absence concerning the most unusual and important element of the film's portrayal of transracial adoption: the fact that the Cumberbatches are *a black adoptive family who have adopted a mixed-race child*. The chances of such a family forming in 1960s Britain would have been quite rare due to the dearth of prospective black adoptive parents at the time, primarily due to reasons of class. Most adoptive parents in Britain historically have been middle class. But in the post-war years, Britain did not yet have a sizeable black middle class, so sourcing parents for racial 'matching' was particularly difficult. Owen Gill and Barbara Jackson report that at the time 'there was a failure to recruit adoptive parents from [Britain's] black community' (3), something also due to the cultural bias of white-oriented adoption agencies and the 'unwillingness of black parents to submit themselves to the investigations of a white bureaucracy' (3). Their survey of transracial adoptive placements found that the 'majority of workers appear to accept the desirability of finding black homes for black children and yet in practice such placements did not occur. All but a few of the workers we contacted said that they had difficulty in recruiting enough "suitable" black families for their waiting black children' (3). Sue Elliott points out that the adoption of black and mixed-race children into white homes happened because 'non-white adopters were not being specifically targeted' (204) during the 1960s. Such reasons explain why, in Derek Kirton's words, there was 'small-scale recruitment of black adoptive families' (15) by adoption agencies and social services at the time, to the extent that in 1975 there was launched the Soul Kids Campaign as a consequence of, in Ravinder Barn's summary, the 'growing awareness of the high numbers of black children in the care system, and the low recruitment of black substitute families' (119). We might note, too, the homogenizing of mixed-race and black adoptees, and the assumption that mixed-race children cleaved more to black rather than white families when racial matches were sought. For example, of the fifty-three adoptees that featured in the British Adoption Project of 1965 (see Introduction) concerning transracial placements, thirty-four were of mixed race.

These important material conditions enable us to regard as a serious blind spot the absence in *Secrets and Lies* of an account of the exceptional status of the Cumberbatches as an adoptive family. If we accept the basic premise of the film that a migrant couple from Barbados adopted a mixed-race child in the UK in the late 1960s, then they would have had to overcome some considerable challenges concerning class and race prejudice. While Hortense's status as a mixed-race adoptee born in 1968 is entirely plausible, her adoption into a Caribbean migrant family at this time is remarkably unusual. Given the exceptional circumstance of the Cumberbatches as an adoptive unit – black, migrant, middle class – one wonders why the film has nothing to say about any of this. Leigh seems either unconcerned about or simply does not know of the *rarity* of adoptive families like the Cumberbatches. Given its lack of concern for these matters, *Secrets and Lies* singularly fails to attend to the racial and class specifics of post-war adoption in Britain and so ends up, through its lack of cognizance, keeping secret the prejudicial constraints which circumscribed adoptive arrangements at the time.

Consequently, Leigh's film does not enquire into the consequences for subjectivity and being that result from Hortense's discovery that she is genetically mixed race. The film acknowledges that tracing can be upsetting for adoptees without ever really plumbing the emotional depths that are recorded in virtually all search and reunion narratives. Hortense cries quiet tears as she reads her adoption file for the first time, when she peruses it at home later and when she talks with Cynthia on the phone. Indeed, the film's first sight of her is in tears at her mother's funeral. These quiet displays of emotional upheaval suggest an uneasy equivalence between different kinds of grief. Their silence marks the limits of the film's capacity to articulate the phenomenon of transracial adopted life. Hortense literally has nothing significant to say about the discovery of her mixed-race history and her birth-mother. She does not talk at length to others about her trace, while the revelation of her racial heredity seems not to impact on her everyday life. When she initially raises the matter of her birth-mother's racial identity with her social worker Jenny, who is rushing to an emergency meeting, she has no answer when Jenny asks 'it's perfectly feasible that your mother was white, isn't it?' In the long conversation with her friend Dionne, Hortense's upheavals are hardly given a mention. Instead she appears convivial and in high spirits, fortified by a good meal and wine, and talks about her adoption with a degree of cryptic philosophical detachment: 'We choose the parents in this life that can teach us something; so that when we go into the next life, we get it right.' At no point does the revelation of Hortense's racial heredity preoccupy her, trigger a crisis or epiphany of selfhood or provoke any kind of discernible weighty reaction on her part. When set against Catherine McKinley's similarly surprising discovery of mixed-race biogenetic heredity described in her memoir *The Book of Sarahs: A Family in Parts* (2002) (which I discuss in Chapter 3), this elision is all the more conspicuous.

Repeatedly in *Secrets and Lies*, Hortense and indeed the film go silent when the consequences *for her* of her adoption are broached. In the famous reunion scene between Hortense and Cynthia set in a Central London café (which Leigh films in one brilliant eight-minute-long shot), Hortense's vital questions concerning the mysterious identity of her black birth-father come to naught, and she is left sitting silently while Cynthia changes the subject back to herself. The scene ends with Hortense recalling the moment she was told that she was adopted, on a plane returning to the UK from Barbados, and her silent reaction: 'I just looked out at the clouds.' This key comment, to which

I'll return, captures the ascendency of silence and the cloudiness of vision from which the film suffers whenever it approaches the emotional marrow of adoptee experience. At Roxanne's birthday party, Hortense tries further to discover her biogenetic paternity, once more to no effect. Again she ends the scene silently, comforting Cynthia while quietly subordinating any upset she may be feeling to her birth-mother's histrionics. While some might argue that Hortense's silences capture the inexpressibility of her identitarian crisis and emotional pain, their regularity, interchangeability and blandness keep her character's experiential depths unplumbed. She is never depicted experiencing the kind of emotional turbulence faced by her birth-mother. Rather, Hortense's ready tears and frequent silences evidence Leigh's film's poverty of concern for the specifics, stresses and standpoint of a transracial adoptee confronted with the mystery and surprise of her mixed-race biogenetic heredity.

I am concerned, then, that *Secrets and Lies* sidesteps the significance of race to the matter of adoption and remains silent, like Hortense, on its ramifications for the mixed-race adoptee. In one of the film's most troubling moments of adoption amnesia as Hortense and Cynthia dine together at an Italian restaurant, Hortense comments that 'I've got so many things to ask you, but I can't remember what they are'. The story of Cynthia's conception of her child and her surrendering is never adequately told. Trifling like this with race and adoption can bring unfortunate consequences. Consider the fact that *Secrets and Lies* never reveals the manner in which Hortense has been conceived, despite Hortense's repeated questions. At the reunion in the café, Cynthia claims that she has never 'been with a black man' until she locates a stray memory that prompts her to break down into uncontrollable tears and admit that she is 'so ashamed'. But she firmly answers Hortense's questions about her birth-father's identity with 'you don't wanna know that' and 'I can't tell you that, sweet'eart, I'm sorry', and determinedly keeps his presence a secret. At the climactic birthday party, when Hortense asks once again, she receives another emotionally fraught answer: 'Oh, don't break my heart, darling'. Hortense's question is never answered, and so the film concludes by revealing everyone's secrets except this one. This refusal to identify the black birth-father and the details of Hortense's conception creates troubling responses. It is worth noting that several critics have tended to presume that Cynthia must have been involved in sexual assault or abuse, even though there seems scant evidence to support this in the film. Graham Huggan argues that 'Leigh skilfully manipulates racial stereotypes of marginalization and rejection, recoding these in terms of sexual abuse (the abandoned single mother) and, particularly, the anxieties surrounding perceived differences of social class' (78). Richard Armstrong summarizes *Secrets and Lies* as 'a story of a girl conceiving a child through her rape, giving it [*sic*] up to adoption, and left to bring up another alone' (113). Even Tony Whitehead, who is sensitive to the deliberate mystery of Hortense's nativity, wonders '[c]ould it, even, have been a rape? Whatever, the memory is obviously traumatic, painful and long-suppressed' (121). At least Paris De Soto chooses to resist reading Hortense's nativity in terms of rape 'because such a reading resorts to simplistic and harmful stereotypes of black manhood and fatherhood that I do not think the film intends to perpetuate' (206). Yet the fact that she mounts this commendable argument evidences the spectre of sexual assault that surrounds Hortense's conception.

The film's inability to clear up the incident makes the film susceptible to perpetuating the figure of the black male as a sinister sexual predator. If, like De Soto, we think the film intends no racial aspersions, then the keeping secret of Hortense's birth-father's identity is clearly counterproductive to this aim. Leigh may want to link Cynthia's unhappy life to her forbidding past with sensitivity by not exposing the details of her teenage encounters, especially if she was subject to sexual assault at the age of fifteen. Such events may be too traumatic to articulate. Notwithstanding, the absence of any specific information about Hortense's birth-father runs the risk of identifying the threat of sexual assault not with the criminality and faults of any single person but with black men in general. Onyekachi Wambu has forcefully argued that in the film 'the Black man remains somewhere on the edge of the abyss, a dark shadowy figure who in this movie cannot be brought in from the cold' (qtd. in Bourne 63). Nowhere is this more true than in the spectral figure of Hortense's birth-father, the concealing of whose identity maintains worrying assumptions about black male sexuality and behaviour that come to toxify Leigh's film.

We might account for Leigh's uninformed approach to the materiality of transracial adoption by deciding that, in *Secrets in Lies*, adoption is meant primarily to function figuratively rather than phenomenologically, and as a catalyst for dramatic action rather than a material predicament worthy of cinematic exploration. But this means that the film comes close to deleting adoption's materiality by treating it as an opportunistic device to announce ethical truisms – clinched in Maurice's lament at the birthday party about secrets and lies – rather than an opportunity to unseal transracial adoption histories. Just as Cynthia forgets Hortense's birth-father (and indeed Hortense's birthday), Leigh's film frequently forgets to consider the consequences of the transracial adoptee's materiality and experiential horizon. It stubbornly subordinates the predicament and needs of the transracial adoptee to the arrested emotional development of the white Purley family, whose problems Hortense resolves by enabling the possibility of admitting their secrets, not hers: Monica's infertility, Roxanne's heredity, Cynthia's conceiving of two children rather than one. Hortense provides the means for Cynthia's regeneration and for mending relations between Cynthia, Roxanne and Monica. But the Purleys do not become a transcultural family by learning of Hortense's presence. As the film closes, there is little sense that Maurice and the others will meet with Dionne or Hortense's brothers, or with those mourners glimpsed at the funeral. As Graham Huggan moots, 'it is the self-assured, dignified Hortense who ends up "adopting" her emotionally fragile birth-mother, nursing her slowly back to health and providing the unlikely catalyst that allows her dysfunctional family to resolve their differences and, eventually, to reunite' (78). Roxanne's birthday party in effect marks the Purleys' rebirth and regeneration, against which Hortense's needs remain less pressing. The Purleys emerge as an improved rather than a transformed family, with Hortense's racial and cultural difference having had no significant impact of how they might now think of, or situate, themselves transculturally.

To be sure, if Leigh's neglect for the particulars of Hortense's adoption experience reveals the limited horizon of *Secrets and Lies*, there is something to be said about his attention to Cynthia, the white birth-mother. Leigh appears laudably to expose the emotional complexity and pain of this member of the adoption triad who is least explored in adoption representations, usually because, as Margaret Homans put it, her de-ontologizing 'erasure' (252) is required both legally and emotionally in adoption contracts. Pejorative representations of birth-mothers are not unusual in clinical studies, which sometimes account for the decision to surrender children as the result of psychological or personality traits rather than the consequence of disenfranchising cultural and social conditions. In their book *Being Adopted* (1992), David M. Brodzinsky,

Marshall D. Schechter and Robin Marantz Henig suggest that the 'intrauterine environment for many adopted children might have been one in which the birth mother was casual about using cigarettes or alcohol or drugs, failed to get prenatal care' and that 'whatever personality traits led the birth parents to the pregnancy in the first place – impulsiveness, immaturity, poor judgement – may themselves have a genetic component, which could be passed on to the child. [… T]his genetic component and prenatal legacy could explain the increased problems in psychological adjustment later in [the adoptee's] childhood' (39). This biocentric rendering of 'personality traits' distracts attention from those political and environmental matters that have produced adoption circumstances and behaviours, to the extent that a birth-mother's predicament appears entirely her own doing. As Betty Jean Lifton writes, '[I]t is only after getting to know a number of birth mothers as real people that we begin to perceive relinquishment not as a rejection but as a result of social and personal pressures that the young mother could not withstand' (*Lost and Found* 208).

So often the missing person, the birth-mother's painful existence is importantly placed to the fore in *Secrets and Lies*. Yet the character of Cynthia does not fully detach from prevailing assumptions about birth-mothers, and arguably only Brenda Blethyn's outstanding performance saves Cynthia from descending into familiar cliché. One concern is Cynthia's frequent presentation of herself as a sexual creature, promiscuous when younger and awkwardly in competition with her daughter Roxanne now that she has reached her forties. In an early exchange while admiring her legs, she reminds Roxanne that when she was younger she 'could have had the pick of the crop', and she asks repeated questions about Roxanne's boyfriend, Paul (Lee Ross), much to her daughter's discomfort. Later we see Cynthia silently contemplating herself in a mirror, drunken and depressed, pushing her breasts together in a sadly provocative fashion as if to recall the young attractive woman she once was. In another upsetting scene, she tries to dole out advice on contraception to Roxanne who is not in the mood to have a discussion about such private matters, and the discussion ends badly when Cynthia offers to raise any child which Roxanne conceives ('I'll give up my job', she pleads). Such moments situate Cynthia ambivalently. On the one hand, Leigh calls attention to Cynthia's abbreviated adolescence due to her pregnancies when younger and the loss of her mother at an early age. In her fraught concern with Roxanne's love-life, we might detect her attempt to reclaim that loss by proxy – just as Cynthia's peculiar declaration that she could raise Roxanne's offspring speaks to a repressed longing to raise a lost child. And when compared to both Roxanne's and Dionne's 1990s sexual behaviour, which is less constrained by social stigma or by the threat of unwanted pregnancy and moral taboo (Dionne boasts to Hortense that she recently has had sex with a stranger), Cynthia's lost youth and painful act of surrender point to the unhappy conditions under which women like her laboured in the 1960s when it came to matters of sexual agency.

On the other hand, Cynthia seems persistently concerned with the sex lives of others and speaks of little else. When Maurice visits her at home the conversation soon turns to memories of his previous girlfriends (Maxine had 'nice thighs', she remembers). While having a drink with Hortense, she asks her newly discovered daughter about her preferred male type, if she sleeps only with black men and which contraception she prefers. These may be reasonable conversations and concerns. But if the cultural cliché of the birth-mother fundamentally anchors her to her sexual behaviour and prioritizes this above all other elements of her character, then the figure of Cynthia (whose name unhelpfully carries the phoneme 'sin') does not readily displace this primary association. Matters are scarcely helped by her explanation to Hortense in the café that 'I didn't know you was black', not just because she was not allowed to see her but because 'I thought you was born six weeks premature'. This may be a reference to another sexual relationship which Cynthia had aged fifteen, and greatly complexifies the charge of sexual assault presumed by some against Hortense's birth-father. The point at stake here is *not* Cynthia's promiscuity but the fact that, as Leigh depicts her, she is associated with little more than sexual affairs. This primary association does little to open up a more three-dimensional rendering of the birth-mother figure that contests or detaches from received notions of her as primarily a casual or impulsive sexual figure.

Cynthia's cliché characterization is not helped by her child-like neediness and craving of attention which drives her drinking. Her alcoholic proclivities index the measure of her unhappy life, struggling to make ends meet amidst a milieu of misery and loneliness; but they also evidence and accentuate forms of behaviour that can appear irresponsible and unconcerned with consequences. Her revelation of Hortense's consanguineous connection at Roxanne's birthday party is not the product of a considered decision or one taken with Hortense's consent, but happens due to Cynthia's drink-infused jealousy of Monica and Maurice's financial gift to Roxanne. Arguably, Cynthia's actions here are selfish and self-centred. She tells of Hortense's relation to her while Hortense is in the toilet, absent from the scene and without any warning. When Hortense returns and realizes that the secret is out, she admits that 'it wasn't meant to happen like this'. Cynthia makes it clear that Hortense's role is subordinate to her own and commands her to back up her up: 'Yeah, well, it has, ain't it? So you tell them – go on'. In the ensuing family conversations, Hortense speaks hardly at all, and even then mainly to support the truth of the revelation, while her question of paternity, as we have seen, goes unanswered. Cynthia's behaviour and motivation, again, do little to shift the perception of birth-mothers as defined by 'impulsiveness, immaturity, poor judgement'. Dispiritingly, the birthday party is another cloudy episode in the film. While it may offer a release of Cynthia's pent-up pain and open the way to refreshed relations with Monica, Maurice and Roxanne, the resolution on offer perpetuates the pain of the adoptee for whom paternity remains a sealed-up secret, a matter which, for the sake of others, Hortense must let lie.

As I briefly noted, when Hortense tells Cynthia that she learned of her adoption while flying back from Barbados, she describes a silent moment of airborne recollection: 'I just looked out at the clouds.' Richard Armstrong reads Hortense's words, a little bizarrely, as 'a beautiful metaphor for her history' which resonates with Leigh's interest in 'the consequences of traditional English reserve' (112). Leaving aside the matter of whether or not an adoptee's silent response to the revelations of their biogenetic genealogy constitutes 'reserve', I would propose instead that the clouds metaphorize the film's ultimately foggy incomprehension of adoption and race which remain obscure, obfuscatory matters, beyond the limits of its horizon of knowledge. The clouds mark the limits of the film's ability to see into and say something about the concrete, material particulars of transracial adoption, the experiential and emotional depths which remain throughout distinctly hazy and significantly silenced. It is a revealing metaphor in a film which otherwise stresses the need for clarity and truthfulness over secrets and lies, and indexes its commitment to vision in details such as Hortense's career as an optometrist and Maurice's life as a photographer of family portraits. Indeed, the arrival of the optometrist

Hortense into the home of the photographer Maurice is meant to suggest a clearing of vision as secrets are brought to the light of day. Hortense's arrival brings focus, sharpness and clarity of insight to the Purleys who are made at last to see that which has been covered up. This is the film which Leigh believes he has made. But as regards the matter of transracial adoption, the film's vision remains distinctly cloudy.

Ultimately, *Secrets and Lies'* lack of vision concerning transcultural adoption is summed up by an early scene that concerns an anonymous little girl whose sight Hortense is testing. When invited to look through a lens and read a series of letters, the girl reads out the largest but then admits 'I can't read anymore'. In a similar fashion, *Secrets and Lies* can only discern in bold, unsubtle terms the serious matter of adoption and race, and so it makes up a feel-good fantasy which stands in for the complex material circumstances of transracial adoptive attachments. Its appropriation of adoption to argue for an ethical rejection of family secrets is contradictory and too detached from the material particulars it evokes but ultimately evades. Too much remains unspoken or blurred. With the historical circumstances of Hortense's adoption left unexplored and her paternity unresolved, *Secrets and Lies* cannot effect a transfigurative articulation of adoptive being as vital signs of multidirectional connection are not adequately tracked. Instead, and fatally, they remain sealed secrets.

One could defend Leigh from the critique I have offered by pointing out that his work, rightly or wrongly, never pretends to prioritize race in Britain nor offers profound representations of it because his focus is primarily elsewhere. In turning now to the fiction of Andrea Levy, British-born daughter of Jamaican migrant parents, one might expect a greater sensitivity to matters of race in adoption contracts because Levy has often centrally thematized issues of migration, racism and black British identity across much of her writing. In her novel *Small Island* (2004), we discover a representation of transcultural adoption that appears much more knowing of adoption's racialized materiality, but one which also remains complicit with biocentric norms, especially the rarefied role granted to consanguineous kinship. As we shall see, *Small Island* is a highly contradictory representation of transcultural adoption. On the one hand, it articulates an important cognizance of the cultural and historical specifics of adoption for colonized and minoritized people, and invites us to think how the assimilative act of transcultural adoption might be productively activated in situ as a resistant rather than fully compliant endeavour that contends with prohibitive constraints such as race and gender. On the other hand, however, the novel maintains a privileging of consanguineous relations that keeps in place racialized notions of cultural attachment and so rules out the possibility of rethinking consanguineous and adoptive relations as equivalent. *Small Island*, then, is a paradoxical text when it comes to its representation of transcultural adoption, and its paradoxical condition hinders it from thinking more creatively and incipiently about adoptive being. Ultimately, the novel is compromised by the fact that its narrative turns on the keeping of an important secret about blood-lines.

At the end of *Small Island*, set in the talismanic year of 1948 when the *S. S. Empire Windrush* arrived at Tilbury docks, Queenie Bligh, the Midlands-born white landlady of lodgings in London's Earls Court, gives birth to a mixed-race child whom she conceived with a Jamaican member of the RAF, Michael Roberts. Michael had passed through London on his way to a new life in Canada. Queenie enjoyed her brief relationship with Michael, believing that her husband, Bernard, a white British RAF serviceman, had died in action overseas, and she is stunned by Bernard's unexpected return in 1948 only a few days prior to her going into labour. The child is delivered at home with the help of Hortense Joseph, one of Queenie's Jamaican tenants, who has just arrived in London to join her husband Gilbert Joseph. Coincidentally, Michael is the biogenetic son of Hortense's father's cousin in whose house Hortense was raised as a consequence of her being born 'out of wedlock' (31) in Jamaica. The birth of Queenie's son (also called Michael, and to whom I'll refer as 'baby Michael' to keep things clear) prompts a number of secrets to be confessed: Queenie's intimacy with a Jamaican serviceman, the bodily evidence of which she has sought to conceal beneath layers of painful bandages; Bernard's decision not to return immediately to London after being demobbed in 1945 as he believed he had contracted a fatal case of syphilis from an Indian prostitute; Bernard's imprisonment for deserting his post and losing his weapon during a fire at his Calcutta *basha*. Unaware of the identity of the infant's father, Hortense and Gilbert agree to adopt baby Michael in the final pages as Queenie claims she cannot look after him for reasons of race. She believes her son's life will be more secure as the black-looking child of Jamaican parents rather than the mixed-race progeny of a white woman. While the Gilberts agree to this arrangement and everything seems settled, Hortense's biogenetic links to the elderly Michael (and hence to her newly adopted son) are never revealed to the characters. In a final loving gesture, Queenie sews into the child's clothes a substantial sum of money and a picture of herself. Hortense discovers them and decides to set them to one side for 'good use when they were required. [...] I determined to keep a secret of both the money and the photograph' (438). *Small Island* closes, then, with the revelation but also the keeping of secrets.

As in the account of Tim Brannigan's adoption mentioned at the beginning of this chapter, baby Michael's transcultural adoption is intended to keep concealed the realities of cross-racial sexual relations in post-war London. Such liaisons were considered transgressive and threatening on the grounds of racial 'miscegenation' in the eyes of those keen to bind tightly together the ideas of race with nation in a country soon to be transformed by postcolonial migration. The novel's adoption arrangement appears at one level as an assimilative act as it remains complicit in the racial separatism that would become more and more central to discourses of British nationhood in the wake of post-war migration from the New Commonwealth. Rachel Carroll has noticed that the Gilberts' willingness to adopt the mixed-race child evokes 'a racial politics of reproduction which is troubling' and reminds us that 'in ways which are historically familiar a black woman is placed in service to white women's reproductive sexuality, and her willingness to nurse and rear another woman's child attributed to altruism rather than to economic or political hierarchy' (75). In writing about the racism of British life through a narrative of transcultural adoption, Levy valuably and critically brings to light the constraining agency of normative discourses of race and nation. She exposes the unequal and prejudicial material conditions which pressed women like Queenie into becoming birth-mothers not as parents and rendered mixed-race children adoptable. Baby Michael's adoption is soberingly assimilative, and Levy wishes to expose the ideological conditions that underwrite it. But she also invites us carefully to recognize the ways in which these ultimately assimilative filial rearrangements are not fully determined by imperious protocols but might also bear the traces and tactics of postcolonial agency in situ. Transcultural adoption, certainly at one level, is a complex affair in *Small Island*, both a means of prejudicial control and a site of resistant intervention: an occasion where disenfranchised people might act resistantly in a very tight space.

Levy's strategy of exposing racial and class inequalities through telling a tale of transcultural adoption as assimilation is threaded throughout *Small Island*. Baby Michael's adoption is not the only one which happens in the text. Hortense, too, experienced an informal adoption arrangement as a young girl. Her conception in Savannah-del-Mar was the outcome of exploitative colonial desire. Her father, Lovell Roberts, was a government man who worked overseas and whose fame was much cherished in the town: 'His picture was pinned to parish walls – cut from the newspapers of America, Canada and England' (31). His race is never specified, but the lightness of skin suggests significant European ancestry and therefore important social standing. He conceived Hortense with the unmarried Alberta, a 'country girl who could neither read nor write nor perform even the rudiments of her times tables' (31), and left her to deliver the child in a wooden hut. Inheriting her father's complexion – 'the colour of warm honey [...] not the bitter chocolate hue of Alberta and her mother' (32) – Hortense possesses the racial capital to do well in early twentieth-century Jamaica with its close alignment of social class with perceived racial gradations based on the shading of skin-colour. And so she was despatched with her maternal grandmother, Miss Jewel, to be raised as a 'lady worthy of my father' (32) by her father's cousins, Philip and Martha Roberts, with Miss Jewel in attendance as the Roberts' servants. Their son, Michael (whom Hortense calls her brother), becomes Hortense's childhood companion and first love. Informal adoption makes possible social advancement for Hortense within the discursive parameters of normative social relations. The light shading of her skin colour matters more than her attachment to her birth-mother Alberta, and permits Hortense to be relocated within the family to access education and social opportunities which result eventually in her training as a teacher. This relegation of maternal attachment is never problematized by Hortense, who hardly mentions Alberta again once she has recounted her conception.

Levy's exposure of adoption as a means of upwards mobility in Jamaica situates baby Michael's adoption in 1940s London as framed by colonial as well as metropolitan antecedents. In becoming adoptive parents, the Gilberts are replicating a not untypical practice in the Caribbean. Their actions are not fully determined by British racism. Hortense's informal adoption also enables

Levy to draw a line of connection between the colonial exploitative attitudes of the past and their replication at the heart of the Empire at the very talismanic moment – 1948 – often posited as marking the beginning of the unfinished postcolonial transformation of London triggered by a new generation of colonial migrants settling in the motherland. Transcultural adoption becomes one of the means by which Levy complicates '1948' as signifying a rupture or moment of transition, from London as colonial centre to postcolonial metropolis. In emphasizing the rearranging of Hortense's family in order to facilitate social opportunity, Levy underlines adoption as an act of racial and class assimilation which functions to sustain colonial and race relations. It is by no means an inherently radical act.

Baby Michael's adoption in London complexifies matters by exposing the more resistant and defiant possibilities that transcultural adoption might enable. When Hortense accepts the offer to mother baby Michael, she takes an opportunity in situ to enact transcultural adoption as a postcolonial tactic rather than a colonial practice, in defiance of British racist attitudes which would have the child expelled from the nation. Queenie is frightened that if she surrenders Michael to an orphanage he will be sent with other mixed-race adoptees to the United States (although, as we will note in Chapter 4, very few such surrendered children were ever adopted by American families in the 1940s). In adopting baby Michael, the Gilberts are negotiating cannily with the racist attitudes which cannot countenance Queenie acting as the mother of a racially marked child and threaten to void him of his familial and national attachments which his nativity in London empowers him to claim. While baby Michael's adoption ultimately will not contest the authority of race thinking, Levy's narration of these two families rearranging their filial attachments asserts the agential and defiant capacity of transcultural adoption to find ways round, if not through, racism's authority that structures domestic as well as public environments.

When faced with the news of his wife's pregnancy, Bernard initially proposes a new future away from Nevern Street in London's suburbs, but Queenie wonders how baby Michael will fit in to his plans for them to move, noting that as he speaks of the future Bernard 'wasn't looking at the baby, he had his back turned to him and he spoke it in a whisper' (424). In arguing that they can raise the child, Bernard turns to adoption counterintuitively as a solution for keeping the facts of baby Michael's nativity from being socially scandalous and disruptive: 'There's been a war on, all sorts of things happened. Adopted, that's what we'll say. An orphan. Quite simple' (431). Queenie acknowledges the 'caring' (431) impulse behind this idea but challenges Bernard regarding the persistence of race thinking in which he is frequently culpable:

> 'You might think you can do it now', I told him, 'while he's a little baby saying nothing. But what about when he grows up? A big, strapping coloured lad. And people snigger at you in the street and ask you all sorts of awkward questions. Are you going to fight for him? All those neighbours … those proper decent neighbours out in the suburbs, are you going to tell them to mind their own business? Are you going to punch other dads 'cause their kids called him names? Are you going to be proud of him? Glad he's your son?'
>
> 'Adopted, that's what we can say', he said, softly. This was blinking daft.
>
> 'Bernard. One day he'll do something naughty and you'll look at him and think, The little black bastard, because you'll be angry. And he'll see it in your eyes […].' (431)

Bernard's solution involves fictionalizing consanguineous attachments as adoptive in order to maintain the guise of racial and social propriety (as did Tim Brannigan's mother in 1960s' Belfast). In announcing baby Michael as the Blighs' adopted son, Queenie's biogenetic attachment to her son would be kept secret in order to maintain the normative social discourses that find fault with a white English woman enjoying relations with a black man. These are discourses which Bernard would himself struggle to subvert, as quickly proved by his disgracefully racist response to the idea that the Josephs act instead as adoptive parents: 'That poor little half-caste child would be better off begging in a gutter!' (434). Queenie's rejection of Bernard's solution indexes Levy's forceful exposure of the depth and perversity of race thinking which extends from public to private space. The scene also functions to add weight to the provocative perception that a cannily arranged transcultural adoption provides a better opportunity to protect baby Michael from racism than keeping the child with his biogenetic mother.

Levy can countenance the resistant stratagem of placing baby Michael at a remove from his birth-mother, but only so far. The tactics of transcultural adoption upon which the plot depends necessarily tilts the novel towards considering the possibility that family-making need not then be a matter of consanguineous attachment. Rather than think through or approach the creative and transfigurative possibilities that might result from the unhappy prejudicial materiality of adoption's circumstances, Levy pulls back towards the very race thinking against which the novel otherwise protests. To put this bluntly, Levy cannot have Michael raised in an adoptive family which is not legitimated consanguineously. In so doing she secretes her own concerns about adoptive families, with the result that her novel falls some way of short of thinking of adoption in terms of the multidirectional vectors of adoptive being. These anxieties are betrayed in three ways: in the biogenetic proximity which Levy draws between Hortense and baby Michael, in the increasing incidence of images of blood which stain the novel's climactic pages and in the keeping secret *from the characters but not the reader* full knowledge of the novel's entangled biogenetic and adoptive relations.

In a skilled reading of *Small Island*, Michael Perfect notices that as an adoptive family the Gilberts are both filial and affiliative: that is, related genetically as well as contracted adoptively. In commenting on the fact that baby Michael shares a distant blood relation with Hortense as the offspring of her presumed-dead brother-figure, Michael Roberts, Perfect suggests that '[t]his coincidence is a rather improbable one, and the fact that Levy shows such an uncharacteristic disregard for verisimilitude here certainly emphasises the importance of the connection which, it seems, none of the four protagonists are ever to grasp' (70). Perfect's observant reading of the novel underscores just how reluctant is Levy to let the Joseph family bond without letting consanguineous personhood play a definitive role. As the novel heads towards its climactic contracting of a transcultural adoption, we might notice that this desire for consanguinity further expresses itself in the advent of the Gilberts' sexual relations and through the repeated appearance of images of blood which implicate Hortense in family-making and biogenetic motherhood.

In heteronormative models of family-making in 1940s Britain, heterosexual couples would be expected to court, marry, have sexual relations safely within wedlock and conceive children, in strict sequential order. It is intriguing to note that Hortense and Gilbert's relationship has not progressed through this sequential narrative arc. In Jamaica, the couple come together in a marriage of convenience. Financially adrift after a business venture in beekeeping goes badly wrong, Gilbert agrees to marry Hortense in exchange for the price of a ticket on the S. S. *Empire Windrush*. '[S]he let me know that I would have to marry her for the money', he recalls: 'This woman was looking for escape and I was to be the back she would ride out on' (174). Hortense has fixated upon Britain as delivering her the socially comfortable life which her surrendering by Alberta was intended to realize. The couple do not consummate their marriage in Jamaica (Hortense is horrified by Gilbert's arousal on their wedding night) and on Hortense's arrival in Nevern Street, Gilbert grumpily vacates his bed and sleeps in an armchair. So why, we might ask, does Levy synchronize the couple's first sexual encounter just *after* baby Michael's birth – the two events are separated by three short chapters – and, additionally, why must Hortense play the part of Queenie's impromptu midwife? In terms of narrative progression, Levy significantly reverses the usual sequence of consummation followed by reproduction, and closely approximates baby Michael's birth with the Josephs' first sexual congress. Levy presents the birth as intimately aligned to their coupling, so that the Josephs' new life as adoptive parents is bound very closely indeed to an act of biological conception. The semantic consequences of this resequencing are highly revealing. Levy cannot imagine the novel's transcultural adoptive family-making as being contracted at a remove from the provenance of biogenetic creation.

Further to the proximity of baby Michael's birth with the Josephs' act of consummation, Levy is keen to strike another symbolic proximity by having Hortense bizarrely appear in her wedding dress while Queenie is in labour. She had worn it to a humiliating job interview earlier in the day in an effort to appear smartly attired, and returns to Nevern Street as Queenie begins her labour. As Hortense tells it, baby Michael's birth soils her dress significantly as she assists Queenie with the delivery:

> Soaking pink with the bloody spattered tissue, my poor dress wept. I picked up [the afterbirth] and dumped it in the bowl of boiled water. [...] Mrs Bligh tutted at the sight of my spoiled dress, then said, 'Come and look at him, Hortense'. She was crying again. 'He's a lovely little boy.'
>
> And I said to myself, Hortense, come, this is a gift from the Lord – life. What price is a little disgust on your best dress? I decided to pay it no mind. (399–400)

Baby Michael and his two mothers are in this intimate moment conjoined by the child's blood. Queenie's tears and Hortense's weeping dress figuratively bond the two women at the moment of birth, but we might note, too, how the blood-stained wedding dress also beckons an image of virginal sexual activity and marital consummation – 'a little disgust on your best dress'. The pink-stained dress engenders associations of intercourse, conception and birth at exactly the moment as baby Michael is delivered. The synchronization of conception and birth in one image consecrates Hortense's forthcoming role as adoptive mother in the blood of labour and ensures that she has played a key part in the visceral experience of conception and childbirth. Additionally, in an especially revealing detail, Levy has Queenie evacuate Michael's afterbirth into Hortense's lap: 'Looking like a piece of best liver it burst on to me as if I was some bullseye in a game. My anguished cry had Mrs Bligh straining to look beneath her knees at the commotion' (399). Hortense's cry fuses the sounds of sexual congress and of birthing, each a kind of commotion near the knees, if you will, and seals the synchrony of sex and reproduction. Levy's narration of baby Michael's arrival inducts Hortense into the visceral matter of reproduction that ultimately legitimates her impending motherhood through the proximate experiences of sexual congress and midwifery, providing her with the memory and the bloody, bodily traces of baby Michael's birth.

Hortense's wedding dress and its blood-soaked condition rhetorically normalize the transcultural adoptive relations which Levy puts in place as the novel closes. These relations are not exclusively adoptive, as Perfect notes, because there is the distant but firm consanguineous line of connection between baby Michael and Hortense. It seems, then, that Levy cannot countenance a domestic environment for her migrant family without traces of consanguineous kinship. The novel's inability to relinquish the conventional understanding of biogenetic attachment as privileged origin marks the limits of its critical agency. For these reasons, *Small Island* ends up reinforcing exactly what it seemed, cosmetically, to take apart via the narrative trope of transcultural adoption: racism, biocentricity, prejudice. Like Hortense in her stained wedding dress, *Small Island* is marked by blood.

Levy's advocacy of consanguinity is the half-hidden secret at the centre of her novel. Because *Small Island* does not fully relinquish an adherence to biocentric discourses of racial and cultural belonging, it cannot imagine blood-lines as one significant vessel of being amidst others that materialize matters of historical and cultural struggle rather than bodily proximity and cultural (Jamaican, black) authenticity and origin. The compounding of blood and secrecy is expressed in the novel's narrative design which keeps Michael's biogenetic relation to the Gilberts a secret from her characters but reveals this connection to readers. Only we can see the lines of attachment that are unknown by the characters. The consequences of this subterfuge are problematic. In mobilizing narratologically the much-contested mechanics of secrecy in adoption contracts, *Small Island* is rendered ethically suspect in its narrative design. One of the most important aspects of the 2009 BBC television adaption of the novel concerned its closing sequence where a now-grown-up Michael shows his grandchildren a photograph of Queenie he keeps in an album, just after the audience discovers that *he* has acted as the narrator whose voice-overs have described the action from the start. This remarkable moment, where a mixed-race man celebrates his connection with his white birth-mother, ensured that the television series did not remain complicit with the agency of secrecy left uninterrupted at the novel's end. On television, Michael ends the tale in the same place as the audience: in full receipt of the multidirectional histories which characterize the story, cognizant of Michael Roberts's paternity as well as Queenie's act of surrender (although *how* he has come to know the facts of his paternity is not entirely made clear). In the novel, things are different. Only we as readers can tell, and so we are left in the morally questionable – and, for me at least, highly discomfiting – position of knowing more about an adoptive contract than do its participants. For these reasons, *Small Island*'s unsteady and equivocating representation of transcultural adoption's attachments, agency and subversive potential is unable to facilitate a transformative conception of adoptive being like those we will witness elsewhere in *Life Lines*. While transcultural adoption's resistant potential in situ is certainly glimpsed and prized in the novel, its transfigurative possibilities ultimately remain unrealized and concealed.

As we have seen, the complicity of both Leigh's film and Levy's novel in keeping secrets in transcultural adoption contexts stymies their transfigurative agency and renders each text problematic rather than progressive. In turning now to the work of Mei-Ling Hopgood, I want to think about Hopgood's commitment to challenging secrecy as part of a wider rendering of adoptive family-making which is subversively transcultural rather than assimilative and normalizing. Hopgood's search and reunion memoir enables us to begin to think at length about blood-lines in material rather mystical terms, part of a wider fabric which weaves together myriad connections and knots the adoptive, biogenetic and experiential in a singular plural turn. The toxic agency of secrets in adoptive life is given a very different rendition in *Lucky Girl* (2009), Hopgood's account of her tracing and meeting her Taiwanese birth-parents and birth-siblings. The ethics of secrecy are central to Hopgood's memoir, not least because her book asks us to challenge not only the practice of secrecy in adoption contracts, but also the *adoptee's* complicity in keeping lines of attachment a secret. *Lucky Girl's* determined quest to expose and face the consequences of some dark and unhappy secrets in Hopgood's biogenetic Taiwanese family, the Wangs, pivots upon her coming clean in the first instance with herself and relinquishing her long-standing decision to build a primarily American selfhood by prohibiting thought about her biogenetic relations.

Prior to her trace, Hopgood's attitude to her birth-parents' historical and cultural domain is out of step with the ethical practice of her parents who always wished to conjoin their daughter's multidirectional histories. As a young girl, Hopgood kept disconnected her Taiwanese nativity and American life, thinking almost exclusively about the latter. But this tactic of separation gives way in the memoir to a coterminous and commensurate rendering of Taiwanese and American relations in situ, which propels Hopgood from an imperious position as an American with an Asian 'background' towards a distinctly transcultural standpoint, both material and noumenal, where the commitment to understand imperfectly (rather than to judge) the cultural behaviours of biogenetic relations is a central element of the ethical agency of adoptive being. *Lucky Girl* offers a particularly compelling response to one quandary of adopted life: *what might we do* when we unearth the little-discussed and painful material circumstances which produced adoptability in the first place, and which adoptees' behaviour might be helping keep secret?

Lucky Girl tells the story of Hopgood's birth in Taiwan in August 1973 and adoption by her mother Chris and father Rollie a few months later; her young life in Taylor, Detroit, and later St Louis; and her virtually accidental tracing of her Taiwanese birth family when she reaches her early twenties. It also reveals the early life of her birth-parents, Ma and Ba, and the impoverished conditions in which they raised their family before working their way into the Taiwanese middle class. The particulars of their past, while grounded in Hopgood's research, are inevitably imagined and the product of a complex process of translation. In the Acknowledgements, Hopgood thanks her biogenetic siblings and her brother-in-law 'for patiently answering, asking, and re-asking questions on my behalf and for translating to and from three languages' (np). From the beginning, then, Hopgood's cognizance of her birth-parents' lives is inevitably constrained by her displaced position as a transcultural subject. Her trace narrative, like so many others, engages in an inevitable fiction-making process even as it quests for truth, as ultimately it must picture a set of material and cultural circumstances which Hopgood cannot ever know securely. In Margaret Homans's words, 'even the most stringently honest memoirs cannot fail to resort not only to fictional techniques in telling their stories but also to fiction in constructing the very origin whose truth is so painstakingly sought' (122). Hopgood's commitment to pursuing truths which are ultimately beyond her reach is an important element of the book's ethical agency that is also expressed in its form. *Lucky Girl* shifts between a number of narrative modes that include autobiography, documentary record (letters, emails, etc.), fanciful fantasy, journalistic investigation and historiography, blending empiricism and conjecture, the verifiable and the imaginary. In terms of its narrative composition, *Lucky Girl* searches for an appropriate mode of representation to express the adoptive particulars of being-with.

Hopgood first travels to meet her biogenetic relations in 1997 and builds links with her many siblings during this and subsequent visits, but soon detects that the Wangs have been keeping secrets from her in order to maintain a benign image of their parents. Trained as a journalist, she makes the quest for these secrets the major preoccupation of the memoir. This requires her to face some unpalatable truths about her genetic parents' behaviour which have rested upon Ba's obsessive desire to father male heirs. The difficulties she experiences in dealing with her birth-parents as she discovers their secrets, both past and ongoing, not only complicate her attempts to bond with each, but also create surprising new possibilities for understanding, compassion and humility as Hopgood faces up to the dilemmas which the situation presents for her as a transcultural adoptee. These possibilities also extend to notions of being, as Hopgood's trace propels her to revise her narrative of selfhood in which she thinks of herself as a liberated American woman luckily free from the constraints of gender perceived in Chinese culture. Instead, *Lucky Girl* moots a mode of adoptive being in situ which operates transculturally, and which thinks past the lineaments and lineages of insistently consanguineous models of roots, heritage, resemblance and identity. In its final pages, as I will show, *Lucky Girl* seeks to express adoptive being by resequencing notions of time and space – intercalating diverse yet related historical and cultural relations – to suggest a way of being singular plural captured in an image of a textile: the 'collective tapestry so intricate that one string cannot be untangled from the other' (238).

Lucky Girl makes no secret of Hopgood's struggle as a young girl with an uneasy consciousness of her Taiwanese past. Its early stages chart her initial disavowal of the past that contrasts with the ethical position taken by Chris and Rollie. Hopgood's adoption was handled by Maureen Sinnott, the sister-in-law of a family friend who trained as a nun and was working as a midwife in Taiwan. Having made contact, Chris and Rollie Hopgood worked with Maureen over several months, dealing with the complex bureaucracy in both Taiwan and the United States, before the seven-month-old Mei-Ling was able to leave by air in the care of an airline representative and meet her parents at San Francisco Airport. Hopgood narrates these events in fine detail because she has at hand the correspondence between Maureen and her parents, some of which she reproduces in chapter titled 'The Odd Couple'. This openness towards documentation, between Chris and Rollie and their daughter and between Hopgood and her readers, underpins *Lucky Girl*'s openness to narratives of all kind, come what may, as part of its aversion to prohibition and hiding. Hopgood's parents' decision not to change her given name, Mei-Ling, helps secure transcultural adoption as a mode of multiple attachments and not erasure, refuses to set at odds biogenetic and adopted links and points to the necessary multidirectionality of transcultural adoptive life.

As part of their refusal to prohibit the past, Chris and Rollie appropriated 'adopted' and 'adoption' as the textual signs of an everyday existence. Hopgood remembers asking her mother if they sought not to speak about the conspicuous reality of their daughter's adoption:

'No', [Chris] told me. They always called me their 'beautiful adopted baby'.
    'But *adoption* was just a word', she said. 'We used it so you would know it, but it meant nothing to us. Everyone makes such a deal of it. I think it's crazy. Adopted is adopted. "So what?" was always our feeling.'

> Never once in my life did I have a problem with that. I never felt separation
> pains that I can recall. I felt isolated racially at times, but the fact that I was
> not my parents' biological child was never an issue. Being adopted was just
> an obvious fact. (69)

Innocuous as this explanation might seem, it is by no means straightforward or
without its complexities. Chris and Rollie's determination *not* to exceptionalize
adoption is a significant tactic that maintains the ordinariness of adoptive
relations in the face of those in 1970s Detroit who 'gawked' (68) at the sight
of the infant Hopgood – those who, despite never offering 'an intentionally
offensive remark' (68), perceived the Hopgood family unit as unusual. In
seeking to negate its meaning, Chris and Rollie empty 'adopted' and 'adoption'
of primary explanatory status. Hopgood is a 'beautiful' baby who is adopted,
not 'beautiful' because she is adopted. The adjective 'adopted' marks the nature
of parental attachment rather than claims special status. It is one of the most
important secrets which *Lucky Girl* ordinarily tells: in contrast to official
knowledge on the subject, being adopted is in many ways nothing special.

Chris and Rollie's ready use of adoption's vocabulary might be seen as
colour-blind or assimilative, or as avoiding the singularity and emotional
turmoil of adoptive life, especially when we recall Hopgood's remark about
feeling racially isolated. Yet as *Lucky Girl* proceeds, Hopgood exempts them
from any such responsibility and bravely foregrounds instead *her* complicity
in disarticulating her links with her Taiwanese past. Actually, Hopgood
tracks her parents' absolute commitment to keeping open the matter of
Hopgood's polycultural ancestry not least through their unequivocal support
of her subsequent trips to Taiwan to spend time with her birth-family. On one
occasion they accompany her, as we shall see, as part of a wider attempt to
function collectively as a transcultural family rather than as an American family
that includes a transcultural adoptee. The dissidence of their 'So what?', as Chris
indicates, is not at all directed against their daughter's transcultural credentials
but targets the assumption of adoption as a proximate term for 'substitute',
'second-hand', 'unreal', 'inauthentic' and so forth. Indeed, the lexical symmetry
of 'Adopted is adopted' refuses entirely any room for metaphor. It evidences
the Hopgoods' attempt not to emblematize their family unit as a version of
assimilative filiation, or of multiracial America, or transcultural harmony and
other such confections. This insistence on the tautology of adoption might

be taken as a determinedly radical act rather than an evasion of transcultural adoption's specificity. Chris and Rollie refuse to hide from themselves or from others the nature and circumstances of their relations which are asserted as pointedly ordinary and never made glibly symbolic.

It might seem that Hopgood inculcates such principles from an early age. She refuses the clinical pathologizing perspectives of those professionals who believe 'that adoptees must automatically, deep down, feel part empty or abandoned, that we must suffer some hole in us that will never be filled because our birth parents did not raise us' (151). Choosing to discuss adoptive relations as 'normal parent-child, relations' she powerfully asserts that in her view the 'only difference is how we became parent and child' (151). Yet as a young girl, she has mobilized this 'obvious fact' more as a means of prohibition, to cover up rather than open up the diversity and transcultural provenance of her early life. Her parents often encouraged her to engage with Asian cultural activities, although in a generalized sense, and in a fashion which, driven by decent intentions, trafficked in cliché snapshots of cultural difference. Hopgood recalls them hanging Asian art on their home's walls, hiring Asian babysitters and eating Chinese food regularly. Nonetheless, Hopgood sought to play down her Taiwanese nativity by refusing to attend Chinese school and pursuing American life with ardour. Her teenage years were marred by racist epithets at high school – nicknamed Chinky, she made no major protest – but she continued to expunge any connectivity with Asian life as an anchor of identity, choosing not to befriend other Asian Americans of her age. It is an isolating strategy born in part out of necessity and due to the lack of positive transcultural role models. Hopgood remembers that '[a]side from Pat Morita on *Happy Days* and *The Karate Kid*, there weren't many Asian American stars, no Lucy Lius, no Amy Tans or Michelle Kwans. There were no rainbow casts like you'd see later on popular television series such as *ER*, *Lost*, or *Grey's Anatomy*. I felt isolated, and that would not change until my final years of college' (80). Things change when she attends the University of Missouri at Columbia and becomes involved with an Asian American group on campus which, despite the diversity of its membership, is brought together in Hopgood's eyes through their shared experience of 'feeling harassed or isolated' (158). Later she joins the Asian American Journalist Association as her career progresses. Yet the moniker 'Asian American' marks Hopgood's consciousness of sharing a vague affinity with minoritized others rather than a detailed, granulated and empowered sense of investment in a distinctive Asian terrain. Other than her ownership of a Chinese Shar-Pei dog, Delilah, her pre-trace identity seems little inflected by a prolonged engagement with Taiwanese life.

This is the first truth which *Lucky Girl* must admit: Hopgood's glib disregard for the cultural provenance of her nativity and the prejudicial society in which she has lived. Indeed, her memoir is an unusual trace narrative because her search and reunion were not impelled by a strong sense of loss or a yearning to know one's biogenetic origins. It is as if Hopgood cared little for such things and was quite content with being adopted. She comes into contact with the Wangs almost by chance, due to an off-the-cuff enquiry she makes about their whereabouts in a Christmas card message to Maureen Sinnott. When she learns from Maureen, in 1997, that her birth-family is alive in Taiwan and has invited her to visit for Chinese New Year, her reaction is mixed: 'There were too many unknowns, and deep down I was a little afraid of being too curious. I preferred *not* caring about my biological past' (9-10). Ignorance acts as an emotional defence and a way of living, which might be understandable; but it also casts Hopgood as complicit in the keeping of secrets in order to make life as an adoptee more manageable and tidy, unconcerned with the materiality which produced her adoptability. When asked as a youngster about finding her biogenetic relations, Hopgood's answer was always no: 'As a teenager, I practically took pride in my ignorance' (7). This way of living sets her out of synch with her parents' commitment to facing facts, and as a young girl aligns her position with that of advocates of closed adoptions who believe that prohibiting pasts secures tidy futures. Hopgood's trace, then, stems from a crucial decision no longer *to keep secret from herself* the unruly past which made her transcultural life possible and, due to the correspondence from Taiwan which begins to arrive in her St Louis home after her card to Maureen, starts to impinge upon her American life 'no matter what I had to say about it' (18). It is the first component of the wider journey that Hopgood takes from the exclusionary tidiness of being adopted to the edgy, imperfect, challenging and taxing productivity of adoptive being.

Hopgood's decision is arguably one of the biggest challenges facing many adoptees: are we willing to admit the people and circumstances which produced us and which may make us uncomfortable today, or do we keep these secret even from ourselves? In confronting the circumstances of her surrender, Hopgood vitally discharges herself from prohibiting knowledge and opens herself up to the tangled and chaotic ties that transport her beyond the parameters of her adopted life in the United States. This is done without idealization and with a ready cognizance of the risks involved in pursuing hard truths:

> My biological parents and I were joined by blood [...] but we did not know each other. I did not speak Taiwanese or Mandarin, their native languages. We may share genes, but we came from different cultures, different worlds. [...T]here was always the chance that I would return to the place of my birth and see my face in their faces, but we would make no connection. Or even worse, the blissful slumber would have been broken, the Pandora's box of the House of Wang would fly open and the ghosts of regret and sorrow would spew forth. As a reporter, I understood how tragic family secrets could be once unleashed. (18)

Importantly, Hopgood does not present an encounter with birth-relations as a tryst with truth or the discovery of authenticated being that would contrast with the fraudulence of adoptive identity. As these prescient comments anticipate, tracing transculturally exposes her to cultural incompatibilities and failures of communication, to fault lines of cultural divergence that override the safe passage of selfhood promised by consanguinity.

These reflections, along with the history of Chris and Rollie's articulation of adoption, come to inflect Hopgood's subsequent trace narrative in profound and significant ways. *Lucky Girl* proceeds from a commitment to truth-telling in order to discover the secrets still held at the so-called origin, while all the time mindful of the inability to discern fully the past and the explanations that might reside there. Ethically, this obligation to truth cements a commitment to others. Hopgood's investigation of the lives of her birth-parents, Ma and Ba, is not primarily routed for her own benefit as a solipsistic attempt to compose self, but engenders a commitment to face her birth-parents' decision-making that was indebted to the cultural and gendered provenance of post-war Taiwanese life, especially for the poor.

Hopgood's encounter with the Wangs surprisingly reveals that the truth of her adoption was not a secret in Taiwan. Prior to opening contact with the

Wangs, she believed 'I was just another one of the endless unwanted baby girls born to and discarded by poor Chinese families' (4). The discoveries of her trace dispute the flippancy and convenience of this sentiment by revealing Hopgood's surrendering as deeply upsetting, especially for her birth-mother who was traumatized by the decision, driven by her husband and her mother-in-law, to place her in the care of others. For two decades, Ma kept by her bedside a photograph of the infant Hopgood. As the Wangs progressed from poverty to financial security, both Ma and Ba made enquiries at the hospital where they surrendered their daughter as to her fortunes, without success. Their other children, including five daughters, knew of Hopgood's existence due to the photograph. When one of them, Jin-Zhi, writes to Hopgood just prior to her first visit to Taiwan, she accounts for Hopgood's surrender in terms of gender: '*Why our parents gave you up. There are many reasons. First, all of the traditional Chinese consider that to have a boy is better than a girl. Our father is very traditional man, and he was affect deeply by Chinese culture and society*' (29). Hopgood was the Wangs' sixth daughter and another disappointment for Ba whose obsession for a son had become all-consuming. The impoverished condition of the Wangs at the time also contributed to the decision to surrender both Hopgood and the next child born to the couple, who would become Irene and be adopted to Switzerland.

The fact that Hopgood was never made a secret helps make for an enthusiastic reunion, on the surface at least, as she is enthusiastically and emotionally welcomed by the Wangs when she makes her first of many visits to Taiwan in 1997. But two changes are triggered. First, Hopgood is forced to relinquish her youthful arrogant view that her American life represented a lucky escape from the agency of gender inequality and confront instead the materiality of her adoption history. Her American self was formulated through the cliché counterpointing between the assumed gender inequalities of Taiwan and the liberal environment of the United States as a land of opportunity. 'Instead of enduring poverty and prejudice against girls and women', she confesses to thinking as a youngster, 'I had been raised to believe I could do anything I wanted. I had a close family, a rich life, and the endless opportunities of the great United States of America' (7). Such temporal and spatial divides are transgressed as Hopgood's trace proceeds, as she realizes that the agency of gender oppression which made possible her adoptability in the past retains the power to shape her life as an adult. Chinese patriarchy is not so readily relinquished but continues to claim her present: 'It was part of my distant past, and I thought that's where it would stay. It did not come to life for me until the day I met my sisters' (31). The prohibitions of patriarchy are embodied by the figure of Ba with whom Hopgood struggles, not least because his behaviour shapes the sobering secrets that result from his belief that '[o]nly a son could perpetuate the name and bloodline, and worship and care for a father's spirit' (29). As Hopgood comes to realize, her Taiwanese sisters do not want her to delve too deeply into Ba's attitudes or behaviour. Rather than the adoptee figured as a secret kept in and by the family, in *Lucky Girl* it is around the birth-parents where secrets and their revelation cluster.

Hopgood discovers that her birth-family includes three sons alongside the eight daughters which Ma delivered. The first was born in 1965 with a cleft lip and, as Hopgood is initially told, died of illness a few days later. The second, Nian-Zu, was not born to Hopgood's birth-parents but adopted 'in secret' (39) by the Wangs in the mid-1960s, despite their poverty, when a local couple in even worse dire straits surrendered him as they could not afford to feed him. Nian-Zu is never told of his adoption or of the quest for a son which fuelled Ba's desire to raise him. Towards the end of the book, Hopgood learns that Ba has very recently fathered a son and a daughter with an unnamed woman who has been struck down with cancer. He has insisted that the male child, Wei-Sheng, is raised in the family home for much of the time despite the clear distress this causes to Ma and her daughters. Ba's behaviour corrupts the Wang family unit, especially his relationship with Ma, and complexifies his relationship with Hopgood who is faced with the challenge of trying to understand her birth-father's ongoing obsession with sons. The stakes are raised when perhaps the most troubling secret emerges late in the book: that the death of the unnamed son born with a cleft lip was premeditated. Ma confesses to her daughters that she had no choice but to agree with Ba and her mother-in-law's decision not to feed the child so that his death would prevent the 'crueller fate to let the child live a cursed life, in which he would be sick and shunned and could not be a normal functioning member of society. Back then, the Chinese called these children monsters' (231). Hopgood, then, is required to face two deeply troubling and persistent truths about her family: her mother's submissiveness to her husband and his family and her birth-parents' complicity in child neglect.

The emergence of these secrets might well play into Hopgood's pre-search narrative that her adoption to the United States was a stroke of good fortune and spared her the perceived tribulations of growing up a Taiwanese female. Instead, the response that Hopgood chooses becomes the fulcrum for her transcultural commitment to the people and pain of the Wang family that, through seeking to understand why her parents behaved as they did, brokers critical compassion for her biogenetic relations, even though full understanding remains partially out of Hopgood's reach. The more secrets which Hopgood discovers about her parents, the more she comes to realize that her knowledge of their lives is provincialized and irredeemably imperfect, and she cannot dismiss or judge them with recourse to the standards of her own upbringing. Her ethical commitment to try to understand the complexity of the particulars that rendered her adoptable requires her to think bloodlessly not indulgently about the merits and failures of Ma and Ba. Hopgood's upset at her birth-mother's lifelong suffering – her many pregnancies, her enforced surrendering of children, her cervical cancer, her husband's adulterous attempts to produce a male heir – is leavened by her frustration with her 'submissiveness' (231), and it requires an act of the imagination for Hopgood to accept that 'Ma was bound by culture and tradition' (231), a fact that her biogenetic sisters realize much more readily. She struggles to accept that Ma cares for Wei-Sheng and so elects to remain 'in a hellish situation, in a sense condoning our father's obsession and prolonging the worry and agony of the people who loved her. While Ba's behavior sickened me, Ma's submissiveness, and ultimately her resignation, broke my heart' (232). The reunion with birth-parents multiples rather than stabilizes the emotional conundrum of adoptive life, as Hopgood's trace plunges her into an emotional tumult triggered by the disappointments of her birth-parents' actions. It shows, too, that the encounter with birth-parents provides no stabilizing origin which is readily legible or which resolves the missing puzzle-pieces of self.

In this regard, Hopgood's relationship with Ba is particularly important. Her delight in meeting him in 1997 is quickly soured by the revelations about his sexism and his contradictory manner. Ba takes pleasure in his American daughter's achievements but puts her 'always on display' (162), presenting her as part person, part curiosity. He also has no qualms in criticizing her publicly for being 'so black' (163), much to Hopgood's annoyance (as a consequence of living for a spell in Hawai'i, her skin tone has darkened). In one particularly raw moment she condemns him as 'the man who cheated on our birth mother and broke my sisters' hearts. Ba embodied some principles I could respect, but he was also a living and breathing example of others that I abhorred' (178). Nevertheless, Hopgood wilfully embraces rather than dismisses the predicament of having to forge relations with a birth-relative whose behaviour she regards as inexcusable:

> This is how people live on. Life forces you forward. You can hate your family, you can try to forget, hide, ignore them. Or you can try to understand the impossible people that you are doomed to love. Maybe you count your blessings and forgive. (189)

'Doomed to love': this unsentimental phrase captures the ethical predicament of Hopgood as a transcultural adoptee, refusing to indulge or reject the affective bonds she accepts with her biogenetic relations. Her commitment 'to understand the impossible' describes the challenge of her precise transcultural vantage. Dislocated from language, culture and a shared past with her birth-family, she nonetheless chooses to pursue the truth of that which exists beyond her comprehension. Her desire always 'to know the real [birth-]family, not just the version that they wanted me to see' (153) is constrained by the realization that her displacement from Taiwan thwarts this possibility. Hopgood cannot comprehend fully the people who surrendered her or the solidity of the cultural protocols attached to gender that cost one sibling his life. Reunions with biogenetic relations can underscore rather than erase distance. Hopgood muses that however adept she became in Mandarin or Taiwanese, or how long she spent in Taiwan, 'my birth mother and I would never have a fraction of the relationship she has with Min-Wei or Jin Hong or my other sisters, or that I have with my own mom in the States. Ma will never be able to tell me one-on-one the stories of her youth. I would never know what she preferred to eat without asking. [...] Ma would remain an enigma to me' (211, 212).

In working with the predicament of being 'doomed to love' one's consanguineous family as enigma not origin, Hopgood's book fashions two important responses. The first is its attempt to resist ready judgement in a context which is never fully legible to Hopgood's transcultural eye. The second is a refashioning of the transcultural adoptee's unsteady yet productive standpoint discovered amidst historical and cultural cross-currents, in situ, one that requires the imaginative intercalation of biogenetic and adopted attachments in shaping a consciousness that can cope with their compulsion.

Hopgood foregrounds her dislocated transcultural position as an ontologically productive one. Her inability to understand fully the Wangs' cultural provenance, for example, opens a space for thinking more generously and with critical perspective about Ba's corrosive impact on his family. Her eventual envisioning of Ba seeks to make something generative from her complex feelings towards him. Generously, Hopgood regards him as responsible for her biogenetic sisters' 'stubborn strength that has helped them rise above his indiscretions' (236). She comes remarkably to think of Ba as an enabling figure in the midst of his destructive propensity:

> In a funny way, Ba's lunatic behaviour helps to unite us. We are all distinct products of this man's muddled logic. I am finding that tragedy is as strong a bonding agent as triumph – maybe even stronger. As we gossip about the last unbelievable thing that Ba did, we are joined in our amusement, horror, shame, and despair. We endure him and our past, together. (237)

When aligned with his representation elsewhere in *Lucky Girl*, this view of Ba works to present him ultimately as 'ambiguous' (237), situated somewhere between the demands of cultural compulsion and his own ruthless belligerence. If she is 'doomed to love', then Hopgood's representation of Ba, voiced from the vantage of transcultural negotiation, enacts how this might function productively, without her avoiding any unpalatable truths that an indulgence of sentimental consanguinity might invite. Ba may well have shaped a past that must be endured collectively, but in the above quotation he has become the object of others' representations not the author of their fate: to be gossiped about, written and rewritten, acknowledged and critiqued via his children's discursive reckoning with his legacy. *Lucky Girl* ultimately pulls back from stern judgement, however justified we might think it, and looks instead for creative ways of shaping transpersonal relations in situ where compassion might be housed despite difficulty, enabled by the productively imperfect understanding of the transcultural adoptee who can never fully encounter, and cannot be securely contained within, the cultural domain from whence she was surrendered. *Lucky Girl* exposes the ethical requirement to search for a mode of engagement with the difficulties and complexities discovered at the assumed biogenetic origin that constitute the material not mystical characteristics of consanguineous attachment.

The transformative propensity of such searching is captured in the productively chaotic, edgy and cacophonous textualization of transcultural adoptive being which is clinched in the book's final pages. Hopgood's trace shifts the tectonic plates of her transcultural self-perception gradually but radically. Initially she tries 'to be Chinese' (159) and indulges in fantasies of homecoming on her first visit to Taiwan: 'As foreign as all of this seemed – the food, the smells, the places, the faces, the language – I felt at home' (100). But the feelings do not last and this fantasy of Taiwan as home quickly recedes, so by the time her first visit comes to an end she confesses to feeling 'relieved to be on the plane. I was worn out and wanted to go home' (112), back to America. As her narrative proceeds, there emerges instead a fledgling and fleeting form of transformed being where the seemingly disparate provenances of Hopgood's various cultural inventories – Taiwanese, American, Asian American – are replaced by productive if hazardous entanglement. This is both material and abstracted, locatable for a while in the world but also a mode of consciousness, transportable and relatable, and engendered by the commitment to truth-telling that has led Hopgood not to idealize her Taiwanese relations but face instead the family's 'dark side that crippled the hearts of its women' (102).

Its first manifestation occurs when Hopgood visits the Wangs in 1998 accompanied by her parents Chris and Rollie, so that her biogenetic and adoptive relations are brought together. The coming together of the two families is a noisy and hectic happening, and at one point Hopgood seeks relief by sitting down and surveying the chaotic scene in Ma and Ba's living room:

> *My God*, I thought. *Everyone, every person, every movement – all the chaos in this room is related to me in some way.*
> The noise, the smells, and the faces blurred together and seemed to crescendo into some raucous masterpiece, dissonant yet harmonic, foreign yet familiar. It all seemed so unbelievable, yet it somehow made sense. I shook my head in wonderment and could do nothing more than take a deep breath and let the cacophony crash over me. (141)

Throughout *Lucky Girl*, Hopgood has sought to indulge in moments of physical recognition with the Wangs (she is delighted to find that her toes are just like her sisters'), but the epiphanic recognition made available in this passage is much more durable and transformative than the quirks of biogenetic resemblance. The self-reflective context of the scene ('related to me') makes its unruly encounters suggest a different way of thinking about being, one which intercalates productively the new and familiar, alien and domestic into a cacophonous, unruly, unfinished whole. The resulting 'raucous masterpiece' denies the tidy lineaments of blood-lines and harmonizing biocentric ancestry, and defines another way of being singular plural with an emphasis on movement, chaos and a blurring of selves so that conventional semantic patternings wondrously give way to a new kind of sense: re-cognition as much as recognition.

Such transformations are not at all easy. This is an edgy envisioning of adoptive being, to be sure, as suggested in the chaos and cacophony which threaten to overwhelm Hopgood as much as stimulate her. Just prior to the party, she is greatly distressed to learn that Chris and Rollie may have been injured in a car accident due to Ba's poor driving skills. Although this proves a false alarm, the perception of the adoptive and the biogenetic as on a collision course is nonetheless given an alarmingly literal expression. Soon enough Hopgood is keen for her parents to leave Taiwan, fearful that their encounter might turn incendiary: 'I felt as if I were crossing these incongruent currents of my life, pinching together two live wires that were never meant to touch, and if I held them together much longer, they might explode' (143). This image of electrification captures the precarious position of Hopgood as transcultural adoptee who connects currents that are not necessarily in parallel, while also suggesting how the predicament of being adopted transculturally can short-circuit selfhood. But these dangerous cross-currents are also energizing and vital – live wires as life lines, if you like – with the propensity to spark into existence adoptive being. They surprise Hopgood in situ at the party and charge Hopgood with the task of living outwith received paradigms of American, Asian American, adopted and other such prefabricated signs of identity, even if only for a moment.

It is not for nothing, then, that the main narrative of *Lucky Girl* concludes with the depiction of another precarious place, both material and ontological, that we also might envision in terms of adoptive being. Whereas the scene just discussed opens a space for cacophonous cultural confluence, the book's last chapter ('The Lucky Eight') effects a moment of temporal interweaving after Hopgood boards Northwest Airlines flight 70 bound for the United States and immediately imagines the first time she travelled by air, as an infant en route to Chris and Rollie's parenthood. As she travels she metaphorizes the manifold passages of her families' travels in terms of a tapestry in which their myriad routes are synchronically spun:

> The list of departure and arrival cities seems endless: Kinmen, Taitung, Taipei, Taylor, Zug, Seoul, St. Louis, Honolulu, Brisbane, Washington, D.C., Guilin, Buenos Aires, and on and on. We have both chosen and been forced down so many paths and found ourselves in so many diverse directions, but with every journey and turn each of us has woven part of a collective tapestry so intricate that one string cannot be untangled from the other. Reunified, we are a remarkable road map of fate. (238)

This figurative textile weaves together travels forced by impoverishment (Ma and Ba's migrations within Taiwan) as well as privilege (Hopgood's student life in Hawai'i); compounds agency with compulsion ('chosen', 'fate'); reorients diverse centripetal journeys as collective centrifugal steps. It is also a moment where singular reflection gives way to plural recognition, as Hopgood's thoughts proceed from 'the many plane rides I've made in my life' (237) to the itinerancies of her family clinched in the confluent 'we' that has drawn 'the remarkable road map of fate'. At this moment, the transcultural adoptee is neither isolated nor exceptional, not a typical Asian American nor a long-lost Taiwanese. The reunification mooted here, as the bulk of *Lucky Girl* has proved, is not one of unity nor the reconstitution of an incomplete biogenetic family unit, but an intricate and ever chaotic one, involving facing dark secrets as much as celebrating human relations that find their source across the full range of Hopgood's myriad attachments. In shaping a vision of adoptive being, Hopgood reformulates a family unit no longer divisible into biogenetic and adopted but constituted through the cross-currents of wonder and wounding, making for 'special scars and beauty marks' (238). Her trace narrative recasts the tryst with consanguineous relations not as the elated discovery of the withheld truth of one's origins that completes self, but as an encounter with prohibited knowledge, the truths of which the transcultural adoptee is fated always to understand imperfectly but are no less part of the imperative of adoptive being to face hard facts.

The transformative potential of adoptive being which *Lucky Girl* enables in these key moments is discernible when Hopgood fantasises about her infant departure from Taiwan in the care of an airline hostess many years previously, who in her imagination tells the other passengers that the 8-month-old Mei-Ling 'is going to live in America' (239). It is tempting to read these words which close the chapter as a climactic, celebratory and patriotic endorsement of American opportunity that supports Hopgood's teenage sense of having luckily escaped a Taiwanese life of female drudgery – and, to be fair, *Lucky Girl* might more determinedly ironize this standpoint as it closes. Yet such patriotism is undercut by the discussion of the familial tapestry that immediately precedes it, so that this journey is recast as 'a new route' (239) which will become part of many others to come, rather than a one-way journey to American contentment. We have seen that no such future awaited Hopgood, of course. In imagining herself 'suspended high above the Pacific Ocean, between countries, between families, between destinies' (239), she offers a precarious and 'extraordinary' (239) moment of unsteady being-with, quite distinct from the vertiginous liminality of the diasporic subject forever freed from the pedagogical preconditions of family, culture and nation. What awaits the adult Hopgood, like most transcultural adoptees perhaps, is that tapestry of transcultural texts very much rooted in and routed through the world. It requires living *amidst* – chaotically, cacophonously – rather than living in-between. *Lucky Girl* eschews the guarantees of consanguineous *relations* in favour of the productive and constrained transcultural contingencies of *relating* – telling new truths of how life might be, otherwise. 'I am not the son who can perpetuate the family name', Hopgood writes, 'but I can tell our story. I am not the heir that Ba wanted, but I, too, can be a keeper of our history. I choose to continue the narrative in my own way, using what I've learned to build our family' (244). Through the encounters with adoption's vexed material histories ('what I've learned') and narrative creativity ('I can tell'), adoptive being may be forged.

The combination of Hopgood's airborne reflections on narrative with her image of the tapestry brings together the notions of text and textile. This figurative expression of adoptive being expresses something of the phenomenology of living adoptively, for all concerned. It is another reason why the memoir form of *Lucky Girl* becomes pluralizing and transpersonalizing. Its weaving together of matters of documentary record with imagined lives and fantasized journeys makes this transcultural adoption trace narrative a particular kind of plaited text that crosses over and strikes out ready distinctions between fact and fantasy. Appropriately, *Lucky Girl*'s epilogue concludes with an enabling act of reading, as if to emphasize the centrality and agency of creative textual production in living and being otherwise. Hopgood describes herself reading with her infant daughter, Sofia, in a mutually explorative and intimately humdrum act of textual proximity, oriented to unguessed futures: 'I sit in bed with Sofia balancing in my lap, surrounded by fantastic tales of hippos, bears, and dinosaurs. Then I open a book and let her turn the page' (244).

In *Secrets and Lies*, as Hortense flew en route from Barbados and learned the secret of her adoption, she could see only the blur of clouds through her window. As *Lucky Girl* nears its conclusion, Hopgood's airborne contemplation of her entangled and imperfectly understood transcultural particulars makes up a multidirectional tapestry from her biogenetic and adoptive genealogies into which – and in contrast to baby Michael's infant clothes in *Small Island* – no secrets will be sewn. As I have argued in this chapter, in transcultural adoptions secrecy maintains its problematic agency despite the adoptive status of such families often appearing more readily discernible due to perceived differences in racial or cultural 'matching'. The conspicuous family does not by default interrupt consanguineous norms. As we have seen, transcultural families may function assimilatively rather than transformatively and refresh the prejudicial milieu through their maintenance. *Secrets and Lies* leaves the racial and cultural dispensation of late twentieth-century Britain in place and does little to bring to light the historical and experiential actuality of transracial adoptive contracts. We have seen, too, and more radically, how transcultural adoption can be marshalled to tell other tales about disinvestment and disenfranchisement, not least through Andrea Levy's attempt to use a story of transcultural family-making to expose and challenge the deeply racist constraints of post-war Britain at a moment of talismanic change. Yet these political aims clash contentiously with the ethical consequences of *Small Island*'s ill-advised privileging of consanguineous attachments and the ill-considered deployment of secrecy as a narrative strategy. Instead, and as Hopgood's work suggests, adoptive being emerges from an ethical determination to face material facts, however uncomfortable or hurtful they may be. *Lucky Girl* captures the transfigurative truthful consequences of determinedly pursuing blood-lines, *not* to secure transcendent attachments to self and origin but instead to understand imperfectly the material and multidirectional particulars that produced adoptability and might be claimed creatively as one fibre of vital connection amongst commensurate others. The transcultural adoptive family does not by virtue of its presence trigger critical insight into the norms of family-making. Secrets can be hidden in plain sight. Instead, we have to learn to tell.

2

Histories: E. R. Braithwaite,
Toni Morrison, Sebastian Barry

What can we make of the histories of transcultural adoption? What possible futures might be struck from adoption's disenfranchising incidences? Can a better knowledge of its pasts encourage a progressive encounter with its legacies?

In Chang-rae Lee's absorbingly written novel *A Gesture Life* (1999), an elderly retired medical-supply storekeeper called Franklin Hata, living in the small American town of Bedley Run, narrates with deceptive formality his emotionally troubled life. Dr Hata, as is he known (although he never actually qualified as a doctor), was born to Korean birth-parents and adopted by a Japanese couple. During the Second World War, he acted as a medical officer where he witnessed the tribulations of the so-called comfort women incarcerated in a Japanese military camp to satisfy the sexual demands of the military. Having emigrated after the war to become the proprietor of a successful local concern, Dr Hata is allowed to adopt a Korean-born girl, Sunny, and he also begins a courtship with Mary Burns. But his relationship with each becomes strained. By the time of the novel's contemporary setting, Mary has died and his relationship with Sunny (who now has her own child) is at breaking point. Dr Hata lives lonely and isolated, having sold his business and, soon, his home, mulling over his unsettling past. Lee shapes his story to bring to light the oft-hidden history of the dehumanizing exploitation of women sanctioned by the Japanese military. Pirjo Ahokas reads Dr Hata's story as also illuminating the repression of Asian histories and racial difference required by the 'assimilationist expectations' (113) of the 'Color-Blind American Dream' (111). But on the whole, Lee's use of a transcultural adoptee as narrator serves predominantly figurative purposes. Dr Hata's troubled life has consisted of going through the motions of attachment rather than risking emotional entanglements. He has attempted dutifully to control his fortunes by playing parts – son, lover, father, 'doctor' – and has lived a life of gesture and duty, 'outside looking in' (356), rather than participate in the hazards of emotional investment and capricious chance. Dr Hata's adoption history is primarily a metaphor for his gesture life driven by a paralyzing fear of 'failure' which has ultimately displaced him from 'human comfort or warmth' (229). Lee does not explore too deeply Dr Hata's fears as the psychological consequence of his adoption, nor does he enquire into the material particulars which rendered Dr Hata and Sunny adoptable in the first place. If representations of transcultural adoption are always located between the historical and the imagined or figurative, *A Gesture Life* opts to instrumentalize adoption as metaphor rather than as a concrete matter, uncoupling it from its referential provenance. Lee's adroitly crafted and profoundly moving novel nonetheless tells us nothing much about the specific histories of transcultural adoption to which it makes only the slightest of gestures.

In this chapter, I am interested in how representations of transcultural adoption negotiate between their concrete historical specifics, embedded in the wider political travails of the moments they depict, and the figurative and projective possibilities that emerge from their narration. As we shall see, a care for referentiality need not circumscribe the transfigurative potential with which transcultural adoption is endowed. For some, representing incidences of transcultural adoption is the means to expose the intimacies of family-making as shaped by the political dispensation of racist politics and chauvinistic nationalisms and, at the same time, the chance to write *against* their continuing agency by making something new out of the historical conditions that compelled acts of surrender and the production of adoptability.

If we wish to understand why transcultural adoption contracts become possible, we must realize the close connections between the seemingly private realm of transcultural family-making and the often dramatic international conflicts and discriminatory racializing practices that always hit home. As I argued in the opening chapter, transcultural adoption is central and not marginal to wider global tensions. David L. Eng considers such adoptions as a particularly 'post-World War II phenomenon associated with American liberalism, post-war prosperity, and Cold War politics', and as constituting 'one of the most privileged forms of diaspora in the late twentieth century' (94). In her work on transracial and transnational adoption in the United States, Laura Briggs argues forcefully that in studying adoption

> we also follow the traces of all the big stories of the last seventy or eighty years, because people lost their children in circumstances of exceptional vulnerability and powerlessness and because adoption was implicated in them. [...] Families are where we live our economic and social relations, and in families formed by law the fiction that families are 'private', constituted in opposition to the 'public', is laid bare as the fairy tale that it is. (24)

Briggs's list of the particular histories which such adoptions bring into focus includes African American civil rights and the politics of indigeneity, the rise of the Christian Right, the ever-shifting terrain of race and the rise of neoliberalism and much more besides. As I touched upon previously, the history of black British politics in the late twentieth century can certainly be witnessed through the prism of adoption. The rise of militant opposition to transracial placements by the Association of Black Social Workers and Allied Professionals (ABSWAP) and others is connected to the wider organization and politicization of black Britons, many of whom were British-born rather than migrant, protesting against the increasingly hostile and tense race relations which found riotous expression at a number of moments during the Thatcherite 1980s. And as we shall observe presently in this chapter, the proximity of the Catholic hierarchy to state politicians and policymaking in post-Independence Ireland serviced a distinctly chauvinistic nationalism within which Ireland's women were freighted with, and made vulnerable by, their prescribed roles in moral and political discourses for much of the twentieth century. Women deemed to have jeopardized these discourses could face the loss of dwelling, family, social position and newborn children. Briggs concludes her work with a sombre reminder: 'If adoption has often been a symbol of hopefulness and new beginnings, it is worth noticing that it is also an event in which long histories of inequality and social marginalization are sedimented, frozen in time and then made into family stories' (283). As her research implies, transcultural adoption may maintain global inequalities of power and resource. New stories are needed which perceive rather than hide these histories.

In shaping stories of transcultural adoption, creative writers have taken the opportunity to engage critically with 'public' histories from the vantage point of 'private' family-breaking and family-making, to the extent that (and as Briggs voiced) it no longer becomes possible to make a distinction between intimate and impersonal histories. In his novel *The Lost Child* (2015), Caryl Phillips imagines the fortunes of an impoverished former slave, marooned near Liverpool's docks in the early nineteenth century, and her mixed-race son who is left destitute when she dies. In recounting with chilling sobriety this sorry tale, which is influenced by the story of Heathcliff in Emily Brontë's *Wuthering Heights* (1847), Phillips points to the complex and central contribution made by the slave trade to British lives and literature. Elsewhere in the novel, his imagining of a young white woman in post-war England who surrenders her two mixed-race sons into care brings into focus the toxic concoction of racism, anti-colonial politics, sexual exploitation and the clinical confinement of unsupported women that obtained in the latter decades of the twentieth century, and with reference to which the losing of children in the novel needs to be understood. It is exactly this kind of attention to the historical locatedness of matters of vulnerability, surrender and adoptability which is missing in Chang-rae Lee's otherwise admirable novel *A Gesture Life*. There the pursuit of transcultural adoption as metaphor happens without too much concern for its historical provenance or referentiality, effectively hiding transcultural adoption's material circumstances as it makes adoption a matter of metaphor.

That said, in arguing for creative imaginings of transcultural adoption to reckon responsibly with the often concealed conditions which produced adoptability, I suggest that transcultural adoption writing often functions transfiguratively when it is materially concerned but not mimetically constrained. As we shall see in Chapter 4, in his novel *Crossing the River* (1993) Caryl Phillips imagines one especially sobering transcultural adoption history as a proleptic fashioning of post-racial adoptive being. Cynthia Callahan reminds us that 'fictional adoptions are not simply mimetic; as a literary trope, adoption allows authors to metaphorically speak to broader questions about identity and belonging' (1–2). In analyzing the three texts which preoccupy this chapter, I am keen critically to pursue two concerns: how each writer articulates a critique of 'public' history through adoption stories in order to reveal and challenge the prejudicial operations of race and nation; and how each writer attempts to make something iconic or symbolic from the rendering of history, which we might consider in terms of the creative potential of adoptive being. In proceeding with an attention to 'both the mimetic and symbolic functions of adoption in literature', as Callahan counsels, we open up through an attention to historical materiality one of the key questions which Callahan asks in her study of American writing: 'what other cultural work might these adoption plots do, beyond contributing to the culture's understanding of adoption at a given moment?' (3).

The three transcultural adoption texts I read in this chapter are more successful than Lee's – although not necessarily less problematic – in negotiating between the mimetic and the symbolic: between the historical incidences of transcultural adoption and what can be made from them imaginatively. The historical contexts at stake are quite different: black and mixed-race British adoptees of the 1960s, informal adoptions amongst African Americans in the late nineteenth and early twentieth centuries and the demonization of unwed mothers in post-Independence Ireland. In proceeding thus, I want to keep in play a sense of the mimetic and symbolic very much as hinged categories rather than discrete or at odds. All creative texts summon the concrete and the tropological, ostensibly in different measures, no matter how realistic or remote they might seem. In what follows, I quite deliberately combine a non-fictional text with two formally complex novels in order to note, first, how reading a memoir of transcultural adoption administration in post-war London as an intervention in history allows us to encounter one writer's highly (and slyly) skilled attempt to metaphorize adoption for solipsistic and symbolic ends. Second, I wish to witness how representations of historical disinvestment as seen through the lenses of adoption in the United States and Ireland, respectively, offer two novelists the means to shape a progressive futurity from an obscene past. While Laura Briggs's research ultimately prioritizes the sedimented histories of inequality and marginalization above narratives of adoption as incipient hopefulness, some of the writing we will think about in this chapter daringly insists upon making transfigurative possibilities wrought from the bleakest tales of emotional desolation.

The first historical incidence of transcultural adoption which I explore concerns transcultural adoption practices in England in the late 1950s and early 1960s. The emergence of a considerable constituency of migrant-

descended black and mixed-race adoptable children during this period caught
the attention of a number of sociologists and social workers at the time, who
were keen to place children in families and also study the consequences of
transcultural placements (as we saw in Chapter 1, nearly all adopting families
were white). Publications from the time which dealt with, in Diana Kareh's
phrase, 'the very new phenomenon of mixed-race adoption' (128) have titles
which reflect the particular racial vocabularies and assumptions at large, such as
Kareh's *Adoption and the Coloured Child* (1970) that appeared in the same year
as Lois Raynor's *Adoption of Non-White Children: The Experience of a British
Adoption Project* (1970). Yet they were often written by those keen to alleviate
the predicament of children in care and challenge wider prejudices, despite
their complicity with many of the assumptions of race thinking. Each book
raised the issue of what has become known today in adoption studies as colour-
blindness: the view that racial and cultural specifics do not significantly matter
to the emotional craft of family-making which ideally transcends or does not
recognize such differences. Kareh spoke to many adoptive parents who firmly
eschewed prejudicial attitudes but were worried about the racist world with
which their children would engage in later life. 'The delicate balance between
family "oneness" and an awareness of racial origins must be maintained if
shocks are to be minimized' (115), she concluded. 'However strong the home-
tie may be, and however good a job the adoptive parents may have made of
rearing the child, they cannot protect him from the attitudes of others, nor
from his involvement with these attitudes' (121). Lois Raynor records the
conversations of a self-support group of adoptive parents (a rarity in the 1960s)
which struggled with the question of cultural difference: 'Would a child being
raised in an English family be as English as anyone, or would he have a special
interest in the culture of a faraway land in Asia, Africa or the Caribbean? [...]
Some felt that teaching a child pride in his race would help him to withstand
discrimination. [...] Other parents felt this was stressing the difference and
that they could only bring up the child as English. One adoptive mother
said, "We have a little English girl in a brown skin"' (141). By the 1980s, the
practice of colour-blindness had been appropriated by ABSWAP as evidence
of damaging political deracination and cultural disenfranchisement, as part
of a wider attempt to fragment the black community in Britain. Some of these
claims were not incontestable. While acknowledging the need for more black

adopters, in *Adoption and Race: Black, Asian and Mixed Race Children in White Families* (1983) Owen Gill and Barbara Jackson concluded that the adolescent transracial adoptees they studied did not suffer from isolation within families and were not confused or academically disadvantaged, while there was no general evidence 'that the absence of racial pride or identity was, at this stage, associated with low self-esteem or behavioural disorder' (130). That said, they remained concerned about adoptees' transition to adulthood where they would 'have to come to terms more directly with life in a society where many people will characterise them on the basis of their racial background. They will be moving out into a society which is significantly racist in its attitudes and its distribution of opportunities' (136). Colour-blindness may not lead to poor family-making, it seemed, yet the disconnect between private and public life left many, including its supporters, concerned.

The centrality of race thinking to the militant critique of transcultural adoption left some exasperated, not least because of their perception that a chance was being missed to demythologize race and think more deftly about the politics of prejudice at large in late twentieth-century Britain. Paul Gilroy expressed disappointment in 1994 with the emergent black British critique of adoption and fostering in the UK as obsessed 'with identity as selfhood' (x) and forged in an 'atmosphere of moralism, confusion and fear' (ix). For Gilroy, the assumption that 'simply asserting the strength and durability of black households and kin structures was a disastrous response to pathological diagnoses of black social and cultural life' (x). He did not advocate glib colour-blindness nor biocentric race matching in adoption practices, but demanded instead a braver interrogation of 'a number of highly contentious but usually unstated assumptions about "race", ethnicity, culture, the family and other kin relationships, identity and individuality, selfhood and autonomy' (xi). As we will continue to witness, creative representations of transcultural adoption have at times accepted this challenge, even if on occasions they have not freed themselves from the constraints of race thinking that limit rather than liberate.

From the vantage of the twenty-first century, colour-blindness appears these days a discredited notion, presumed to evade the grimly enduring realities of discrimination through a sentimental vocabulary of 'love conquers all'. It may also be complicit in transcultural adoption as an assimilative act, where colour-blind families absorb difference rather than reconstitute their cultural inventories in polycultural rather than monocultural terms. The extent to which the nominally transcultural family unit interacts with the lived particulars of other minoritized peoples and communities may not reach very far beyond the confections of cultural cliché, if at all. In a discussion about colour-blindness in the United States which readily resonates in British contexts, Julia Chinyere Oparah, Sun Yung Shin and Jane Jeong Trenka warn that an enthusiasm for colour-blind adoptions plays into the hands of the 'neoconservative lobby' as it conceals the ongoing inequalities of race within a discourse of selfless sentimentalism that reaches for post-racial pieties as it traffics in pro-racial policies: 'The underlying common sense notion that "loves sees no color" provides a useful ideological framework for the reframing of the racial script so that those seeking to assert that race matters are recast as segregationists or ideologues' (6). As these words published in 2006 readily testify, the debates similar to those which have raged in Britain since the 1980s have a long history elsewhere, and nowhere have they been concluded. Most commentators recognize, however, that colour-blindness is inextricably invested in the ongoing racialized character of social life in general and transcultural relations in particular, and carries the capacity to cloak rather than cancel the divisive operations of race thinking.

However, if we return the pursuit of colour-blindness in British transcultural adoptions to its historical moment, its political efficacy under certain circumstances can appear more pointed. In certain conditions, a colour-blind approach to transcultural family-making may acquire important anti-racist traction in the public sphere. This is one reason why I want to dwell upon E. R. Braithwaite's non-fictional account of transcultural adoption, *Paid Servant* (1962). Braithwaite is frequently overlooked in literary histories of post-war black British and diasporic writing, despite the success of his 1959 memoir *To Sir, With Love* which in 1969 was made into a successful film starring Sidney Poitier and scripted by James Clavell. His bypassing is no doubt a result, first, of the disciplined autobiographical mode of his writing which sets it apart from the fictional experimentalism of coterminous migrant Caribbean writers such as George Lamming and Sam Selvon; and, second, of the resolutely middle-class and Anglophile envisioning he takes towards life in post-war Britain which aligns him more with an obsequious than a postcolonial standpoint, despite the coruscating record of racism he offers.

Settling in Britain after his service in the Royal Air Force during the Second World War, Braithwaite was turned down for a series of engineering jobs on the grounds of race before taking a job as a teacher in a tough working-class East End School in London, the travails of which form the substance of *To Sir, With Love*. *Paid Servant* concerns his subsequent employment as an officer in London County Council's Department of Child Welfare who is responsible for helping place black and mixed-race children for adoption. The book is unique in offering a literary reflection upon, rather than a sociological study of, the practices of transcultural adoption in the UK as they played out in the immediate post-war years, as seen from the vantage point of a black social worker. In pursuing the argument that the placing of a child with a loving family should always take priority over matters of so-called race matching, Braithwaite's advocacy of colour-blindness attempts a significant political intervention in the prejudicial mechanics he found in social work at the time and reminds us that the political and ethical standpoints one might hold in principle can play out very differently under certain circumstances in practice. *Paid Servant* suggests that colour-blindness should not be simply dismissed as the ideological convenience of neoliberal white adopters whose actions always uphold, in Dorothy Roberts's words, 'the policies and systematic inequities that produce so many adoptable Black children' (54). Understanding the advocacy of colour-blindness in *Paid Servant* requires us to read historically and to consider if there might be a case for a *strategic* deployment of colour-blindness in particular conditions. In Braithwaite's book, colour-blindness makes an important critical intervention in the public realm of policy and is not confined to the private labour of family-making, as Braithwaite pits the anti-racist potential of transcultural adoption against those welfare institutions which considered black and mixed-race adoptees a moral as well as a social threat. That said, while colour-blindness can deliver vulnerable children into loving homes with political efficacy, Braithwaite's representation of it cannot broker adoptive being due to the cancellation of any kind of value or agency for consanguineous relations that might happen beyond biocentric or racialized norms. This happens, as we shall see, because Braithwaite finds in colour-blind transcultural adoption a mode of joining rather than undoing the normative conditions of middle-class British life he so admires.

Indeed, *Paid Servant* commands attention as much for its figurative strategies as for its record of post-war transcultural adoption practices. Braithwaite's book is a fascinating example of how the political challenge it makes to racism through its advocacy of colour-blindness is circumscribed by the much more assimilative and normalizing manoeuvres he makes via his narration. This state of affairs is something which is not readily discernible at first sight, I would hazard. Braithwaite's documentary style, his deference to received English and his avoidance of rhetorical flourishes can make *Paid Servant* seem more like a transparent document rather than a text which shapes a fantasy of class assimilation in its rendering of transcultural adoptive families. Yet the book is deeply involved, albeit tacitly, in combining an attention to the historical matters of transcultural adoption with their imaginative and ultimately problematic requisitioning. These manoeuvres happen through the book's central narrative strand: the colour-blind adoption of a mixed-race infant called Roddy by a white family. Roddy's adoption seems to be the outstanding success story of *Paid Servant* as it evidences the triumph over state-sanctioned racism by the colour-blindness advocated by the narrator Ricky (as Braithwaite is called by his friends and colleagues throughout the text). As such, the political agency of colour-blindness in this moment needs to be recognized, however uncomfortable some might feel about this. But as we shall see, Roddy is appropriated as much as he is supported by Ricky for his own fantastic designs. Actually, through his steadfast attempts to place the child and the challenges he mounts against those who would stand in his way, Ricky displaces Roddy and shapes for *himself* a fantasy of belonging in Britain through the act of transcultural adoption which does not facilitate the transfigurative agency of adoptive being.

According to his case file, Rodwell Williams, aged four and a half, is the offspring of a US serviceman of Mexican origin and a local white prostitute, Angela Williams. When Ricky receives the file and pursues Roddy's biogenetic background with the welfare officer previously in charge of the case, Miss Coney, it soon emerges that the birth-father's Mexican nationality is most likely a fiction as Angela had not offered such information. Ricky is stunned to learn that this alleged information is the result of Miss Coney's visual assessment of Roddy's features. 'Well, when you see Rodwell you will understand', she tells Ricky. 'I've been in this job for a long time and I can tell. It has to do with his colour and his hair and the shape of his nose and cheekbones. I know about these things' (7). The assumptions about Roddy's facial appearance extend to his moral character, as Miss Coney breezily conflates two popular prejudices about birth-mothers and mixed-race adoptees that presume a genealogy of moral degeneracy. When asked why Roddy has not been placed in an adoptive family, Miss Coney raises the issue of sexual licentiousness (despite the fact that Roddy is yet to turn five):

> Well, you know, there is the problem of placing him in a family where there might be girls. After all, the children won't always be young, and we must think of what could happen in adolescence or later. [...] I've had to work among Asians and Africans and West Indians in London and before that in Cardiff, and I know how they feel about things like sex, quite different from the way we English people feel. [...] I'm sure you'll agree that the child would be far better off with people of his own kind. (8, 9)

Roddy's white biogenetic ancestry is swiftly elided in his construction in the file as 'Coloured' (6), while the conflation of racial difference with sexual danger maintains a depressing envisioning of race and sexuality entirely typical of post-war Britain. To this way of seeing, as Ricky acidly notes, Roddy is 'a cretinous gargoyle at worst, a problem child at best' who 'would surely break through the camouflage and emerge as a fully-fledged sex-motivated problem' (9). Ricky's quest, then, to present Roddy as a 'handsome, intelligent, happy child' (9) is part of his larger assault on the ways of seeing that read Roddy's physiognomy in terms of racial and moral degeneracy. Colour-blindness is pursued by Ricky at one level as the means to contest institutionalized racism rather than as an investment in a liberal fiction of loving relations which deny rather than confront the presence of race.

Paid Servant repeatedly calls attention to the social consequences of scopic prejudice. In one early scene, Ricky finds himself interrupted while sitting at a café in Earls Court Road by an unnamed troubled young white woman who asks him to buy her a coffee and proceeds to tell him an unhappy story about her attempts to be a singer, her falling out with her parents and her subsequent work as a prostitute. Ricky's telling of the scene foregrounds matters of sound and vision. The staff and customers at the café looking on have no idea as to the substance of this chance encounter but quickly make a range of assumptions about Ricky as playing the devil's part in the woman's upset (as a dispassionate lover? or a cliché pimp figure?), especially when she flinches at Ricky's attempt to clasp her hand compassionately: 'In her eyes was a look very near terror. I felt confused and humiliated, the more so as now everyone in the coffee bar seemed to be staring at us, at me, the eyes cold and disapproving' (15). Ricky is aware throughout of the waitress's stern gaze, 'looking boldly at me, her eyes bright and hostile' (13).

Set against these visual hostilities are possibilities linked to the sonic. The woman had wanted to become a singer prior to falling on hard times, and this cancellation of a successful career in sound is figuratively resonant. The woman's despair is readily conveyed in the café when 'she rested her head gently on the table and pressed her hands over her ears in the loneliest gesture I have ever seen, as if she wanted to shut out the whole frightening world' (13). Unhappy vision, no sound: in *Paid Servant* this is a condition that results in unfathomable emotional turmoil – one in which the mechanics of transcultural adoption are also ensnared – with the creative possibilities signified here by sound (singing, telling) overruled by the prejudicial ways of seeing that deny human agency.

What would change if one was not to look but to listen? One of the more minor but most interesting figures in *Paid Servant* is Miss Felden, a blind telephonist who works in Ricky's department. Ricky marvels at how she never fails to know him by his step as he walks by, even when he alters it, and unlike many of his colleagues she is genuinely helpful to him in his work. Her physical description is telling. As well as possessing a mouth which is 'always on the edge of laughter', she embodies for Ricky a way of knowing, distinctly sonic, that challenges and inspires him at once:

> The sweetness of smiles was always in her voice, and somehow I could never quite become accustomed to her blindness, or the suggestion of helplessness which the word invoked. Her general air of assurance and independence was so natural that, whenever in conversation with her, I had the feeling that she had just closed her eyes the better to concentrate on some elusive point, or to listen to some faint sound, and that presently she'd open them again, wide. (23–4)

Ricky's uneasiness with Miss Felden's blindness suggests a degree of sympathy for her disability and marks an attempt to acknowledge his difficulties in seeing past assumptions about blindness. But Miss Felden is anything but helpless, and the passage presents her figuratively as possessing, if not sight, then significant insight. Coupled with her assurance and independence is her ability to discern others accurately – she never mistakes Ricky's step for anyone else's – and her excellence of concentration. While the figurative use of disability can certainly be a problematic manoeuvre, the description of Miss Felden presents blindness at one level as a productive mode which sharpens concentration and maintains a commitment to the pursuit of hard-to-realize goals. The result, Braithwaite hopes, is transformed vision. The opening of refreshed eyes is not for Miss Felden, alas, but rhetorically for readers, who might embark upon the relinquishing of the surety of vision that sees the world in racializing terms. If Miss Felden's blindness is a sign not of helplessness but independence, then Ricky's pursuit of colour-blindness also equates liberty with the relinquishment of vision.

Roddy's placing rests on the identification of enlightened adopters who effect the challenging of institutionalized racism. This is not a mean feat. Ricky proceeds to draw up a shortlist of prospective parents whose middle-class credentials would make them seem to possess the financial security required by London County Council to act as adopters. Yet matters of race keep getting in the way. One of these families, from Barbados, is black; the other is Jewish; a third is white South African. Ricky boasts that matters of cultural specificity are irrelevant, and if he 'found a coloured family for [Roddy], it would be because I was fully convinced of their suitability, and that Roddy liked them' (21). The Bajan family, the Ellesworths, are quickly ruled out when Ricky learns that they do not want to adopt a mixed-race child and will consider only West Indian children: '"Sorry Rick", Don said, "but it would cause too many complications. If it was a Negro child we might consider it, but as it is …"' (31). Such racializing reluctance conveniently adds weight to Ricky's pursuit of colour-blindness as at core preferable to the prejudicial protocols of same-race matching. The next couple on the list, Hannah and Hardwick Rosenberg, fit Ricky's criteria much more happily. When told about Roddy's race, Hardwick Rosenberg declares that any problems Roddy might face in the future because of this 'will be faced by us as a family' (61). Flushed with admiration at such vernacular cosmopolitan convictions, Ricky extols the virtues of his friends: 'This was a Jewish couple, but so complete was their involvement with all humanity that neither of them had asked any question about the child's religion or that of his parents' (61). Ricky's use of 'but' here both acknowledges and cancels cultural specificity, and captures the tricky rhetoric of colour-blind transcultural adoption as a means of post-racial filiation. Yet the Department of Child Welfare thwarts the Rosenbergs' application to be adoptive parents. Hardwick telephones Ricky with news of the welfare officer's assessment visit which soon became hostile when the officer began to warn of the 'dark doings' which would occur in the family once Roddy began to grow older (it is noteworthy that the Rosenbergs already have a small daughter). In addition to the dismal denigration of the mixed-race adoptee as a sexual generate in waiting, there is hinted an anti-Semitic element to the welfare officer's dim view of the Rosenbergs. She asks 'a multitude of questions about their religion' (82) and, in her assessment, points to the couple's busy professional lives which meant they had little time to spare for a new child. Ricky's chief in the department is obliged to accept this report due to their faith in the 'experience' of their field officers, and the chance for adoption is lost due to the reinscription of race during the pursuit of public policy.

Roddy's eventual placement depends upon a chance encounter on a train between Ricky and a stranger, Mrs Ella Tamerlane, and is something of a surprise. Ricky is in the midst of dealing with an urgent contingency. Two black infants have been left alone in foul conditions and he is taking them to a children's home in Brighton for urgent care. He has been assisted in collecting and cleaning the twins by a benevolent white taxi driver, whose concern for them offers another neat everyday example of colour-blind transcultural compassion. 'I've got kids of my own, mate', the driver says to Ricky. 'In this world, you never know when you'll need a helping hand' (94). After he explains all this to Mrs Tamerlane while aboard the Brighton train, Mrs Tamerlane immediately nominates herself a prospective adoptive parent. Ricky soon meets her family (which includes two young girls, Jackie and June, and a friendly shaggy dog) in their comfortable Middlesex home and, despite some wrangling with the Department of Child Welfare, Roddy's adoption as a Tamerlane is eventually sealed. This arrangement also makes provision for Roddy's white foster aunt, Miss Keriham, to continue to visit him, while Ricky's personal investment in Roddy's welfare sees him build a modest relationship with the child (who calls him 'Uncle Ricky'). Hence, Roddy ends up as the recipient of a wealth of colour-blind care and part of an adoptive family that functions lovingly and successfully.

Soon after Roddy's adoption is confirmed, Ricky launches into a self-lauding passage in which he redefines his role as the paid servant of the Department of Child Welfare *not* as the representative of migrants and their descendents but of a larger constituency altogether: '"My people" were not only the black ones; they were all the unfortunates temporarily down on their luck, needing a helping hand; [...] all those who did not limit their love and kindliness by the unprobable barriers of colour or caste or creed' (185). Ricky's last sight of Roddy outside a school with his mother and two new sisters is saccharine in conveying the new directions for collectivity that are plotted when race thinking is relinquished:

> Looking back, I saw them going in the opposite direction; Ella and Jackie sedately in step, arms linked; June and Roddy holding hands and skipping along beside them. A family. Each one belonging. (188)

The benign physical connectedness across genders and generations here opposes sinister associations of sexual contact that Roddy was freighted with by institutional racism. The book's final word, 'belonging', not only clinches Roddy's achievement of a family unit but also stands as evidence of the utopian utility of colour-blind strategies that can overcome the privations of race more widely through the refusal racially to limit 'love and kindliness'. Institutional racism here meets its match through the labour of colour-blind family-making. In this historical moment at least, according to *Paid Servant*, colour-blindness has the capacity to intervene in the public administration of transcultural adoption which has so often turned on terrible kinds of prejudices.

Yet the political efficacy of colour-blindness in *Paid Servant* comes at a price: the impossibility of adoptive being and the chance to think transfiguratively. Ricky's antipathy towards race means that he cannot envisage consanguineous relations as possessing the capacity for empowerment when thought of outside of normative race thinking. In opposing biocentric explanations of human character, Ricky cuts off blood-lines from acting as possible life lines, vital strands of connection to histories and cultural provenances with which Roddy might make something in, and as, the future. In the quotation above, 'belonging' does not require any reference to consanguineous attachments because they are rendered as of no value at all in *Paid Servant*. Should readers doubt this point of view, Ricky produces some powerful and highly contentious 'evidence': namely, Roddy's birth-mother, Angela Williams, whose contempt for Roddy is narrated as proof of the redundancy of biogenetic lines of connection.

The unflattering representation of Angela in *Paid Servant* makes the book complicit with the dreadful rendering of birth-mothers more widely and is its deepest flaw. It enables Ricky to dispense with biogenetic attachment as meaningful for Roddy's present and future life. Impulsively, Ricky decides to track down Angela and visits her unannounced one afternoon in her apartment house 'in a dingy side street, not far from Paddington Station' (80). The visit does little to alleviate the stigma of prostitution which has been attached to Angela. She answers the door wearing only a 'thick towel robe' (80), and when she reluctantly admits Ricky inside she closes an interior door 'which probably led into a bedroom' (81). She claims to be unemployed, yet Ricky considers that her flat suggests she is 'doing quite well' (82). When asked about her concern for Roddy, Angela is a model of indifference:

> 'Don't you care anything about him?' I asked her.
> 'No.' The word came out flat and definite. I sat looking at her, wondering about the protracted process which finally made her like this. Something must have been happening inside her also, for now she leaned forward. 'Look.' A new strident note was in her voice. 'I made up my mind before he was born that I would not look at him, wouldn't have anything to do with him. I've never seen him, don't know what he looks like, don't want to know. I've had enough, do you hear, and I'm finished with that.' (81)

Angela's voiding of Roddy from her life is both unsettling and a mode of convenience for Ricky. Although it is clear that she may be a victim of emotional or psychological damage, or driven by desperate circumstances to her current life – the 'protracted process' of which Ricky remarks – neither Ricky nor the book as a whole is especially interested in Angela's fortunes. Her strident decision to be 'finished' with her son is highly convenient and, in the context of birth-mother testimonies which have appeared recently, probably suspect. The encounter, which is narrated about one-third of the way through *Paid Servant*, lasts for less than three pages, and it concludes with

Ricky accepting Angela's judgement that 'Roddy was better off without her' (82). At no point does Ricky try to establish Roddy's paternal genealogy, so the vagueness of his American parentage remains (as in *Secrets and Lies*, the problematic withholding of the birth-father's identity is endorsed by the text). Angela's representation does nothing to dispel cruel myths of birth-mothers as unpalatable, amoral and lacking compassion. At one point in the book, Ricky seems to attend to the often unspoken pain of birth-parents, 'those tragic figures who are sometimes literally pressured into the decision of abandoning a child or children whom they love, choosing that drastic way of ensuring that it received food, clothing and shelter which they could no longer provide' (148–9). But *Paid Servant* thinks rarely about these people and is much more concerned with the belonging brokered through being raised in white adoptive families which need not make reference to the pain of sundered attachments.

In expediently dispensing with Angela, *Paid Servant* also removes the notion that biogenetic relations may retain significance or at least have some role to play in adoptee life, now or in the future. In so doing, Braithwaite keeps race and biogenetics worryingly aligned. His refusal to countenance race becomes a wholesale rejection of biogenetic relations. His advocacy of colour-blindness cancels the potential significance of consanguineous attachments tout court rather than effects the uncoupling of race thinking from the nature of blood. It is revealing that just prior to the book's end Angela crosses Ricky's mind just for a moment so he can replay her earlier dismissal in order to clear the ground for the book's final image of Roddy outside school. 'Did she really forget she had borne a son?', he wonders. 'If tomorrow I saw her and told her the boy was ill and calling for her, would there be a change of attitude? Probably not. After all, she did not know him, could certainly not remember him, so he was merely a vague and rather painful experience' (183). Ricky endorses Angela's previous position without thinking about how her affectless responses might themselves be a symptom of pain or require welfare support and significant care. Rather, he is content to allow Angela's painful experiences also to remain 'vague'. If Roddy's adoption requires Angela legally to give up all claims to her child, then *Paid Servant* clinches its vision of colour-blind belonging by effectively giving up on Angela. The new embrace of the adoptive family erases the physical presence of Roddy's progenitors. Without the opportunity to think constructively, even playfully, about the biogenetic life lines of his existence, there will be no adoptive being in Roddy's future, from whom the particulars of his nativity have been concealed.

As we have seen, Ricky's endeavours on behalf of black and mixed-race children in care means that his colour-blindness plays an important critical role in the administration of transcultural adoptions by the local authority. Under certain circumstances, *Paid Servant* suggests, colour-blindness has productive political agency. In regarding transcultural adoption historically, we need to admit this possibility. But Ricky's narrative account – what he makes these adoptions *mean* symbolically – circumvents this political agency and turns transcultural adoption towards more normative and assimilative ends. Put bluntly, Ricky requisitions adoption as a mode of imaginatively realizing 'belonging' in Britain which ultimately reflects not the political needs of others but the fantasies of the narrator. His unspoken ambition, across both *Paid Servant* and its predecessor, *To Sir, With Love*, is to gain access to the liberal, relatively tolerant environs of comfortable middle-class professional and domestic life. Roddy's adoption is the perfect symbol of this possibility in action: the forging of a race-free mode of filial belonging within a liberal environment, beyond the institutions of racism that are out of synch with vernacular day-to-day life (as proved by the benign taxi driver) and the self-defeating lackadaisical activities of black communities in Britain as Braithwaite finds them. Intriguingly, in his book *Reluctant Neighbours* (1972), Braithwaite remembers being stationed with the RAF in Hornchurch during the War and befriending a kindly white couple, Elsie and Dan Rowlands, in Brentwood. He is encouraged to call them 'Mum and Dad' (30), and collectively they constitute for a while the image of a welcoming and colour-blind transcultural adoptive unit. Demobbed and working in London, Braithwaite repeatedly distances himself from migrant communities and expresses imperious disappointment with them. In one extended passage he decries the conduct of Caribbean migrants who augment the discrimination cruelly visited upon them in the UK with some home-grown prejudices of their own: 'they still find time and energy to maintain amongst themselves the invidious demarcations between manual worker, office worker and student groups; between dark-skinned and light-skinned; between the educated and the unlettered [...]; yet any suggestion that they shoulder some of the responsibility for improvement in inter-racial relationship [*sic*] receives the stock answer, "What can we do in this white man's country?"' (*Paid Servant* 62-3). Theirs is precisely the community and class which Ricky wishes to escape. When Ricky considers transcultural adoption, I would hazard, it appears as an idealized opportunity where the racialized subject can exit the constraints of meagre minoritized life and enter a colour-blind domain of white-middle-class assimilation and acceptability. Roddy's adoption ultimately is so appealing to Ricky because it symbolizes his fantasy of class mobility as much as the 'end' of race. In that closing image of the once-derided Roddy 'belonging' in a white family, Ricky sees an image of the future he craves for himself and has sought to realize vicariously through his administration of colour-blind transcultural adoptions. In sum, Roddy becomes the transcultural adoptee that Ricky longs to be.

As we have seen, in the UK the emergence of a significantly sized black and mixed-race constituency of adoptees was a distinct phenomenon of the immediate post-war decades. In the United States, the history of racialized adoptability is a much longer one, not least because the country has possessed a considerable black population for centuries. As Briggs records, the end of slavery increased the vulnerability of many black children, as former slave owners moved quickly to rid themselves of the cost of providing 'for children who, through whatever legal or extralegal violence, illness, or other catastrophe, were not under the care of their mother or another relative' (50). While the actions of several philanthropists sought to support the growing number of black waifs and orphans, the burden of childcare fell to black families and micro communities 'who never saw themselves as institutions' but 'performed social welfare functions for their neighbors, kin, and strangers, taking in boarders – paying and not – of many ages, including children' (51). While these ad hoc intra-racial informal adoptive arrangements are not transcultural strictly speaking, they are indelibly stamped with the wider prejudicial dispensation of post-abolition America and striated by the steeply hierarchical condition of welfare provision and race relations which, as Briggs argues, have not radically shifted in US adoption practices after the end of Jim Crow and the advent of civil rights.

These particulars contribute to the historical context of Toni Morrison's novel *Jazz* (1992), which is set between 1855 and 1926. It tells of the virulent racism of the South in the nineteenth century, the passage north of many African Americans and the so-called realm of the 'New Negro' and the Harlem

Renaissance of the early twentieth century, ostensibly through the fortunes of its central characters who have experienced intra-racial adoptive upbringings. While the novel's attention to informal rather than 'strong' adoptions might set it apart from the other texts and contexts we explore in *Life Lines*, I wish to bring the novel into my wider critique of transcultural writing for two reasons. First, the adoptive attachments it explores are the result of the racist disenfranchisement of African Americans and need to be situated within the vexed transversal relations between racialized communities rather than approached as discrete. Second, Morrison reckons transfiguratively with the violent histories she tracks in improvisational family-making in order to fashion a reconditioned futurity for African Americans which we might recognize in terms of adoptive being. Indeed, the rendition of adoptive being in *Jazz* resonates productively with other such examples I will discuss later, such as Catherine McKinley's and Jackie Kay's trace narratives. The inclusion of Morrison's work deepens rather than diverges from the major preoccupation of *Life Lines*.

Morrison's exploration of impersonal or public histories through the seemingly private realm of family-making is characteristic of her vivid, exquisitely crafted fiction. In *Tar Baby* (1981), she follows the story of orphan and adoptee Jadine to expose, in Margaret Homans's words, 'the appeal and the risk of romantic fictions of racial origins' (130), while the plot of *Beloved* (1987) revolves around Sethe committing infanticide rather than see her young daughter doomed to slavery. *Jazz* daringly moots how transpersonal relations, damaged by the history of race in America, might be progressively refashioned in order to break the recursive constraints of the past without ever forgetting the past's damaging and often fatal conditions. And while the practice of adoption as a legal contract or state-endorsed rearrangement of filial relations does not centrally preoccupy the novel's historical enquiry, the informal adoptive reconditioning of relations that Morrison explores is given a figurative and richly suggestive purpose.

In an early response to the novel influenced by New French feminist notions of pre-Oedipal semiotics, Andrea O'Reilly proposes that *Jazz* brokers a process of self-healing by reconnecting its central characters with an experience of the maternal previously denied through the sundering of African American families. An indicative example is Joe Trace's journey to his birth-mother

Wild's womb-like woodland dwelling in Vesper County which requires him to clamber through an opening in a rock formation that, to O'Reilly's eyes, appears like another 'birth canal' (374) which enables Joe emotionally to reconvene his relations with the maternal. O'Reilly's approach keeps in place biogenetic motherhood as exclusive and primary, and casts other occasions of nurturing in the novel as 'substitution': as counterfeit stand-in relations that function as 'strategies of denial' (368) rather than as meaningful possibilities of alternative kinship. O'Reilly persistently endorses a distinctly consanguineous model of 'original self' (371) for the central characters which the sundering of blood-lines has violated and which requires recovery. But *Jazz* suggests otherwise. Actually, in the novel such origins are audaciously presented as constraining not confirming. Morrison is interested instead in what might be refigured from the painful past of sundering and severance which scars the history of African American life. In her brief sharp reading of the novel, Marianne Novy rightly questions the assumption that substitution is a secondary means of securing intimate kinship: if love 'is always love of a substitute, the novel suggests, it is still love; this has obvious implications for how we see the substitution involved in adoption' (218). What would happen if we read *Jazz* outside of assumptions of biogenetic primacy or original or umbilical selfhood?

I want to consider the possibilities for *refashioning* intimate kinship which the novel's productive approach to adoption engenders and explore why Morrison does not prioritize biocentric mothering nor privilege the linking of birthing to motherhood visualized by the umbilical hyphen in 'birth-mother'. The lost body of the birth-mother remains unrecoverable in *Jazz*, and repeated attempts to reconvene this particular relationship significantly remain unfulfilled. Wild's woodland dwelling, when Joe eventually discovers it, is empty. There, Joe experiences but a fantasy of reunion with Wild – 'She will hold out her hand, walk towards me in ugly shoes, but her face is clean and I am proud of her' (183) – rather than encounter at last her missing person. At the vignette's end he is still wondering, '[b]ut where is *she?*' (184). Joe's trace discovers only more traces and does not deliver the missing maternal body. Instead, Morrison makes from her characters' regrettable histories of sundering, loss and pain an improvisational mode of adoptive being. These regenerative aims are captured in the novel's changing weather. In the narrative present of 1926, we move from the chill of winter to the first buds of spring,

away from cold darkness towards the 'Sweetheart weather' (195) with its 'pure
and steady light' that inspires the jazz musicians on the rooftops, whose music can
be heard 'from Lenox to St Nicholas and across 135th Street, Lexington, from
Convent to Eighth' (196). As in Jackie Kay's novel *Trumpet* (1998), jazz becomes
the sonic signature of fledgling modes of adoptive being, of emergent kinds of
transpersonal relations scored by unhappy histories but resyncopated by the
agential possibilities which adoption delivers up to all – just as the impromptu
jazz music performed on the rooftops of Lenox Avenue circumnavigates the
neighbourhood and lifts the spirits of those who hear it down below.

As is often noted, the formal design of *Jazz* is clearly indebted to the
disciplined and inventive form of jazz music, particularly the ways musicians
improvise musical passages within a repeating chord structure or recurring
notation, often returning to join the other band members at key moments of
refrain. Gurleen Grewal has described the narrative's polyphonic artistry in
musical terms and proposes that 'the novel strains to gather in the rhythms
of a jazz narrative the experience of black collectivity' (128). The disciplined
adventurousness of jazz – of going out on a limb but never off key, improvising
a score but often coming back into alignment with a repeating chord sequence
or phrase – clearly inflects Morrison's novel. We are reminded many times that
fifty-year-old Joe Trace, partner of Violet, has shot his new young lover Dorcas
in a seeming fit of jealousy, and that Violet has attacked Dorcas's corpse with
a knife as her body lay in its coffin at the funeral. As the unnamed narrator
fleshes out the circumstances behind these incidents, the narrative shifts to
and fro to recount the younger lives of these central figures, always returning
to the present of 1926. Less often recognized, however, is the novel's structural
indebtedness also to the patternings of adoptive relations, specifically the triad
of birth-parent, adoptee and adoptive parent. The prevalence of references to
triads or the number three is worthy of note and provides *Jazz*'s musical form
with a distinctly adoptive rhythm. As well as the triangular relations between
Joe, Violet and Dorcas, several other threefold arrangements appear: between
Dorcas and the Miller sisters; between Violet's grandmother True Belle, Vera
Louise and Golden Gray; between Joe, Violet and Felice. Joe's relationship with
Dorcas lasts for 'three months of nights' (28); Dorcas has three dolls (Rochelle,
Bernadine, Faye) that perish in a house fire; Violet attacks Dorcas's body at
the funeral held 'three days into 1926' (9); Joe searches for Wild three times in

Vesper County. With the concluding triad of Felice, Violet and Joe, Morrison shifts away from the adoption triad as a sign and consequence of violated connections and instead reshapes triadic relations as an improvisational concert – resembling something like a jazz trio, if you like. A constraining fixation upon the past's irrecoverable losses gives way to a sense of personhood as constituted *not* by its missing pieces but as an unfinished harmonious plurality, a concerted 'being-with' (31) in Nancy's parlance.

The consanguineous losses suffered by *Jazz*'s three central figures damage the lives of each. Joe is the birth-son of a mysterious African American woman, known only as Wild, who lives rough in the woods of Vesper County, Virginia. He is raised adoptively by Rhoda and Frank Williams and always knows that he is not genetically related to them. He names himself 'Joseph Trace' at school to reflect his adoptive status because Rhoda told him that his biogenetic parents left without a trace: 'The way I heard it I understood her to mean the "trace" they disappeared without was me' (124). As well as perpetually positioning Joe in relation to missing birth-parents and maintaining the cognizance of loss, 'Trace' also holds out the promise of recovering that loss through an act of tracking down the departed. It is not for nothing that Joe is one of the best hunters in Vesper County, 'more comfortable in the woods than in a town' (126), who builds a sense of self out of his capacity to search out the most elusive of creatures. This compulsion to trace comes to animate his adult relationships. His consciousness of having failed to find Wild three times creates an interiorized sense of incompleteness that he takes into middle age and which is significant in his relationship with both Violet and Dorcas. His marriage to Violet is entangled with his inability to find Wild, as if his relationship with his wife will compensate for the loss of his mother. Frustrated that Wild will not give him a sign of maternal acknowledgement by waving her hand through a bush, Joe looks elsewhere for love: he declares, '"All right, Violet, I'll marry you", just because I couldn't see whether a wildwoman put out her hand or not' (181). His marriage to Violet does not divest Joe of feelings of emptiness derived from biomaternal absence but remains to fuel his pursuit of Dorcas. As the narrator puts it after telling of Joe's failure to find Wild, 'the inside nothing he traveled with from then on, except for the fall of 1925 when he had somebody to tell it to. Somebody called Dorcas with hooves tracing her cheekbones and who knew better than people his own age what that inside nothing was like' (37-8). Joe's repeated attempts to live in the present always with reference to his unhappy past block his maturation and keep him curiously boy-like despite his being aged 50. The narrator imagines him as 'one of those men who stop somewhere around sixteen. Inside. [... H]e's a kid, a strapling, and candy could still make him smile' (120-1). This touch of infantilization recurs across the novel's three key characters and indexes the recursive relation between past and present which the novel, in its jazzy narrative manoeuvring, seeks to put on the move.

Dorcas is raised in the City by her aunt, Alice Manfred (her mother's sister), after her parents are killed when she is a child. Her father dies, presumably in a racist incident amidst the tense racial atmosphere of East St Louis in 1917, 'pulled off a streetcar and stomped to death' (57), while her mother is killed in an arson attack as Dorcas sleeps at a friend's house across the road. Dorcas is also linked to the dangers of repetition, especially as regards jazz music. She is thrilled by the seductive excitements of the City, especially its music and dance-parties, which stir her body with their sensual and ennobling promise. If, for Alice, jazz is proximate to 'dirty, get-on-down music' (58), a sign of disorder and a contributory factor to the fatal happenings in East St Louis, then for Dorcas it is the City's passionate affiliative possibilities sculpted in sound. She hears the drums as the beat of 'a beginning, a start of something she looked to complete' (60) and thrills to the erotic subtexts in the popular songs: 'a knowing woman sang ain't nobody going to keep me down you got the right key baby but the wrong keyhole you got to get it bring it and put it right here, or else' (60). In presenting Dorcas as convinced 'that life-below-the-sash [is] all the life there was' (60), the narrator significantly turns to the image of the firebombed house in order to strike a metaphor for Dorcas's passions, writing that a woodchip from the house's collapsing porch 'must have entered her stretched dumb mouth' (60) eventually to settle 'comfortably somewhere below her navel' (61). This image of smouldering desire keeps fused together jazz, passion and violence, and in a very important way ensures that jazz is not unthinkingly idealized in the novel. Like Dorcas's body figuratively aglow with the heat of the woodchip, jazz makes its own record of abuse which has damaged African American life. There is always the danger of maintaining the conflicts of the past in the repeated performances of jazz music or indeed in the repetitive elements of its composition. At one point, the narrator compares the past to 'an abused record with no choice but to repeat itself at the crack' (220).

Jazz – and, ultimately, *Jazz* – must do more than spark up older passions and conflicts.

To put this point another way, if jazz can keep old scores and is darkened and weighed down by 'a complicated anger' held in the 'belt-buckle tunes vibrating from pianos and spinning on every Victrola' (59), then its innovative capacity to process and reformulate is severely thwarted. Joe may live his life with an 'inside nothing', but Dorcas's 'inside something', her wood-chip glow, is not a ready alternative but another rendition of a sorry past taken firmly into the present – one that has the agency to overwhelm innovation and impromptu performative creativity with its recursive incendiary score.

The emphasis placed on the repetition of the past in the present is strengthened by the image of Dorcas's body in her coffin which recalls the fate of her three favourite dolls burned in the fire, made from wood and resting in a cigar box. Morrison makes the connection explicit when she warns early in the novel that Dorcas may release her figurative woodchip, 'let it loose to leap into fire again, [and] whatever happened would be quick. Like the dolls' (61). As with Joe, these important details also craft an infantilized sense of Dorcas, doll-like and childish despite her longing for mature experience.

Violet's adoption context is as troubling as Dorcas's and beckons another version of living tied to, and by, the past. Violet's mother, Rose Dear, drowns herself in a well not long after she is left destitute in Vesper County, while her father is frequently absent, returning periodically with presents and trinkets for his children but offering little enduring love and even less commitment. Violet is raised by True Belle, her grandmother, who had recently returned from service in Baltimore. There she helped raise Golden Gray, the mixed-race child of a white woman, Vera Louise, who was effectively banished from Vesper County as a consequence of her sexual relations with a local black man, Henry LesTroy. Golden Gray's champagne-coloured skin saves him at birth from being surrendered to the local Catholic Foundling Hospital, where 'white-girls deposited their mortification' (148). Additionally, and as O'Reilly has noted, True Belle's absence due to her enslaved condition (she has to pretend to be dying in order to be released from service to Vera Louise) robs Rose Dear of a vital means of maternal support, evidence again of the transversal damage done to African American filial relations by slavery's operations. Violet's traumatic loss of her mother becomes a significant reason in her own decision never to have children. 'Whatever happened, no small dark foot would rest on another while a hungry mouth said, Mama?' (102). We are told that she has experienced two miscarriages, but a fleeting reference to 'soap, salt and castor oil' (109) suggests that her pregnancies may have been aborted. Yet later in life, Violet suffers an unbidden change of heart. Despite appearing beyond child-bearing age and 'just when her nipples had lost their point, mother-hunger hit her like a hammer' (108). She undergoes a 'panting, unmanageable craving' (108) for a child – another 'inside empty', maybe – that on one occasion leads her to start sleeping with a doll and, as reported early in the narrative, momentarily to take a stranger's baby from a pram. By 1926, Violet appears as a child without a mother and like a mother without a child. Her body seems distinctly pre-pubescent (she binds her breasts to look flat-chested). This doubling of middle-aged and child-like bodies indexes the extent to which Violet too is stuck in, and animated by, a painful history that dictates and constrains her fortunes, arresting the possibilities for regenerative acts of reproduction for her own being as well as of another's.

Violet's increasingly acute feeling of missing an unborn child poignantly emerges when she wonders in 1926 'how old that last miscarried child would be now'? (108). Such feelings figure too, and with crucial significance for *Jazz*, when she links the figure of the deceased Dorcas to her unborn child. This linkage provides a clue as to how to read the triadic relations between Violet, Joe and Dorcas:

> Who lay there asleep in that coffin? Who posed there awake in the photograph? The scheming bitch who had not considered Violet's feelings one tiniest bit, who came into a life, took what she wanted and damn the consequences? Or mama's dumpling girl? Was she the woman who took the man, or the daughter who fled her womb? [...] [B]itch or dumpling, the two of them, mother and daughter, could have walked Broadway together and ogled the clothes. Could be sitting together, cozy in the kitchen, while Violet did her hair. (109)

Violet's rendering of Dorcas's dead body as the image of an unborn daughter, seen in the coffin or remembered posthumously in the photograph she purloins from Alice, has considerable consequences for the novel's transfigurative aims. Violet's childlessness is a response to the loss of her mother, and her fantasies of bearing a lost child perpetuate that initial maternal absence. Read figuratively, Violet's unanticipated and unrealizable desire to bear a child of her own reconfirms the capacity of the death of Rose Dear to dictate her adult behaviour. With Dorcas cast as the latest manifestation of the unrecoverable or unavailable – Violet can only assault her corpse, not confront her rival – Violet's attack at the funeral is not solely motivated by jealous rage but also a symbolic attempt to end once and for all the traumatic and recursive wounding of Rose Dear's suicide. It is an attempt to destroy in the present an older constitutive act of destruction from the past, a potential moment of release which might make transformation more possible.

Violet's *action* of striking out, rather than the act itself, is what matters. Dorcas's body is not violated by the stabbing: '[the knife] bounced off, making a little dent under her earlobe, like a fold in the skin that was hardly a disfigurement at all' (91). Violet does not penetrate the corpse but scores it, impressing a groove in the skin rather than cutting it open. She uses a knife taken from her parrot's cage at home, where she had left it after scraping 'the parrot's claws and beak weeks ago' (90). Another image of recurrence, the parrot mechanically repeats the words 'I love you' (24), suggesting the absence of love and reciprocity in Violet's life that rendered her emotionally void. Within the complex figurative framework of the novel, the act of Violet's assault on Dorcas using a knife taken from the parrot's cage symbolizes the attempt, once and for all, to relinquish the reiterative agency of traumatic loss. It is a necessary act that will empower other forms of possible kinship in which the memory of biological maternal connection can be *redeployed* generatively as one line of attachment amongst others. The fact that Violet releases the birds she keeps at home from their cages immediately after her assault on Dorcas's body thematizes this attempt to be free, to locate elsewhere a better kind of loving which, like jazz music, can shape something creative by working with, rather than repeating, a set score.

The same transfigurative process is at work in Joe's pursuit and violent attack on Dorcas. As we noted above, Joe's relationship with Dorcas is entangled with the disappearance of Wild. So when Dorcas slips from Joe's sight and takes up with Acton, Joe's pursuit of her in the City effects the repetition of his tracking of his birth-mother and his memories from his childhood (such as his brother, Victory):

> As he puts on his coat and cap he can practically feel Victory at his side when he sets out, armed, to find Dorcas. He isn't thinking of harming her, or, as Hunter had cautioned, killing something tender. She is female. And she is

not prey. So he never thinks of that. He is hunting for her though, and while hunting a gun is as natural a companion as Victory. (180)

The words 'She is female. And she is not prey' echo the words of Hunters Hunter, the man who trained Joe in Vesper County (and is probably Golden Gray's birth-father) and who used to warn him against injuring Wild, something which Joe always interpreted as evidence of Wild's maternity. Joe's rather dubious declaration of his intention not to harm Dorcas assists in accentuating the figurative significance of his pursuit as one which not only partially recalls his youthful quest for Wild but shapes an opportunity for Joe to succeed in the present where he failed in the past. But in successfully tracking Dorcas to the party, Joe is instead brought to realize once and for all that tracking missing persons does *not* lead to their recovery but sustains destruction and loss. The outcome of his pursuit is the death not the recovery of Dorcas, shot through the shoulder causing a fatal loss of blood. Tracing does not recover the missing, just as Dorcas does not recover from her wounding. In shooting Dorcas, Joe symbolically terminates the assumption that tracing consanguineous origins secures the bedrock of being. Dorcas's loss of blood at a moment which promised to fulfil Joe's earlier quest to recover blood-lines indexes the mortal rather than mystical condition of consanguinity. Just as Violet's assault is a displaced attack on the constraints of maternal loss, Joe's attack is a figurative termination of the primacy of the notion of the trace as restoring and preserving consanguineous relations.

In these readings, the symbolic role assumed by Dorcas in the narrative – especially the bloody nature of her death – is both complex and crucial. Her orphaning tells of the long, ongoing history of racism in the United States, while the circumstances of her death foreground the sexism that has characterized African American female experience and points to the particular predicaments within which women have found themselves when African American men act chauvinistically. In a manner which recalls her beloved childhood dolls, Dorcas is considered a marionette by men who seek to sculpt and style her as they choose. Keen for love and attention, she is vulnerable to the whims of others. At one of the first parties she goes to, aged sixteen, she seeks the attention of two handsome brothers and is crushed when one of them dismisses her by wrinkling his nose and turning away from her:

'Dorcas has been acknowledged, appraised and dismissed in the time it takes for a needle to find its opening groove. The stomach-jump of possible love is nothing compared to the ice floes that block up her veins now' (67). For Joe, as we have seen, she doubles for the lost mother-figure, someone to alleviate his 'inside empty'. Her new beau, Acton, also has his own designs for her, as she describes it: 'he tells me when he doesn't like the way I fix my hair. Then I do it how he likes it. I never wear glasses when he is with me and I changed my laugh for him to one he likes better' (190). Her death is prompted by male covetousness and violence. The antagonisms of racism and the jealousies of men incline destructively and are frighteningly fused in an image of Dorcas's attenuated mortality. But just as adoption is more than the painful conditions which enabled it, Morrison daringly uses the manner of Dorcas's dying as contributing to a new way of thinking about transpersonal being *adoptively*, without forgetting or sanitizing these conditions.

As we have seen, both Joe and Violet perceive Dorcas in terms of consanguineous relations: missing mothers and unborn children. Her symbolic connection to blood and blood-lines is very particular. She dies from a loss of blood from her shoulder wound, and, according to her friend Felice she rebuffed the chance to receive medical attention and so effectively chose to bleed to death: '"Dorcas let herself die. The bullet went in her shoulder, this way." I pointed. "She wouldn't let anybody move her; said she wanted to sleep and she would be all right" [...]' (209). At the party, blood is referred to several times as a sign of inflamed or warring passion, leading to conflict rather than congress. It is anything but a symbol of intimate relations or filial safety. The party is 'like war. Everyone is handsome, shining just thinking about other people's blood. As though the red wash flying from veins not theirs is facial makeup patented for its glow' (191). This remarkable image of blood as cosmetic, prettifying the handsome bodies whose ruthless pursuit of each other will render '[p]artners and rivals devastated' (191) is turned to again soon after, when Dorcas witnesses Acton seeking to clean his blood-soaked clothing with the assistance of a nameless woman: 'Blood is on his coat jacket and he is dabbing at it with a white handkerchief. Now a woman takes the coat from his shoulders. He is annoyed by the blood. [...] Acton looks angry; the woman brings his jacket back and it is not clean' (192). These traces of blood on the clothes and the body mark Morrison's attempt to expose and disrupt sanguinity not as substance but as a style – a way of acting, relating, thinking, appearing – the pursuit of which stains the self rather than sustains being. Morrison challenges a notion of blood as vital or nourishing by exposing its cosmetic, confected 'glow' and figuratively connecting it to conflict rather than confluence, corruption rather than fulfilment. Dorcas's death literalizes the novel's relinquishment of received ideas of blood as the primary substance of transpersonal relations and emotional well-being.

In the context of sundered filial relations, this giving up on thoughts of blood is concomitant with Morrison's renouncing of the primacy of biogenetic origins as vital to transpersonal well-being. When we recall that Joe's pursuit of Dorcas is animated by his displaced desire to realize his previously failed attempts to locate his birth-mother, his explanations of his longing for Dorcas take on particular resonance. In one speech, he casts her as another Eve:

> I told you again that you were the reason Adam ate the apple and its core. That when he left Eden, he left a rich man. Not only did he have Eve, but he had the taste of the first apple in the world in his mouth for the rest of his life. The very first to know what it was like. To bite it, to bite it down. Hear the crunch and let the red peeling break his heart. (133)

The novel's triangulation of Dorcas with Eve and Wild presents a biblical context for Joe's discovery of Wild's woodland dwelling in Vesper County. The attempt to reunite with his birth-mother is equivalent to a return to a prelapsarian state of unsundered innocence, before 'the crunch' when the heart breaks, as the apple (significantly red, not green) is lost as it is consumed. Its taste is part of the 'empty inside', the residue of which recalls the original object, forever gone. If we follow this figurative line of thought, then we might think of Dorcas as like the life-long 'taste' that carries the memory of what is lost, and Wild as the 'apple and its core' always missing but ever-present in Joe's consciousness. Dorcas offers a route to an Edenic origin, to the return of Eve and the unsullied red apple. According to Felice, as Dorcas is dying she sends Joe a cryptic message: "'There's only one apple.' Sounded like 'apple'. 'Just one. Tell Joe'" (213). At the moment of death Dorcas returns us to the point of (human) origin only to rule out the possibility of recovering that origin, of escaping heartbreak, just as Joe happens upon Wild's dwelling only to realize that she remains remote, ever a question – 'where is *she*?' (184) – and never an answer or an end to the conundrum of a self phrased as an 'inside empty'. Indeed, Wild's dwelling is the ultimate 'inside empty', a natal refuge devoid of life. Like others, Joe has to start looking elsewhere if he is to move away from sundered selfhood towards reformulated being.

Felice plays the vital role in effecting this shift towards adoptive being as the novel works through these figurative meanings towards a transfigurative end. She not only brings the news of Dorcas's significant last words but also helps beckon into view possibilities for reconstituted relations. She, too, has something of an informal adoptive past, raised in the City by her grandmother and seeing her parents usually once every 'three weeks' (198). Her character empowers the rescripting of blood-lines as life lines: modes of material connection from which much might be made or improvised. We might wonder why, after Dorcas's death, Felice arrives at the Traces' abode holding a record under one arm and 'a half pound of stewmeat wrapped in pink butcher paper' (197) in her hand. These details moot a relation between the embodied and the aesthetic, between weighty matters of blood-staining flesh and the lightness of musical creativity. Her news of Dorcas's final words clinch Joe's redemptive realization that he cannot ever recover all he feels that is lost, as indexed by his 'sad' smile (213). Felice also engenders conversation with Violet which enables her to relinquish her pent-up distress about Rose Dear's death. Rather than crave for a child that will take the place of the lost mother, Violet begins to talk instead of the need to bring a new version of herself into being, related to but not defined by the actions of others: 'I want to be the woman my mother didn't stay around long enough to see. That one. The one she would have liked [...].' (208). This singular plural mode of living locates the 'one' transpersonally in the midst of missing others (Violet's mother and grandmother) but does not prioritize those relations as primary, exclusive or healthy. These consanguineous attachments resource an ontological task – 'I want to be' – and contribute to an improvisational rather than a prescribed future, critical of as well as concerned with the past. As Violet explains, True Belle's ardent nurturing of Golden Gray, the mixed-race 'little blond' (208) child who passed for white, helped redirect the energy and agency of nurturing away from Violet and her siblings and towards the racially privileged, to the extent that he 'lived inside my mind. Quiet as a mole' (208). Because of the historical circumstances involved, consanguineous relations can be complicit in the maintenance of racialization, even unwillingly. They do not necessarily offer the means to safeguard self. As Felice understands, Violet must jettison the emotional and identitarian baggage which violates or gazumps being, of 'having another you inside that isn't anything like you' (208).

The powerful consequences of turning sundered blood-lines into sustaining life lines are captured at the novel's conclusion when Felice witnesses Violet and Joe respond surprisingly to the sound of music which is heard in their apartment one afternoon through an open window: 'Mr Trace moved his head to the rhythm and his wife snapped her fingers in time. She did a little step in front of him and he smiled. By and by they were dancing. Funny, like old people do, and I laughed for real' (214). This image of a new transpersonal choreography, dancing 'funny' to raise a smile, signals the moment when the creative propensity of jazz and the future-facing chances of adoptive being come together. After Felice's visits, Violet and Joe craft new relations with each other which recall but do not reinstate the painful pasts from which they have emerged. They spend time at home 'figuring things out, telling each other those little personal stories they like to hear again and again' (223). In bed together, their emotional intimacy is animated by their imaginative improvisation with the images and rhetoric of their filial histories. Violet 'rests her hand on [Joe's] chest as though it were the sunlit rim of a well and down there somebody is gathering gifts' (225), recalling her mother's death and her father's largesse. In a spin on Joe's previous metaphor of the Edenic apple, together they think of the 'pears they let hang on the limb because if they plucked them, they would be gone from there and who else would see that ripeness if they took it away for themselves?' (228). This moment reconfigures an image of singular loss, the Edenic apple, into one of plural engagement (the pun on pears/pairs is especially sweet here). Joe calls his wife 'Vi' (223), a word denoting life, replacing her previous nickname amongst the locals, 'Violent'. Violet and Joe move from a siloed and prescribed existence, founded and foundering on the past, to an improvisational and collaborative mode of being-with, remaking themselves and their relationship, putting on the move their painful experiences of filial severance without forgetting their traces. Like jazz musicians, they improvise with the scars and scores of their histories, making something anew from cross-hatching the genealogical with the contingent, no longer parroting the past. In Violet's words, 'What's the world for if you can't make it up the way you want it?' (208).

Jazz's movement towards springtime, light and music underwrites its highly ambitious brokering of adoptive being. The 'abused record' (220) of the past is replaced with a new vitality, so that Violet and Joe are no longer infantile but 'dangerous children [...] thinking other thoughts, feeling other feelings, putting their lives together' in ways the narrator 'never dreamed of' (221). In a generative and loving space at home and under the covers, where one can '[s]ay make me, remake me' (229), *Jazz* clinches the literary occasion it has fashioned where adoptive and biogenetic notions of existential creativity generatively entangle; where the dialogic exchange of lives clasped lovingly together replaces the 'inside empty' with an embryonic form of adoptive being which *makes* as it moves palpably within: '*Talking to you and hearing you answer – that's the kick*' (229). Out of the traumatic histories of sundered relations striated by the privations of racism, Morrison imagines a refashioned futurity in terms of adoptive being.

My final example of a literary text which makes possible futures from bleak histories is Sebastian Barry's novel of twentieth-century Ireland, *The Secret Scripture* (2008). Here too is a text which refracts public affairs through the private prism of family-making, one which looks back critically across the history of post-Independence Ireland from the vantage of the early twenty-first century to admit the failures of the postcolonial nation and consider new prospects. The novel joins Barry's wider creative project, as evidenced by fictions such as *A Long Long Way* (2005) and *On Canaan's Side* (2011), in exploring the problematic complexity and untidiness of key issues and moments in Irish history especially for those Irish whose memberships of class, nationalist or denominational groupings were complicated by cultural and professional particulars. In many such texts Barry offers a rewriting of Irish history, which demands a critical reckoning with the doings of Irish politics and the authoritarianism of the nation as they are made manifest in everyday life. He draws upon a longer tradition of Irish writing (and, I would suggest, postcolonial literature more broadly) which challenges political designs, however laudable they might be in principle, by exposing the damage they may inflict on those considered suspect, especially women. Writing in 1996, Declan Kiberd contrasted the practical politics of '"green" and "orange" essentialists' after partition with 'the pluralist philosophy espoused by the artists [which] may yet contain the shape of the future' (7). In *The Secret Scripture*, a pluralizing sensibility drives its representation of race and nation as Barry recasts the alleged consanguinity of the former in terms of the itinerancy and hybridity of the latter, so that the essentialist gives way to the adoptive. With Irish blood-lines materialized as life lines of cultural and historical connectedness that may be appropriated amidst others, a post-nativist futurity for Ireland can be threaded. Barry brings to light an horrific history of Irish women, to borrow a phrase from J. G. Farrell, '"undergoing" history' (147). He rewrites that history from the margins and edges where those deemed politically corrupting or morally corrupted, like Barry's heroine Roseanne McNulty, were banished.

'I was born on the edges of things', reflects Dr William Grene, one of the two narrators of *The Secret Scripture*, 'and even now, as the guardian of the mentally ill, I have by instinct pitched my tent in a similar place' (310). An adoptee from England working as a psychiatrist at a crumbling mental hospital in twenty-first-century Ireland, Dr Grene describes himself at the novel's conclusion as a 'ridiculous, sober, ageing, confused English Irishman' (307). His involvement in the closing of the decrepit hospital, Roscommon Regional Mental Hospital, exposes readers to the secreted lives which have been pushed to the edges of Ireland's twentieth-century history since the War of Independence (1919–21) and formation of the Irish Free State, especially those women deemed to be 'fallen' by pursuing sexual affairs or having children out of wedlock. In combining the narrative of Dr Grene with that of the 100-year-old patient Roseanne, Barry's novel exposes and challenges, to use James M. Smith's terms, 'postindependence Ireland's nativist national imaginary' (3) and its indebtedness to the twinned notions of sexual and cultural purity which the realities of illegitimacy and adoption transgressively complicate. Barry demands that the violence visited upon unmarried mothers and their children by the aligned authorities of church and state be 'admitted' in two senses of the term: confessed as part of a redemptive act of atonement for the suffering of the past, and granted access to the centre of modern Irish history as part of a constituted imagined community for the next century.

Bronwen Walter records that oral Irish culture is replete with family stories of lineage and descent often told by women, but these tales are usually selective:

'some parts of the story have been hidden by collective agreement, for example stories about adoption or "illegitimate motherhood", particularly resonant in the Irish case because of punitive religious regulation' (5). Barry's novel is turned precisely to these lacunae. In foregrounding the ill-treatment of those Irish women stigmatized as sexually deviant through the figure of Roseanne, *The Secret Scripture* mounts a wholehearted critique of Irish chauvinistic nativism with the history of adoption at its heart, as a way of refusing romantic notions of cultural purity and national distinctiveness that have driven national fortunes. While the bringing together of an adoptee and his birth-mother at the novel's climax might seem to prioritize biogenetic connection over adoptive relations, Barry's *refusal* to narrate this moment as a reunion or as reconfirming the primacy of consanguineous attachment is of the upmost significance. In *The Secret Scripture*, adoptive and biogenetic genealogies interweave commensurately as Barry challenges biocentric notions of kin and kind that serve the advocacy of nativist blood-lines.

The Secret Scripture is part of a steadily growing body of recent cultural work about the fortunes of Irish women socially ostracized as sexually deviant and morally 'fallen', often as a consequence of them conceiving children when single. These women were banished to mother and baby homes, as recorded in June Goulding's memoir *The Light in the Window* (1998), which depicts her years as a nurse at Bessboro home for unmarried mothers in 1950s Cork. Stephen Frears's film *Philomena* (2013) visualizes the daily life of these homes and the unceremonious and brutal wrenching of babies from their mothers that regularly took place when the children were adopted by wealthy American families happy to make a charitable donation. Other women were confined in Ireland's notorious Magdalene Laundries, often for life, as depicted in Peter Mullan's 2002 film *The Magdalene Sisters*. As a birth-mother of a missing child and a patient in a mental hospital, Roseanne focalizes the history of these women kept away from public view. *The Secret Scripture* makes of this history a distinctly transcultural tale. Roseanne occupies more than one kind of liminality as a Presbyterian daughter of an Irish father and English mother living in the edgy social environment of Sligo in the immediate aftermath of independence and civil conflict. Meanwhile, Dr Grene is a Catholic-raised English adoptee born to an unknown Irish birth-mother, who has come to Ireland to take up a professional position at Roscommon. These details keep to the fore the culturally pluralized condition of the modern and contemporary Irish. Indeed, *The Secret Scripture*'s critique of decolonizing Ireland's public history troubles the invention of Ireland in terms of moral and cultural purity. It admits instead the transcultural encounters between different peoples and faith communities that confound the goal of establishing discrete, flawless Irish and Catholic lineage which services an atavistic nativism.

The Secret Scripture takes the form of two intercalated fictionalized narratives, neither of which is produced for public consumption. The first is 'Roseanne's Testimony of Herself' which she writes in secret while awaiting the closure of the increasingly ruinous Roscommon buildings. She recalls her early life in the post-Independence decades as a young girl growing up in Sligo, the vexed life and death of her father Joe Clear and the mental decline of her mother Cissy, after which Roseanne took to working in a local café having shunned the suggestion of the authoritarian local Catholic priest, Fr Gaunt, that she marry a recently widowed and much older man to help alleviate her straitened circumstances and join the Catholic faith. During this time she meets and marries Tom McNulty, from an influential Sligo family, much to the disapproval of Tom's strict Catholic mother. Following a clandestine meeting with an Irish insurgent, John Lavelle, which is witnessed by Fr Gaunt, Roseanne finds herself accused of sexual infidelity, shunned by her husband and confined to a tin hut on the edge of town, where she eventually learns that her marriage has been annulled on the grounds of her 'insanity' as a nymphomaniac. Later, wretched and lonely, she experiences a chance liaison with Tom's brother Eneas during the early 1940s and becomes pregnant. She bears her child by the sea as a terrific storm rages in Sligo. Waking after her ordeal to find her child gone and an ambulance present, she is accused of infanticide and confined in mental institutions for the rest of her life.

The second narrative, interspersed with Roseanne's, is 'Dr Grene's Commonplace Book' which records the facts of Dr Grene's adoption, his reflections on the decline of his marriage to Irish wife Bet and her death, the problems he faces in assessing which Roscommon patients continue to need care and who might be moved back into the community once the building is demolished. He also reflects upon his past in England, his mother's suicide, his growing care for Roseanne and his attempts to track down the files which tell of her history of confinement. As Dr Grene pieces together the official version of her life, elements of which do not entirely tally with Roseanne's account, the novel works towards its climactic revelation: that Roseanne's baby was not washed away by the sea but was secretly taken by John Lavelle's son John Kane (who now works in Roscommon), given to an orphanage and adopted by a couple from England, who turn out to be Dr Grene's parents.

These two narratives are precisely historically situated. In *Ireland's Magdalen Laundries and the Nation's Architecture of Containment* (2007), James M. Smith lays bare the centrality of notions of sexual purity – and, by default, sexual deviance – to the collaborative activities of the Catholic Church and Irish politics from the nineteenth century to the establishment of the Free State and long afterwards, until at least the late twentieth century. Smith notes how in the wake of colonial rule and civil war, 'Catholic morality became at once a hallmark of Irish identity, differentiating the national community from its near neighbors, and an emblem of the uncontested political territory, enabling politicians to eschew party affiliations and seek unanimity through religious conformity' (3). Catholicism was a means of forging common nativist identification and healing the rifts opened between Irish communities during the War of Independence and the civil strife that followed after 1922, and helped cement a close partnership between the mechanisms of the Free State and the machinations of the Church. The moralism pursued by this partnership had consequences for women, for whom any divergence from the expected behaviour of marital respectability was framed as a criminal action against the broader expanse of family, community and nation. Smith explains how the emergence of the mother and baby homes and Magdalene laundries set up by the Catholic Church to house and imprison so-called fallen women enabled a strategy of containment which went directly to the heart of post-Independence Irish self-fashioning:

> the availability of this containment infrastructure empowered the decolonising nation-state to confine aberrant citizens, rendering invisible women and children who fell foul of society's moral proscriptions. In this way, I argue, the state regulated its national imaginary; it promoted a national identity that privileged Catholic morality and valorized the correlation between marriage and motherhood while at the same time effacing nonconforming citizens who were institutionally confined. (46-7)

In these terms, the conjoining of church and state in post-Independence Ireland happened along one direction through the disciplining of female sexual agency, which made alleged sexual impropriety a menace for 'the fiction of Irish cultural purity' (19). Extra-marital sexual relations not only disconcerted religious precepts, they also posed a threat to the distinctiveness, particularity and propriety of the newly minted nation and its citizenship. Sexual transgression threatened the reproduction of cultural character, so that to pursue intimacy outside marriage was to fall (short) both as a woman and as an Irish citizen.

Maryann Gialanella Valiulis has argued that the decolonizing Irish state, along with several other once-colonized locations, consolidated its fragile new authority by 'asserting its power *vis a vis* restrictions against women' (127) and crafting a post-Independence model of Irishness in which 'women would be a badge of respectability for a new state' and safeguard the values, ironically derived from Victorian Britain, of 'respect, sobriety, hard work, self-help, thrift, and sexual puritanism' (128). This seeking of a higher moral high ground was a reflex response created out of Ireland's colonial history: 'the Free State used gender ideology to demonstrate moral superiority [...]. It was an opportunity for an Irish government to vindicate itself from unflattering stereotypes and degrading portraits that had been so much a part of their colonial experience' (129). Within this cultural environment, a great deal was at stake in the scandal of the so-called fallen woman, sexually deviant and morally degenerate, bearing children outside of wedlock. Chillingly, and as Smith reminds us, the image of the disrespectable Irish woman was perversely *required* by Irish self-fashioning: 'The spectre of the Magdalen penitent must always be available; she represents a stark contrast that enables women in the outside world, regardless of class, to secure their respectability based on religious, social, and sexual conformity' (36). The fallen woman's unhomely figure carries simultaneously a sexual and societal threat. In her impropriety she conjures the ghosts of the colonial past, traces of that wider colonial attachment of old. She reminds the Irish of their previous subservience to, and congress with, a foreign colonial power, and recalls Empire's colonialist representation of Ireland as morally and intellectually lax, uncivil and lacking culture. The unwed mother in post-Independence Ireland signifies a scandal and a threat that supersedes exclusively moral or religious insubordination.

She also serves as a reminder of the cruel colonial cliché of the degenerate Irish, and her presence at large threatens to corrupt those attempts to fashion a new culture of Irishness that repudiates the imperious imaginary of its near neighbour.

In *The Secret Scripture*, Roseanne's unhappy fortunes find their historical provenance in these particulars. She is constructed as both culturally and sexually perverse within the provincial world of Sligo during the transitional period of postcolonial independence and civil war. Roseanne is a disquieting presence in Sligo for her gender and her demonization. She is perceived in sexist terms as dangerously beautiful – Fr Gaunt calls her 'a mournful temptation' (98) – and she is transculturally troubling as a Presbyterian of Anglo-Irish descent who refuses to become Catholic. 'Presbyterians were not much loved in Sligo' (41), Roseanne recalls. '[I]n the old days there was a lot of that proselytising going on, with a Presbyterian mission to the west and the like, which though it had not been a raging success, had yet gathered a number of Catholics to the fold in a time of terrible hunger and need, and thereby increased the level of fear and mistrust among the people' (41). Given this account, Roseanne symbolizes an edgy, dual menace to Irish nativist harmony and purity. Her Presbyterianism recalls long-standing divisions within the nation which trigger the traumatic memory of the Irish Famine, while her English heredity points to the persistence of perceived foreignness within. This heredity can also be traced through her father's name as well as her mother's side of the family. She tells Dr Grene that her maiden name Clear 'is a Protestant name and maybe comes out of England long ago' (118), although Dr Grene wonders if it may be connected to Cape Clear (Ireland's southernmost inhabited island). Looking at her aged body in Roscommon, Dr Grene can still discern the difference she represents, 'a sort of manifestation of something unusual and maybe alien in this provincial world' (18). Her eventual confinement in a mental institution, declared guilty of improper sexual relations and infanticide, has everything to do with her unwillingness to conceal and contain the cultural provenance of her biogenetic heredity by refusing to be absorbed into a nativist confection of the proper Irish woman at the bidding of the sinister Fr Gaunt.

Importantly, Roseanne's life story emphasizes exogamous connections, to England and Ireland, beyond the Catholic faith. As will become apparent, an important element of Barry's ethical envisioning of a reinvented Ireland is his decoupling of biogenetics from biocentrism, voiding consanguineous guarantees of identitarian and cultural constancy. As *The Secret Scripture* is at pains to emphasize, blood-lines do not provide guarantees of stable identity or connections to people of similar kin or kind. In constructing images of nativist purity, the Free State's Irish Catholicism seeks to produce a vision of endogamous nativism which compensates for and conceals polycultural plurality, which is the vernacular condition of Irish life, primarily through the mechanisms of marriage and motherhood. Women are so threatening to this vision because their agency to reproduce outside of cultural confinements threatens the private reproduction of public national concord. Women threaten the procreation of a united Ireland which, when biogenetic heredity is actually scrutinized, never existed in the first place.

Fr Gaunt, the novel's key figure of nativist provincial authority, is deeply uncomfortable with the religious and cultural multiplicity of Roseanne's Irish-English filial links and takes every chance possible to contain and erase them through the mechanism of marriage. Just after her father Joe dies, the priest visits Roseanne to suggest that she marry a widowed gravedigger, Joe Brady, so that she can at last be received 'into the fold' (99). Catholic womanhood will conceal her unsavoury ancestry as well as contain her attractiveness by aestheticizing and disembodying it in terms of beauty. 'I can find you a good Catholic husband', states Fr Gaunt, 'and he will not mind your origin eventually, as, as I also have said, you are graced if I may say again with so much beauty. Roseanne, you really are the most beautiful young girl we have ever seen in Sligo' (99). Within the confines of Catholic marriage, cultural attachments can be disinherited and attractiveness can be graced. The alternative, as Roseanne fatefully discovers, is the conversion of her cultural liminality into a sexual criminality. Reading Fr Gaunt's deposition regarding Roseanne's unhappy fortunes, Dr Grene notes how the priest regards Roseanne's religious leaning 'as a simple, primal evil in itself' (239). Under the priest's influence, Roseanne's cultural difference is reshaped in terms of sexual threat, so that her liaison with Eneas McNulty and subsequent pregnancy appear as proof of her predictable moral vacuity, foreign at root. Indeed, during a key scene when Fr Gaunt tells Rosanne of the annulment of her marriage to Tom, he significantly connects her 'crazed' condition as a nymphomaniac to the madness of Roseanne's English mother Cissy, who suffered a breakdown after her father's death, through images of biological attachment: 'Madness, Roseanne, has many flowers, rising from the same stem. The blooms of madness, from the same root, may be variously displayed. In your mother's case an extreme retreat into herself, in your case, a pernicious and chronic nymphomania' (232). The 'stem' of Roseanne's heredity roots her 'madness' to a place outside the close quarters of both Sligo and Ireland – the erstwhile colonial motherland, no less – effectively banishing it (and, ultimately, her) from the domestic scene.

Roseanne's act of recording her history as an elderly woman exposes her abuse at the hands of those in positions of authority who demonized and criminalized women perceived to be fallen and immoral, denying them their rights as women and mothers. It moves against the designs of nativism to uncover and centralize the diverse cultural genealogy of decolonizing Ireland which threatened church- and state-sponsored myths of cultural purity and provoked their stern authoritarianism. Roseanne's narrative tactically re-centres Irish history in terms of its political, cultural, denominational *and biogenetic* admixture, as Barry uses her fortunes as a birth-mother as a catalyst for this wider, urgent project of transcultural revelation. Counterintuitively, he appropriates blood-lines to the task of delegitimating consanguineous national community, with the nation rescripted in terms of the pluralized attachments found in transcultural adoptive families. In *The Secret Scripture*, blood-lines are as culturally capricious as enacted affiliative attachments and do not essentially possess privileged or primary explanatory power. The trope of consanguinity, so beloved of biopower, is set against its disciplining design.

The Clear family's ancestry offers one example of culture's complex capillaries, but it is not the only one in which the singular plural agency of transcultural trespass can be found. Roseanne is conceived only because Joe Clear spent his young life as a sailor and encountered Cissy in England's port town of Southampton, where she worked as a chambermaid in a sailors' boarding house. Cissy distinctly embodies transatlantic and transcultural difference. She possesses 'that darkhaired, darkskinned Spanish sort of beauty, with green eyes like American emeralds' (8), while her religious leanings are towards the 'Plymouth Brethren' (99) and not Catholicism. As her husband's fortunes decline, Cissy turns for support to Mr Fine, a local Jewish figure and another embodied manifestation of cultural diversity in provincial Sligo. The McNulty family, a powerful presence in the town, are no less immune to the impact of the influences of the world beyond, culturally and biogenetically. In Roseanne's narrative, they too exemplify Sligo's transcultural rather than nativist provincial environment despite their investment in the nativist politics of the Free State and the stringent Catholicism pursued by the family's matriarch known imperiously as 'the mother'. Roseanne first meets Tom at the Café Cairo, with its 'elaborate carved doors, and the touches of an Egypt no one had ever seen' (140), and they begin their romantic attachment by the sea during a 'hot Irish day [that] is such a miracle we become mad foreigners in a twinkle' (149). The McNultys build the Plaza ballroom on the beach at Strandhill where the locals dance to the latest jazz music from overseas, featuring Tom on the trumpet and occasionally Roseanne at the piano. Tom's musical attachments blend Irish and transatlantic musical traditions. He thinks that Cavan O'Connor – child of English and Irish parents, born in Ireland but raised in England – 'was the greatest singer that ever breathed' (153), while he admires the trumpet playing of African American Bubber Miley. His elder brother Jack has spent time in the British Merchant Navy and has seen 'every port from Cove to Cairo' (153). Jack frequently works overseas in Africa and possesses a 'halo of Hollywood about him' (153) and brings into conversation various phrases he has used while working abroad.

The McNultys have made their fortune from the export business and are no strangers to the sea passages and exchanging with the world beyond Ireland. Yet their parents, Old Tom and the mother, compel the family to adhere to the narrow tenets of Catholicism. They promise their daughter, Teasy, to a mendicant order and often they liaise closely with Fr Gaunt about matters of faith and family. The mother dresses entirely in black made of a material that shines 'like the elbows of a priest's jacket' (167). Roseanne's marriage is not welcomed due to her Presbyterianism which, as she pithily puts it, makes her a Protestant 'but maybe not the right kind of Protestant' (155). Barry attends relentlessly to the hypocrisy of the mother's imperiousness. As well as having familial links to Irish Protestants – Jack claims that he is a cousin of the Unionist politician Edward Carson – the mother's nativity is mired in scandal. Dr Grene learns late in the novel that she was rumoured to be an illegitimate child of an army officer and a Presbyterian woman, Lizzie Finn, who was adopted by her father's Catholic batman. In a nativist frame, the mother is no less alien than Roseanne. Her strict Catholicism is represented as a mechanism of concealment that makes secret these transcultural particulars beneath a performance of atavistic purity. Roseanne's narrative subversively derealizes this performance and beckons forth the realities of cultural plurality and transcultural crossings from the edges so that Ireland's cultural bastardization is central and seminal to its history.

Using a significant textile image, Dr Grene notes in a Yeatsian mood that 'we are missing so many threads in our story that the tapestry of Irish life cannot but fall apart' (191). His words not only point back to the histories the novel uncovers but also orient us towards a present and future which depend upon a better knowledge of the past. Irish futurity depends upon a new historical patterning that learns lessons from old stories in order to weave the nation anew. While Roseanne is at the end of her life, Dr Grene is at a transitional moment in his. He has lost his wife and is involved in closing Roscommon, but he is also future-oriented in his care for the prospects of the Roscommon inhabitants and his disdain for the clinical and political practices of the past. *The Secret Scripture* does not only tell a difficult past but, in the figure of Dr Grene, insists upon a productive response to it. Barry emphasizes the necessity of regarding and dealing with Ireland's mixed fortunes not just politically but also ethically: we must act for the future when we face up to shameful pasts. This insistence is central to Dr Grene's characterization, as in the novel it falls to him to act upon the discoveries which the novel brings to light. In turning now to explore his response, I want to consider how adoptive being – the capacity to reconfigure the multidirectional material particulars offered by both biogenetic and adoptive attachments – can be a matter for public participation not just private self-constitution. If Roseanne's narrative reveals the shameful strands that have been missing from Ireland's national tapestry, Dr Grene is charged with the task of projecting an ethical future, specifically as regards how the Irish intend to act upon Roseanne's revelations of everyday Ireland's little-mentioned but always-known cruelties, prejudices and pain.

In keeping with the novel's rendering as commensurate the often-opposed modes of biogenetic and adoptive attachments, Barry makes the cultural provenance of Dr Grene's biogenetic ancestry very similar to his adoptive one. This manoeuvre is important, not least because it is crucial to the revelation that Roseanne is Dr Grene's birth-mother. As the biological product of Roseanne and Eneas McNulty, his blood-lines materialize attachments to Catholicism,

Protestantism, Presbyterianism, Ireland and England, provincial Sligo and seafaring travelling. His adoptive cultural ancestry is similarly plural. As an adoptee he is raised as a Catholic in England and marries an Irish woman, Bet, whose family are suspicious of his English foreignness, as is clear on his wedding day:

> her numerous family ranged on one side of the church, and no one on the other side but my adoptive father, enduring the warlike stares from the other side. My parents were Catholic, which might have stood in their favour, except that they were English Catholics, a people in the eyes of my inlaws more Protestant than the Protestants themselves, and at the very least, deeply deeply mysterious, like creatures from some other time, when Henry VIII was wanting to marry. They must have thought Bet was marrying a phantom. (122)

The resonances between the hostility visited upon Roseanne as a younger women and Dr Grene's experience of Irish suspicion and bigotry are striking. Dr Grene does not need to be biogenetically linked to Roseanne to be circumscribed by Ireland's vexed cultural tensions. He is already implicated in them as a consequence of his adoptive upbringing and his transgressive marriage. His adoptive and biogenetic genealogies are confluent not counterpointed. They are proffered as commensurate life lines that combine myriad forms of material attachment. The discovery of Dr Grene's biogenetic link to Roseanne, then, does not make for an opportunity to swap selves, discover new cultural inventories or shake off a synthetic sense of selfhood or identity in favour of something authentic, stable and pure. Barry suggests that there is nothing particularly special about *either* biogenetic or adoptive attachments. He directs attention towards the confected and transplanted genealogies of both natal and adoptive heredity.

Therefore, when Roseanne and Dr Grene share a meeting at the end of the novel after he has discovered the truth of their biogenetic relation, Barry has prepared for this encounter *not* to be an occasion of consanguineous reunion where long-lost relations are marvellously reattached. His decision to have Dr Grene withhold the news from Roseanne of their relation secures this moment as about something other than recovery and reconnection. It is a risky strategy on Barry's part: as we have seen, the keeping of secrets in adoption is morally contestable and prohibitive of transfigurative agency. But note that Dr Grene delays rather than deletes news of their relation, which is suspended for a future moment. 'I hadn't the words', he thinks, 'I will have to wait for the words' (302). This is a different state of affairs than in Andrea Levy's *Small Island* where the characters will never know of baby Michael's biogenetic particulars. *The Secret Scripture* keeps the inevitability of revelation to hand. Barry renders the scene (narrated by Dr Grene) as one where state-endorsed matters of disenfranchisement are admitted and atoned, with Roseanne and Dr Grene's dialogue acting as a blueprint for refreshed ethical relations at large:

> 'You are blameless' [I said].
> 'Blameless? I hardly think that is given to any mortal being.'
> 'Blameless. Wrongly committed. I apologise. I apologise on behalf of my profession. I apologise on behalf of myself, as someone who did not bestir himself, and look into everything earlier. That it took the demolition of the hospital to do it. And I know my apology is useless and disgusting to you.' […]
> 'I wonder will you allow me to forgive you?' she said.
> 'My God, yes', I said.
> There was a short silence then, just enough of a silence for the breath of a dozen thoughts to blow through my brain.
> 'Well, I do', she said. (302-3)

In this powerful moment, the characters requisition the religious virtues of confession and forgiveness as a secular and reciprocal mode of ethical compassion, putting to work the precepts of Catholicism for principled rather than pious purposes. Catholicism here becomes a usable past rather than an abusive establishment which can be salvaged from the constraining cultural provenances of yesteryear and put to use as a life line to a secular future. Such ethical relations are not prompted by biogenetic attachments or their lack. Nor are they guaranteed by faith or divinity, but shaped by mortal beings who, like Dr Grene, are far from perfect. The lives of Roseanne and Dr Grene as mother and son were lost and this fact cannot be undone. As in *Jazz*, there is no future to be found in searching to recover and recommence interrupted relations, however much we might be angered by the politics which sundered families in the first place. What matters more in *The Secret Scripture* is ethically facing the cruelty that has been visited upon women like Roseanne and bringing them in from the edges of history, while soberly acknowledging the impossibility of fully recovering their experiences and reconstituting their lost lives.

For such reasons, Barry ultimately fashions Dr Grene as a public manifestation of adoptive being and not simply an adoptee or a returning prodigal son of the soil. He functions as a multidirectional conduit where gather matters of cultural plurality, biogenetic 'impurity', denominational multiplicity, national variety, secular imperfection and moral acknowledgement and imagination. In threading a new future by drawing upon these manifold materials that arrive through consanguineous and adoptive routes, Dr Grene allegorizes a transfigurative version of Ireland, secular and post-nativist, that looks to the future entirely cognizant of the historical horrors heaped up behind it. His surname certainly invites us to consider him in such terms because it is a homonym of 'Green', the traditional colour both of Ireland and of anti-colonial Irish insurgency. But at the twentieth century's end, the fabric of Ireland's traditional green is worn and ready to fall apart. The misspelling of 'Green' as 'Grene' signals the insistence upon reinventing Ireland as mixed-up and adulterated, imperfect and at best approximate to orderliness and ideals. As Barry shows (and as Kiberd reminded us), such mixedness and entanglements have ever been central elements of the country's striated vernacular life. As the Irish-born English child of Presbyterian birth-parents raised as a Catholic and married into a Catholic Irish family, Dr Grene is imperfectly attached to a wide cultural terrain within and beyond Ireland and straddles the country's various traditions. His life on the edges of things is a starting point, not a site of marginalization as it was for Roseanne, marooned in her tin hut on Sligo's limits; his 'confused' (307) condition – like the messed-up spelling of 'Green' in his surname – is, like that of the nation, to be embraced rather than feared.

'Dr Grene is like an angel' (104), remarks Rosanne, suggesting a metaphysical trait to her psychiatrist, but in *The Secret Scripture* it is imperfect mortal beings who pursue enabling moral acts. What might be regarded as divine has its origins on earth, in decisions and behaviour. To be angelic is to be a better human, not a heavenly being. For Roseanne, despite everything that has happened, human acts of kindness have the capacity to make manageable a life as abused and her own – acts which include bearing witness and listening to her silenced story, too long a secret:

If you are reading this, then the mouse, the woodworm and the beetle must have spared these jotters.

What can I tell you further? I once lived among humankind, and found them in their generality to be cruel and cold, and yet could mention the names of three or four that were like angels.

I suppose we measure the importance of our days by those few angels we spy among us, and yet aren't like them. (277)

The presence of these 'three or four others' suggests a secret history of selflessness, hidden from view, which gives Dr Grene's standpoint an historical genealogy rooted in the vernacular everyday life of modern and contemporary Ireland. Roseanne is a part of this history, as Dr Grene emphasizes. When Dr Grene expresses his grief for his late wife, Roseanne crosses her room and lays her hand on him. One might read this act sentimentally as the latent support and love of a mother for her son here mystically materializing. But something else is at stake. As Dr Grene recognizes, it was 'an utterly simple gesture perhaps, but more graceful and helpful to me than the gift of a kingdom. By such a gesture she sought to heal me, supposedly the healer. As I do not seem able much to heal, then maybe I can simply be a responsible witness to the miracle of the ordinary soul' (292). Spoken by a psychiatrist not a priest, these words underline the disavowal of divine activity as the cause of human goodness and its anchoring instead in chosen ethical behaviours.

The angelic life-saving gestures of secular compassion, human not divine, constitute the ethical bearing and public agency of adoptive being in *The Secret Scripture*. In sculpting two characters from Ireland's transcultural and adoption histories, Barry calls upon the multidirectional attachments which have defined and been denied in post-Independence family-making as constituting the hub of Ireland's futurity. As such it contributes to a critical process akin to that described by Colin Graham as 'a postcolonial critique of Irish culture [...] able to disrupt the dominance of the discourse of nationality in Ireland, reinvigorating the dissidences of gender and subalternity, undermining the complacencies of historiography, and moving towards a notion of Irish culture which views the dialogic hybridity of "Irishness" in empowered ways' (98). *The Secret Scripture* proposes the end of fictions of nativist purity and asks that Ireland admits those variously deemed native or foreign on equal footing, in terms of adoptive being understood as both necessarily public and a matter of ethical personhood.

As we have seen, the experiential and material particulars of transcultural adoption's history are centrally bound up with matters of public concern, and the fortunes for those inward of adoption cannot be confined to the allegedly private realm of family-making. Bringing to light these often-hidden histories not only calls attention to the many disenfranchised in the interests of biopower. It also exposes the quotidian manifestation of the racism and nativism that structured life in post-war England, post-abolition America and post-Independence Ireland. In turning to these histories with a care for their referential specifics, Braithwaite, Morrison and Barry refuse to hide home truths. But just as important are their narrative approaches, their capacity to find in these histories the opportunities to see past the prejudicial constraints that have ruined very many lives. In Braithwaite's case, his stalwart colour-blind refusal to let race have anything to do with transcultural adoption is productive but ultimately short-circuited by the assimilative designs of his own faulty vision, which sees in the transcultural family a chance to enact a fantasy of belonging which bails out of, but does not break down, the persistence of racism at large. Morrison and Barry are both more pragmatic and more adventurous, imagining something generative from painful contexts. Morrison invites us to relinquish the recursive agency of a traumatic past at the very moment we acknowledge its permanent loss, and fashion being in an improvisational mode using the attachments we cannot recover nor should lose. Barry finds in Ireland's shameful treatment of unwed mothers a creative opportunity to admit the past ethically and shape a future from the plural provenance of the country's transcultural condition. Transcultural adoptions are always made in the context of inequality, as the texts in this chapter show. But what might be made imaginatively from them in situ, as we have seen, can confront discourses and operations of power in order to challenge their precepts. In transcultural adoption writing, 'making history' happens in the affirmative sense by creating other ways to imagine personal and public attachments. Adoptive being, not gesture life.

3

Traces: Hannah Pool, Buchi Emecheta, Catherine McKinley

In his one-man play *Something Dark* (2004), Lemn Sissay reflects upon being surrendered into care just after his birth in 1967 and his subsequent life as 'Norman Greenwood', the name he used until he turned eighteen. As a child, Sissay spent time with a Baptist family and suffered the weekly ritual of being made to kneel on a carpet before a Baptist elder who attempted to cast out the evil lodged in his soul: 'An elder looked at my Dad, both acknowledged the devil was leaving me through my tears. But I was being spat on' (332). Having suffered regular beatings with belts, rulers, slippers and canes, aged eleven Sissay was dismissed by his foster family and subsequently spent his teenage years in children's homes administered by the local authority in Wigan where he was nicknamed 'Chalky White', a racist ironic reference to his black African ancestry. On turning eighteen, he was told by his social worker that his initial name was Lemn Sissay and given documentation from which he learned that his birth-mother, Etsegenet Amare, had only intended for him to be fostered for a short period while she pursued her degree studies, and that she had written regularly for many years 'pleading for me back' (339). The social worker who replied to these letters was called Norman Goldthorpe and had renamed Sissay after himself. Reverting back to his initial name, Sissay tracks down Etsegenet who is working for the United Nations in the Gambia, although their meeting is uneasy: she has concealed his birth from her other children and does not know how to break the news. Eventually Sissay learns that Etsegenet was raped by his birth-father, Berhanu, who worked as a pilot for Ethiopian Airlines. In attempting to trace him, Sissay discovers that he died in a plane crash in 1973. Later he meets his biogenetic paternal family and also forges relations with those on his birth-mother's side. 'So now I have a fully dysfunctional family like everyone else', he declares, having discovered the secrets surrounding his conception through tracing the past. 'Secrets are the stones that sink the boat', he concludes in a poetic couplet: 'Take them out look at them, throw them out and float' (347).

Something Dark articulates one of the primary preoccupations of contemporary adoption narratives: the tracing of biogenetic relations whose identities have often been withheld as part of the legal contracting of 'strong' adoptions. Writing in 1970, Diana Kareh euphemistically explained that in the UK at the time, adoptees' birth records were sealed and replaced with fresh documentation to '[do] away with any embarrassment' (9). Increasingly so since the 1970s, both the administration of and attitudes towards adoption have begun to shift, to the extent that the concealment of the particulars of each adoption contract is regarded these days more as a form of harm. This shift has happened especially through the activities of adoptees who have presented the issue of access to birth and adoption records as a political one concerning rights and empowerment and also as a matter of psychological health. Growing up with 'genealogical bewilderment' – without knowledge of one's biogenetic provenance – may endanger one's capacity to formulate a fully functional sense of self. As such, this shift has by no means been total. Not all American states support the opening of sealed birth records (sealing became increasingly the norm from the 1950s), while in Ireland and the UK the deanonymizing of adoption contracts has been slow and subject to the reluctance of some of those agencies involved (especially religious ones) to make available their documentation. While British adoptees now have rights of access to their pre-adoption certification and their birth-parents' names regardless of when contracts were made, those who surrendered children before the advent of more 'open' adoption practices in the last years of the twentieth century cannot easily find out about adoptees' whereabouts and identities.

The advocacy of rights of access to documentation concerning birth particulars and legal decision-making have been presented in terms of emotional and not just legal self-discovery, so that tracing the identities and whereabouts of birth-parents appears an inevitable and necessary step along the road to emotional completeness and well-being that can only be delivered through reunion. The US adoption reform activist Jean Paton, who campaigned vigorously for more openness in adoption, was always wary of this conflation, as E. Wayne Carp has recognized: 'Paton predicted that, having achieved freedom [to unseal records], adult adoptees would find themselves no better off than before' (39). Nonetheless, others have sourced the achievement of emotional well-being in the enactment of tracing documentation. Betty Jean Lifton's groundbreaking and influential work which, like Paton's, did so much to breach the secretive silence surrounding adoption in North America presents tracing as a crucial pathway to complete selfhood, a laudable 'striving for authenticity and self-autonomy' (78) that adoptees bravely undertake. She argues in the updated edition of *Lost and Found: The Adoption Experience* (1988) that the adoptee who has not traced is not fully conscious but is living in 'delicious sleep, so free of conflict and ambivalence' (72). While Lifton is cognizant of the complex and varied experiences of tracing and meeting birth-relatives, as evidenced by her own trace narrative *Twice Born: Memoirs of an Adopted Daughter* (2006), her representation of those unwilling or reluctant to trace can be notably unflattering. She writes with reduced sympathy of 'militant nonsearchers' full of 'righteousness and loyalty' who have 'absorbed society's negative image' to the extent that their political and emotional needs are damaged by their 'self-denigrating' pusillanimity: 'There is the implication that they don't have a right to rock their own boat, to open their own can of worms. They seem to accept that they don't have a right to their own heritage. We see such internalized guilt in them that even if their adoptive parents should sanction a search, it would be hard for them to follow through' *(Lost and Found* 75). In the light of such thinking, in a relatively short space of time tracing has been transformed from a task which those inward of the triad must be legally prohibited from pursuing to an activity which adoptees in particular often feel under pressure to perform. As I have experienced at close quarters, an adoptee hesitant or reluctant to trace is fast becoming a contemporary curio.

From Lifton's standpoint, the adoption journey is from ignorant loss to illuminating discovery which pivots on the decision to trace birth-relatives. Adoption appears as a lifelong *fort/da* game, in which the adoptee awakens from somnambulant self-denial, achieves agential autonomy by conducting a search for consanguineous relatives and is 'resurrected as their own person' (173), even if the consequences of biogenetic reunion can be difficult and unsettling for all concerned – as Lifton acknowledges with a sensitivity born from her own adoptee experience. Tracing would seem to offer a unique opportunity for an adoptee to comply with the metanarrative of selfhood that prioritizes biocentric particulars in the achievement of consciousness and agency, even if tracing opens up new challenges once birth-relations meet. Whatever the consequences, the normative arcs of identity's narrative broken by adoption must be repaired if one no longer wishes to be 'lost'. John Triseliotis, Julia Feast and Fiona Kyle found that adoptees who had made contact with birth-parents were often primarily concerned with completing narratives, 'finding out why they had been put up for adoption and to obtain background information. [...] Some [adoptees] would add they were not looking for a relationship or emotional attachment, but simply to know "why"' (158, 159). But as we shall see, finding out 'why' does not produce 'the real me' (159). Sissay's *Something Dark* is instructive not only because it attends to the challenges of tracing – the often difficult news which it brings, the 'dysfunctional' biogenetic family which one joins – but also because it points to the ways in which tracing calls into question rather than confirms the agency of normative metanarratives to resolve 'incomplete' personhood and legitimately constitute adoptive being. As the texts I explore in this chapter variously suggest, the phenomenon of adoption tracing brings to crisis the ability of received narrative forms ever to encapsulate and express adoption experiences. They also challenge the assumption that tracing triggers an empowering of autonomous selfhood.

The challenge to narrative form that tracing presents is important. Mark C. Jerng has discussed the upset caused when consanguineous relations are reunited as resulting from the lack of fit between the challenges of these encounters, on the one hand, and the predominant form of 'search and reunion' narratives that 'structure models of personhood built on continuity and an unmediated relationship to home or some original culture' (xxvii). Noting the ambivalence, frustration and misunderstandings which emerge when experiences of reunion 'run against and within this narrative of return', Jerng alerts us to the 'dynamic, reciprocal relationship between the forms and conventions of narration and processes of imagining and constituting adoptive personhood' (xxvii). As we shall see in this chapter, the phenomenon of tracing birth-relatives frequently pulls against the narrative promise of reunions, no matter how hard transcultural adoptees seek or are seen to pursue normative modes of personhood and filial attachment.

As Margaret Homans writes, '[l]ife stories of adopted people have complex narrative lines' (112). Transcultural adoption writing is often keen to capture such complexity in imagining or enacting new lines of narration. Sissay's *Something Dark* is notable for its formal innovativeness which disassembles co-ordinated narrative as it relates the emergence of 'Lemn Sissay' from the discovery of secreted legal documents and the reunion of consanguineous human relations. The play requires a reconditioned narrative form to bear witness to the experiences it presents. Accordingly, on stage Sissay slips between prosaic monologue and performance poetry; he addresses the theatre staff and audience as well as recounts his past experiences; he moves unexpectedly between tales of New York, the English North, the Gambia and the Simeon Mountains where his birth-father's crashed aircraft lies buried. His opening words are repeatedly and distractingly interrupted by changes in the stage lighting. A few minutes into the play he shares an anecdote about catching a taxi in London before abandoning this story so that '*The story begins proper*' (331). Like the infant Sissay moving through his various care homes, families and indeed proper names, *Something Dark* refuses to stay generically or formally in place. It suggests in its design that the prevailing narrative arcs of personhood remain unfit for purpose in adoption contexts *after* tracing and reunion. They neither quell the disquiet of being adopted nor propel the possibilities of adoptive being. Many such representations of adoption tracing take the opportunity to relinquish once and for all received narrative modes and the assumptions of autonomous or complete personhood which they support. They use the representation of search and reunion as an opportunity to look for new narratives so that the experience of tracing is captured as a transgressive rather than compliant activity. It is interesting to note that in the film *Philomena* (2013), director Stephen Frears has birth-mother Philomena Lee speak enthusiastically about popular romance fictions to a bemused Martin Sixsmith (there is none of this in Sixsmith's 2009 book, *The Lost Child of Philomena Lee*), while several scenes concern Sixsmith's worries about the challenges of formulating a narrative from Lee's search which would be readily digestible. These are important tactics which Frears uses to foreground the ways in which the experiences of adoption do not readily fit popular narrative fashions, and they make the problem of *how* to tell a trace narrative a central component of the film's sensitive portrayal of adoption's particulars.

In the context of transcultural adoptions, matters of biocentricity acquire significant weight due to the cultural, racial and national awakenings they might promise. In Kimberly Leighton's terms, the experience of genealogical bewilderment has particular resonance in the contexts of cultural and racial difference where the harms of not knowing one's heredity cut deeply. In proposing the construction of such harms as the post-adoption consequence of a social environment which renders 'incomplete' those who do not possess knowledge of their biogenetic ancestry, Leighton shows how '[w]ithout clear and certain knowledge of biogenetic genealogy, the epistemology of race as a means of assigning categories of identity to groups of individuals, based on their heredity, falls apart' (68). As we have noticed elsewhere in *Life Lines*, biogenetic tracing may be used to uphold the metaphysics of race and the confected clichés of culture that claim to resolve the anxieties and isolation of being adopted transculturally by offering reassurances of identity and origins. But in their different ways the transcultural adoption trace narratives I read in this chapter show how such categories of identity cannot, indeed should not, any more be claimed. In Sissay's case, having grown up in a racist environment, it might be tempting for him to reach for an Afrocentric cultural heritage or race politics to relieve the emotional and transpersonal isolation he suffered while in care, where 'the only proof of my existence was me' (336). But his blood-lines lead instead to tales of sexual violence and political machinations. Much of his consanguineous family history is learned from his birth-mother's husband who was imprisoned for fifteen years when Ethiopia's Emperor Haile Selassie was overthrown in 1974. In shaping a conclusion to his play that is 'not black [...] not white' (347), Sissay eschews an atavistic racial politics and a sense of cultural exclusivity more widely, and resists a metaphysics of race while engaging in a firmly anti-racist politics. *Something Dark* discovers not solid origins or consanguineous reassurance but the chance to think progressively through 'dysfunctional' attachments without recourse to fully functional received forms, both narrative and filial.

Like Lemn Sissay, Hannah Pool was separated from East African birth-parents and grew up in the English North, in the city of Manchester. Born in Eritrea in 1974, she was surrendered to an orphanage when her birth-mother died giving birth to her, and adopted by a white British couple who were working in nearby Khartoum (they were told, wrongly, that both birth-parents had died). After her mother's suicide four years later, Pool was sent to live with family friends in Norway for a couple of years, eventually rejoining her father in the UK, where he had taken up a post at the University of Manchester. Pool arrived in Manchester as a young black daughter of a white father, and whose only language was Norwegian. On completing her schooling she attended the University of Liverpool, moved to London and built a highly successful career as a journalist at the *Guardian*. Just after her graduation, she discovered that her birth-father was still alive and that she had biological siblings in Eritrea. One of these, a birth-brother, wrote to her soon after the news broke, but Pool took several years to decide to act on this information and commence tracing her biogenetic relations. Her memoir *My Fathers' Daughter* is an account of meeting blood-relations in London and her subsequent travels to Eritrea to meet her birth-father, Asrat, and her Eritrean siblings.

The plural possessive in the memoir's title importantly signals Pool's intention not to detach herself from her adoptive relations but to resolve the sense of her British-based life as missing important information and defined in part by unanswered questions. It expresses grammatically an ideal state of affairs with adoptive and consanguineous relations equalized and accommodated, and with the singular and plural neatly aligned. Consequently, *My Fathers' Daughter* is not a quest to trace a robust racial identity or to replace transcultural family-making with endogenous racial belonging. Pool's relationship with her father David is represented as strong, reciprocal and supportive (indeed, the book is dedicated to him). Not untypically of adoptees, Pool is terrified that her desire to trace would be received as 'the ultimate betrayal' (1) of her dad's parenting. Instead, David assists in helping her make initial connections to her consanguineous relations, offers to go with his daughter to Eritrea and patiently waits until she is ready to telephone him on her return and talk about the events of her search and reunion. Her brother and sister, Tom and Lydia, are 'also completely unfazed by my trip, and the fact I now have four other siblings. The idea that they'd mean any less to me, or I to them, simply hasn't occurred to them, or if it has they've immediately dismissed it' (243). Pool's decision to trace is not motivated by domestic difficulties but by the world at large, which presents her with a range of questions that construct and amplify her sense of genealogical bewilderment. She turns not so much to the metaphysics of race but to the cultural and environmental specifics of nation to find answers to these questions and add to her British life a complimentary Eritrean one. But much to Pool's surprise, the transnational and transcultural contact zone she traverses is disruptive and disjunctive. Rather than add a new dimension of knowledge to her sense of selfhood by becoming Eritrean, Pool finds her being unravelling. Bruce King has unfortunately dismissed *My Fathers' Daughter* as one in which 'a story of abandonment, adoption, feeling displaced, and seeking origins [is] trivialized' (105). But as a careful reading of it discovers, Pool's memoir is actually a salutary, valuable and remarkably honest account of the profound uncertainties which tracing birth-relations can multiply and which confound the view that tracing leads to self-autonomy and fully resurrected personhood.

As an adoptee, Pool readily buys into those narratives which pathologize adoptees in terms of emotional and mental precariousness, primally wounded and permanently marked. 'I am certain a good deal of my personality is tied up with me being adopted', she moots. 'Everyone finds it hard to trust people, but adoptees find it nigh on impossible' (80). Her queasiness concerning the unsteadiness of adoptee life is dramatically expressed in the mantra which she claims is 'tattooed' on her psyche: 'love is temporary' (80). Consequently, and akin to Lifton's standpoint, Pool seems disparaging of adoptees who either decide not to trace or say they have no such desire. 'I know they are lying' (92), she writes, and proceeds to claim to know how all adoptees feel about their alleged condition. Much of her own apprehension about tracing, which stalled her decision to act, concerns the scenario it may provide for a repetition of natal surrender should her birth-family resist her reappearance: 'By searching out your birth family, you are giving them another chance to do the very same thing they did all those years ago, to wreck your life all over again. It's like the victim of a vicious attack asking their assailant if they would like another go' (81). This sentiment captures an oft-held sense of adoptee as victim and birth-family as perpetrator, but remains complicit with prevailing myths of adoption that misread the painful particulars of surrender squarely in solipsistic terms of rejection. Such views maintain an a understanding of tracing as a reflex response to failing personhood while locating the problems of being adopted as generated through the act of surrender, as opposed to formed by the social milieu in which adoptees are called to account for their identity.

Ironically, Pool's narrative underscores the extent to which her genealogical bewilderment is indeed produced post-adoptively. Her adopted life is marred by the unanswerable questions she is asked by others. She recounts a 'lifetime of having to excuse myself, of dodging the simplest of personal questions – questions such as "Who do you look like?" – because I didn't know the answers' (26). Tracing promises to deliver 'a proper answer' to the conundrum of self and to discover 'what it feels like to be normal' (26). Pool admits her obsession with 'what I would have been like if I had had a "normal" upbringing' (80), and renders abnormality as a consequence of the adoptee's initial surrendering. Normal existence is predicated on 'not being given away' and a faith that biogenetic families 'are permanent' (80). These stimulate a missing 'sense of belonging' (80) which circumscribes the practical and material contingencies of adopted life. After meeting her birth-cousin in London she imagines telephoning 'the boy who bullied me in primary school, shouting "Famine Victim!" at the top of his voice down the corridor whenever he saw me. I never had an answer because as far as I knew he was right. But now I know he's not. My father is alive and I look like my mother' (26). Just before she flies to Eritrea, when doubting the wisdom of her journey, she consoles herself with the thought that 'when I come back I'll have an answer for all those people who bang on about how it's "important" for me to go "home"' (38). These expectations of consanguineous permanence and mystery-solving problematize Pool's experience of tracing and constrain her responses to it. Instead of enabling her to weave together her adoptive and consanguineous attachments, Pool comes damagingly to fall between selves that appear to her as incommensurate not confluent. Rather than offer answers that complete the mystery of one's narrative of identity, tracing calls Pool's experience of personhood harmfully into question.

In Eritrea, Pool's attempts to participate in the imagined community of national life are thwarted by vexing moments of questioning. On her first morning she is pleased when a woman stops her to ask for directions and so '[pays] me the highest compliment of all – she thinks I look local' (58). But a moment of shared orientation quickly becomes one of divisive disorientation as Pool cannot answer because she does not speak Tigrinya. The woman departs 'laughing to herself and repeating *"Inglese!"* So much for looking like a local' (59). The vignette anticipates her reunion with her biogenetic family in Asmara which also promises participation but requires Pool to entertain the unlikelihood of her traversing British and Eritrean selves. While Pool's encounter with her biogenetic relations is emotionally charged and characterized by the warmth of her relations' welcoming, it offers little opportunity for her to gain the narrative resolution she seeks. At the reunion, her inability to understand Tigrinya means that she has little idea of what her birth-father Asrat says to her. She is quickly stripped of self rather than transculturally clad: 'like a complete con merchant [...] here I stand completely naked, exposed for the bogus Eritrean I am' (97). Her emotional response to the occasion is vacant and neutered:

> All I feel is numb. I've felt more emotionally involved watching *EastEnders*. Maybe I'm just too freaked out to cry. Maybe I could stoke up a little emotion if it didn't feel like there was already more than enough in the room. I've seen enough reunions on daytime television to expect some tears, but not this outpouring. I want it to stop. [...] The only time I let this many people touch me is on the Central Line, and even then it's hardly through choice. I hate to say it, but I never realized how English I was. (98–9)

A moment or two after this, Pool describes her father in minute detail and comments on how similarly shaped are their heads. 'I've seen it all before in the mirror' (100), she remarks, anti-climactically. The banal facts of physical resemblance cannot cancel the blunt realities of Pool's English acculturation which short-circuits filial lines of connection. The reference to London's Underground railway line highlights disorientation and underlines the moment of reunion as one which ironically routes the transcultural adoptee back to their post-adoptive life and away from points of contact with perceived origins. When offered a celebratory drink of *zabib* she finishes her glass in one gulp rather than sip it in small amounts, an incident which prompts odd looks from others in the room. Her physical self-fashioning also fails to secure sameness at a moment of transcultural contact. Pool hopes that her Afro hairstyle will function as a sign of Eritrean authenticity and compensate for her lack of linguistic and cultural literacy: '[i]t is probably the most rootsy thing I've ever done. I can't speak Tigrinya, I can't cook *injera*, but I can at least grow a decent Afro' (129). Asrat comments instead that she 'looks like a bandit' (130). The reunion measures more than it mediates national and cultural displacement. 'I have failed in one of the few things I was confident about for the trip', Pool realizes, 'that I'd at least be able to dress the part, to blend in' (130).

With the reunion experienced in terms of fraudulence and failure, Pool's vocabulary becomes inflected by deathly and spectral images as if to signal the mortality of personhood which she has risked. Prior to the reunion, she had imagined her birth-relations in spectral terms, 'faceless but there, like shadows' (83). The hope that the reunion will exorcise the ghostly presences of her pre-trace fantasies does not result. As her relations discuss the matter of her physical resemblance, Pool thinks she hears her biogenetic brother Medhanie (who has been translating) compare her to her deceased birth-mother, Hidat. But Medhanie has been speaking of Himan, Pool's birth-sister: 'she died on the front in 1984 when she was about seventeen; that is who you look like' (104). The reunion delivers Pool not the chance of a new life but a tryst with death, as she doubles for 'the dead sister I never knew I had' (105). The room rapidly becomes imagined as an asphyxiating, entombing space. She struggles with the incessant crying of her biogenetic relations and feels that her own numbed lack of tears is 'putting up a wall between us' (100). 'I have to get out of this room immediately', she narrates soon after, as '[the] walls are closing in and I need to get some fresh air' (105). She longs to 'go back to my hotel room and shut the door' (111); on returning back to her accommodation she 'close[s] the door and lean[s] against it' (115). Such innocuous details index the enduring emotional and cultural barriers that tracing can consolidate rather than crack.

Given the candour of Pool's account of this first meeting, one might expect *My Fathers' Daughter* to rethink the nature and utility of consanguineous lines of attachment and derealize their privileged function in normative narratives of personhood (as we saw in Mei-Ling Hopgood's *Lucky Girl*). To be sure, Pool does not hide the disappointment and anger generated by her encounter, especially regarding Asrat and his critical view of Pool's perceived immodest clothes: 'This man gave me up for adoption when I was a few days old, I have come all this way to find him and now here he is criticizing the length of my skirt. How dare he? He simply doesn't have the right' (130–1). Her experience brings Pool face to face with the prospect that transcultural reunions thwart mystical notions of biocentric attachment and roots, while measuring the seemingly unscalable heights of national and cultural obstacles.

In Hopgood's memoir, to recap, the ethical commitment to mobilize life lines of transcultural connection that are only ever imperfectly understood seeds the beginning of new singular plural being rather than resolves sundered selfhood. In a similar spirit, Marianne Novy reinscribes her physical resemblance to her birth-mother as a rhetorical figure for the new relations which they must script in the present and future: 'Reunions – or subsequent meetings – often frustrate any wish to find spiritual kin with whom communication is effortless. In my contact with my birth mother, I had to accept her differences, see what I could learn about her as she is, work on bridging the gap between us. [...] Perhaps physical similarity could be seen as a metaphor for that bond' (85-6). But in *My Fathers' Daughter*, Pool recoils from these transfigurative possibilities and decidedly chooses to pursue her fantasy of blending into Eritrean life in defiance of her unhappy experiences. This makes for one of the book's most fascinating and peculiar aspects: namely, Pool's staging of a *second* reunion with Asrat at his village home near Keren to compensate for the disappointments of the first. But the more she seeks to orient her selfhood with recourse to Eritrean belonging, the more she approaches an isolating liminality which breeds disjuncture more than attachment.

Amidst the emotional upheaval resulting from her first reunion, Pool rhetorically turns to familiar images of secure belonging in order to hold them ever more firmly in place. Arboreal metaphors of organic rootedness are despatched to manage the upheavals of tracing's revelations. 'It is difficult to describe the feeling of going from thinking you are an orphan to being told you have a living birth parent', she writes. 'It doesn't just shift the world's view of you, it shifts your entire view of yourself. Suddenly you have a root. A family tree. Something from which you came, and grew. It – your history, your life – no longer just begins and ends with you' (144). These words appear just before Asrat begins his two days' journey back to his village and prior to a chapter in which Pool admits that 'I have lost my sense of self—I no longer feel like a person or like I'm on a personal journey, but like I'm a travelling side show, or a prize cow' (146). A second reunion would authenticate personhood by allowing the stability of roots to triumph over the itinerancy of the 'travelling side show'. Pool also thinks this enables her to act as a 'normal' daughter should: 'Without them in front of me I realized how little I know about them, about their lives. What kind of daughter doesn't know what her father's house looks like? What kind of a sister has never met her nieces and nephews?' (149). Pool's second reunion is her anxious attempt to materialize the fiction of rootedness which both her adoption *and* the first reunion rendered unavailable.

This encounter involves Pool leaving the relative comforts of Asmara and travelling via bus and on foot to Asrat's village of Awogaro and also to the home of her elder birth-sister, Timnit. She will discover the house, and indeed the bed, in which she was born. Her first stop is in Keren, home of her birth-brother Zemichael, which is of particular significance for Pool because Keren is named in her passport as her place of birth. The visit enables her to stockpile answers for those awkward social situations mentioned earlier. Pool triumphantly imagines herself responding to all those who previously pitied her lack of knowledge about her past, and casts the value of her trip in terms of narrative completion: 'I will be able to describe the haze of sunset and the smell of the market. I might even start adopting a wistful tone and a slight air of mystery as I look into the middle distance and say, "Ah, Keren, it means mountain, you know. Beautiful place, beautiful people." That'll put an end to those pitying looks I get when I give my usual response of, "I don't know what it looks like: I left when I was a baby"' (162). The hint of self-parody in this remark ironizes the romantic confection of rooted belonging it indulges, but only so far. Pool seems unequivocal when she writes of Keren that 'no matter how easy my life seems compared to [my siblings'], I'd much rather have grown up here, with my family, with them' (160). Yet her narration of her journey westwards presents such indulgences as momentary, as if she cannot but admit with reluctance the ultimate failure of the quest which, on the surface at least, she completes in staying with Asrat in Awogaro.

The second reunion brings the increasing fissures within Pool's selfhood into sharp focus. In coming 'face to face with the reality of [my family's] daily existence' (180), she participates in the village life of her family and admirably attempts to engage with her biogenetic relations beyond the occasion of the Asmara meeting, which she recalls as 'romantic, a dream come true and other clichés' (180). Her visit brokers one particular moment of fatherly tenderness which seems to capture the desire for intimacy and belonging for which she has quested for so long. As she sleeps alongside her birth-brothers outside her father's house, she awakens temporarily to realize that 'my father has come outside and is covering me with his *gabi*. I turn and whisper "*yekanyeley*", "thank you" in Tigrinya. I have no way of knowing if he has heard me or not, because he silently goes back inside. I pull the *gabi* tighter around me and wonder if I am dreaming' (195). Indeed, this is a moment of realized fantasy with birth-father and birth-daughter no longer divided by the barrier of language, existing within the ambit of warmth and consideration. Its tenderness is all the more poignant for its temporariness. It constitutes the one fleeting occasion in *My Fathers' Daughter* where tracing a birth-parent delivers the transcultural adoptee to the life they might have led had they not been surrendered. But its momentary materialization also underscores, finally, the impossibility of making permanent the fantasy of reconnection which, as Pool knows as she gathers herself within Asrat's *gabi*, remains within the realm of dream. The contact it promises can only be imperfectly connected, just as Pool has no idea if her reciprocal words of thanks have fallen on deaf ears.

Ultimately, Pool turns to face the impossibility of that for which she cannot stop yearning. The morning after brings deeper feelings of displacement and self-loathing when she sadly watches her young biogenetic nieces and nephews at play:

> It's not just that they are so very small for their age, nor is it that I know how hard it must be for their mother, now pregnant with her sixth, to keep them fed. It's that despite the hardships, they have something I have never had. They are slap bang in the middle of a normal, happy Eritrean childhood. [...] My nieces and nephews have never left their village. I can see how poor they are, I can see how hard their lives will be and what little opportunity they will have, yet I am jealous of their few certainties. And I hate myself for it. (198, 199)

Despite her nocturnal intimacy with Asrat, her experience of village life has deepened her sense of loss rather than compensated for or narratively resolved it. Her jealousy evidences the counterproductive consequences of persistently dwelling on the losses of the past rather than mobilizing that past for productive, future-facing purposes.

By the close of *My Fathers' Daughter*, the title of the memoir has come to name a self torn between paternal cultural heredities rather than the singular plural signature of adoptive being rendered from the productive patterning of Pool's biogenetic and adoptive life lines. Pool is unable to imagine how her Eritrean and British environments might be productively negotiated beyond the normative discourses of rooted personhood and biocentric origin. In the memoir's sombre epilogue, she writes stirringly about the difficulties she faced in London in the year after returning from Eritrea. Rather than relishing opportunities to provide answers to the 'usual questions' of birth and belonging, Pool shuns company and lives a cloistered life, concerned about how her father David might respond to her trace and feeling bereft of her biogenetic relations whose presence she now misses. She brings back from Eritrea a troubled self not a wholesome narrative, sundered by the cultural provenances she has moved between, having lost rather than sharpened resolution. The memoir's final paragraph contains her perspicacious if troubled conclusion that finding her natal family 'was a breeze compared with trying to figure out where we go from now' (244). As occurred more than once in her search and reunion, pursuing the compass-points of consanguineous selfhood has led to more disorientation, not less. Pool ends her trace narrative with an arguably bigger question than those she set out to answer.

The value and honesty of *My Fathers' Daughter* resides in its candid refusal not to conceal the unrealizable quest for normative personhood which Pool nonetheless has chanced. The memoir admits what it does not want to face, and paradoxically demythologizes the utopian promises of tracing consanguineous relations in the act of stubbornly seeking them out. It is interesting to note that the closest Pool comes to feeling some kind of permanent belonging in Eritrea is when she writes of the preponderance of Asmara's 'returnees': those of Eritrean origin who have lived in the United States, Canada, the UK, Sweden, Germany, Ethiopia and a number of Arab countries, and who are split as a group internally into those who do and do not speak Tigrinya. Pool indulges their company as something of a 'guilty pleasure' (148) and takes from this community a vital degree of energy (she decides to pursue the second reunion after a night in their company). They constitute an example of how she might live in Eritrea beyond the normatively Eritrean (which she cannot be for very long) or as a European visitor (which she does not wish to remain). That said, theirs is a kind of liminal cosmopolitan living that seems the negative image of adoptive being: caught between cultural and national inventories rather than fashioning futurity from them, randomly polyglot instead of imperfectly polyphonous, semi-detached and siloed in the environment in which they move.

Like many transcultural trace narratives, Pool's memoir suggests that it is the emotional and intellectual discoveries facilitated by searching, rather than the recovery of missing persons through the act of reunion itself, that are often the most significant consequence of tracing. To be sure, the unravelling of normative discourses can be profoundly unsettling, especially when one is invested so heavily in their legitimacy, as is Pool. Her important trace memoir captures the tribulations and pain involved in opening up the self to the realities of one's biogenetic heredity. Indeed, the narrative trajectory of her memoir underwrites the outcome of her trace: namely, the discovery that one's biogenetic heredity does not resolve the serrated selfhood of being adopted, and perhaps inevitably furthers the unravelling not securing of certainty. *My Fathers' Daughter* begins with a map of Pool's Eritrean family tree but ends, as we saw, with an admission of puzzled personhood, 'trying to figure out where we go from now'. In these terms, the narrative proceeds away from the certainties of rootedness which Pool craved and towards the challenge of shaping a futurity which uses consanguineous attachments alongside Pool's British experiences, even though the book does not figure out how she might respond proactively to that challenge. *My Fathers' Daughter* is not able to see beyond normative narrativization and envision how such a future might be phrased. But to my mind, part of its enduring value lies in its frank and candid account of just how extraordinarily difficult it may be to approach the new thresholds of adoptive being when normative narratives of identity hold fast.

My Fathers' Daughter demonstrates that the attempt to settle self by pursuing the narrative arc of search and reunion is both remarkably fraught and may not deliver the vital certainties and answers with which tracing is linked. In this instance, tracing can lead to isolation and morose liminality if it is actioned to broker biocentric nativist belonging. A similar state of affairs is found in Buchi Emecheta's novel *The New Tribe* (2000), which imagines the life of a black British adoptee, Chester, searching for his princely ancestral past in Nigeria. Emecheta offers a relatively unequivocal disqualification of Nigeria as a locale of secure being for Chester, whose indulgence in Afrocentric fantasy appears as a form of life-threatening narcissism. Her novel invites its readers to behold instead the productivity of Chester's adoptive standpoint where his biogenetic lines of attachment might be articulated just in time with the realities of his adoptive particulars, contributing to a sociable community or 'new tribe' more substantial and generative than Pool's liminal Eritrean 'returnees'. Of particular interest is Emecheta's exploration of genealogical bewilderment as the outcome of adoptive parenting rather than primal wounding. Her novel asks critical questions about those determined *not* to embrace colour-blind family-making. *The New Tribe* also brings to crisis the search and reunion narrative as one which resolves adoption's interruptions to the normative arcs of identity but does not fashion an alternative narrative form (in contrast to Catherine McKinley's and Jackie Kay's writing, as we will discover presently). The novel ends instead at the future threshold of adoptive being, pointing to a singular plural being-with that is located beyond the novel's limits.

Set in the fictional UK seaside town of St Simon, *The New Tribe* concerns the life of Chester Arlington, born to a Nigerian mother and surrendered for adoption at the age of eighteen months. His birth-mother, Catherine Mba, had placed him in the care of the Social Services as her new partner (with whom she is expecting twins) would not accept another's child. The social workers approach a local white Christian couple, a young curate Arthur Arlington and his wife Ginny, as they had successfully adopted a young girl Julia who had been discovered in a nearby telephone booth by a paperboy. There is a moment of uneasiness when the social workers make it clear that Chester is black – 'The room was frozen into silence' (7) – but Ginny quickly dismisses it and agrees to foster Chester with a view to adopting him permanently. The Arlingtons' benign Christian humanism ensures that they refuse to regard his race in negative terms – 'The fact that he was black only added to their feelings of having been specially chosen' (7) – although Ginny in particular decides not to pursue a strategy of colour-blindness. Yet the novel's narrative develops from the problematic consequences of her decision to shape Chester's racial identity as a key component of his cultural filiation and sense of selfhood. After researching Nigeria at the local library, she makes Chester 'a storybook based on an African folktale she had read [...]. On the cover she painted green banana trees, and tall, graceful palms, surrounding a mud-walled compound. Inside the compound she painted her own vision of an African village scene, women carrying water pitchers on their heads, men sitting together under a shade tree, and children playing' (8). This practice mimics the use of life-story books in recent British 'open' adoption arrangements, where adoptees are given at an early age an account of their life history that describes their fortunes from birth to adoption. In Sally Sales's summary, '[l]ife story books were predicated on the importance of the recovery and reconstitution of lost histories as an important regime of truth about the adopted person. [...] The necessity to acknowledge the adopted child's different heritage was an increasingly important condition for adopting and life story books were a tool in helping adopters to both recognise and assimilate this difference' (102). In *The New Tribe*, the recoverability of lost histories is rendered suspect, while assumptions about natal 'heritage' are called into question. Ginny's saccharine fantasy of Africa, envisioned by a well-meaning parent with no first-hand experience of the continent, approximates imperfectly for the 'lost' homeland of Chester's birth-mother. Soon the infant Chester 'came to know all the words and pictures by heart' (8). The damage caused by maintaining this narrative of identity and belonging is the novel's major concern. Growing into adolescence with this sense of a missing African legacy, Chester leaves the security of his St Simon home in a troubled quest for selfhood that takes him, first, to live with a Nigerian family in Liverpool and then on to Nigeria itself, where he endures a deeply disconcerting encounter with the realities of Africa which almost cost him his life.

Emecheta's representation of the Arlingtons as adoptive parents is sympathetic to their circumstances, and their representation militates against an unsubtle or thoughtless rendering of transcultural family-making. In many ways, the Arlingtons seem laudable adoptive parents. Ginny is keen to make Chester's adoption an unexceptional matter in everyday life. 'Chester could not remember the exact moment when he knew he was adopted', writes Emecheta. 'It was like learning to feed yourself. You knew you must have been taught while you were in the cradle, but you could not pinpoint the exact minute or the particular hour' (9). But if Ginny's storybook is a part of this tactic of truth-telling, it also concocts a fraudulent vision of the African which Chester internalizes in terms of the instinctual. He admits from a young age to 'a sense of unbelonging. He instinctively knew that broaching the subject with his parents would cause pain, and so he kept silent, but he was sure it would come to light one day' (9–10). Soon Chester experiences a recurring dream that resembles the storybook village from Ginny's fantasy, although it is considerably more detailed and embellished so that it appears as 'a city in microcosm. There were gatemen who collected all manner of foodstuffs from people on their way to the innermost part of the enclosure' (17). This fantasy, which soon comes to haunt his waking hours, displaces him from his family and accentuates his childhood feelings of isolation:

> Chester started identifying this compound as his very own. He didn't doubt its existence, but felt sure it was somewhere waiting for him to come and claim it. He did not however trust himself to tell anyone about it. Sometimes, during quiet afternoons, when he unguardedly drifted into his 'city', a smile would appear on his face, like the smile of an old person remembering childhood. (17)

Chester's catachrestic dream both compensates for and consolidates 'unbelonging' by providing an imaginary location of identitarian anchorage in which he is sovereign rather than stranger. It is a place without a material referent and its growing prevalence in Chester's life accentuates loss through the very strategy which is designed to negate it. In these terms, Ginny's parenting, however well-motivated, propels Chester towards the paradoxes of being adopted and away from alternative ways of brokering adoptive realities. Her attempt to disavow colour-blindness leads to the confection of an origin that functions, to borrow Margaret Homans's words, as 'a back-formation created by desire in the present' (150). In Homans's terms, the novel aligns with other adoption texts and recent social and cultural theory that argue 'against the possibility of recovering authentic personal or cultural origins, whether for the adopted or for diasporic and postcolonial subjects' (150).

In *The New Tribe*, part of the problem is Ginny's lack of care for the realities of Nigerian and African life. Her desire to orient Chester to his biogenetic material provenance is not matched by any significant attempt to understand life beyond Britain. As a child Chester is asked to play one of the three wise men at his school's Christmas Nativity play and is soon known as 'Chester, king of the Orient!' (12). When he asks Ginny to explain the meaning of 'Orient', she first describes it as 'the East, where the wise men came from' (12) before adding that Africa 'is in the East. Where your people come from' (12). In addition to falsifying Chester's genealogy (Nigeria is south of the UK, far from the Orient of biblical myth), her mention of 'your people' drives a wedge within

Chester's domestic sphere by culturally and racially disinheriting him from the Arlingtons' filial nexus. No wonder, then, that at this moment Chester's 'sense of unbelonging strengthened' (12), as Ginny prioritizes unknown people before intimate relations. Yet Ginny has no desire to engage with such people and makes little effort to bring Chester into contact with those who might educate the Arlingtons about Nigerian life. She objects when her neighbour Mrs Miller comments that Chester has met one of his 'own people', a Nigerian-born tourist, while working at a holiday camp: 'What do you mean, his people? [...] We are his people as far as I know' (45). As Emecheta shows, Ginny's knowledge scarcely goes far enough, and her claim over Chester when faced with the presence of real-life Nigerians is disingenuous and contradictory. As such, Emecheta's characterization of Ginny is part of the novel's critique, in Derek Kirton's phrase, of the 'liberal paradigm' (51) of transcultural parenting in which cultural difference is '"taught" rather than "lived"' (52). Kirton praises 'the small minority of white families with strong multiracial networks' (51) for enacting transcultural life sociably rather than purely domestically. The Arlingtons do very much the opposite, to the detriment of Chester's maturation.

Phil Cohen has remarked that '[g]iven the absolute centrality of lack and loss to children who have been abandoned or rejected by their birth parent, it would hardly be surprising if many of them developed a strong emotional attachment to personal myths of origin which function as defence mechanisms' (46). While we might worry about the representation of birth-mothers' constrained decisions in such problematic terms, Cohen alerts us to the crucial role of narratives of normative origin in the emotional management of adopted life. Cognizant of their important role, Emecheta focuses at length on the agency of such myths to disrupt transcultural family-making and perforate adoptive personhood. By the time Chester reaches adolescence, he has refashioned Ginny's African fantasy into a fully fledged narrative of both his lost past and the circumstances of his leaving Nigeria as the endangered son of an African king. This fantasy, which as Brenda Cooper points out is modelled on an ancient story from Benin known as 'the Lost Prince of Idu' (31), concerns a king who attempts to conceive a son with his twelve wives with the help of a special potion concocted by a medicine man. In Chester's version, when the king's first wife, Mpulasi, becomes pregnant, much to the fury of the other wives, she is smuggled out of her compound for her own safety and bears her child in a mission station. The child is surrendered to a white couple who take him to the UK, but when they are killed he becomes the charge of their nineteen-year-old housegirl, Catherine, who came with them from Nigeria. Pregnant herself, Catherine approaches a local Christian couple with a view to surrendering the child yet again. This narrative provides Chester with an imaginary account of his severance from Nigeria and his essential rootedness in Nigeria, but it turns on a crucial and deeply problematic act of rewriting in which Catherine Mba is no longer the birth-mother. Chester dispenses with a crucial element: the fact that he was born to a Nigerian migrant.

In removing the traces of migration history in his refashioned genealogy, Chester indulges in fantasies of African rootedness rather than consider the contingencies and itinerant passages which characterize both his birth and his adoption – the similarities of which challenge the ready counterpointing of genealogical sureness with adoptive entanglement. Throughout *The New Tribe*, Chester repeatedly encounters opportunities to consider and indeed value Nigerian culture in a migratory, transcultural frame. Each time he performs a similar sidestepping by rewriting the migrational as rooted, the improvisational as authentic and certain.

Chester's disavowal of migratory history produces a fixation with continuity and resemblance which perpetually misreads the present. His decision to trace his biogenetic ancestry is presented as a quest 'to find a frame he could fit himself into. He thought of the generations of Millers in the St Simon churchyard. He had no ancestors there through whom he could claim a bond with the place. He was only passing through' (39). In St Simon he experiences two encounters which allow him to configure his relations with Africa, but he chooses to use each as an opportunity to root himself to an African ancestral past rather than see either as evidence of multidirectional passage and the difficulties of transcultural change in which cultural relations to Nigeria are both displaced and deployed. The first concerns Chester's attendance at a local library lecture concerning the life of Olaudah Equiano delivered by a Nigerian historian, Dr Isidore Ogude. The event is revelatory. Chester learns of the history of black people in Britain in previous centuries and is struck by Equiano's narrative as 'an African, who had been taken from his home in Nigeria, and brought to England' (53) that chimes with his fantasy of selfhood. Chester regards Equiano as a fellow adoptee but is only concerned with his

African birth and not the complex passages of his life and work. The full title of Equiano's book, *The Life of Olaudah Equiano, or Gustavus Vassa the African: written by himself* (1789), emphasizes the translations and discontinuities of self which mark Equiano's life across the black Atlantic and suggest the non-coincidence of his being which morphs between 'the African', 'Gustavus Vassa' and 'Olaudah Equiano' as he travels, or is taken, from place to place. Equiano's passage between Igbo and Christian cosmologies, his experience of cultural transition while at sea and his abolitionist, political activism all might offer resources for Chester to think about how to meet the challenge of negotiating across cultures and countries in a vexed environment, of forging being from conditional cultural intercalations. Chester is interested in none of this and instead amplifies 'the African' over everything else, rewriting Equiano as disingenuously as he substituted his birth-mother, Catherine Mba, with the fantasy of Catherine the housegirl.

Second, while helping out at a local holiday camp Chester encounters Enoch Ugwu and his two sons, Rufus and Thomas, visiting from Liverpool. Enoch offers a contemporary example of black British diasporic realities, but Chester persists in misreading the transcultural in terms of nativist certainty. He looks to the migrant Ugwus for guidance on how to substantiate the traces of his self-declared Nigerianness rather than as an example of how one might live as a Nigerian-descended black Briton. He does not look to discover how in Enoch's family one might glimpse at times a transcultural practice of dealing with everyday life and negotiating actively with Nigerian cultural resources from a remove. This is partly because Enoch also indulges in confections of race which serve to stimulate Chester's sense of being Nigerian at root, although Enoch's declarations of racial brotherhood owe something to his implicit understanding of the difficulties of life for black Britons and the necessity of maintaining supportive communities of difference which bond through myths of racial or continental solidarity – difficulties of which Chester has been largely ignorant by living in a small village by the sea within a liberal parenting paradigm where 'African culture' appears only in myths and is never embodied.

Chester is excited by Enoch's identification of himself as Nigerian and is keen to be inducted into Nigerian ways. He agrees to call Enoch 'Uncle' because in Nigeria 'that's how a young person addresses someone older but familiar' (83), is keen to know how to make a Nigerian chicken stew and eventually learns 'to make fufu with ground rice and to eat it with his hands like the others' (88). Yet Enoch's life in Liverpool involves a lack of conformity to cultural protocols. He is separated from his children's mother and acts as their primary carer until he returns from a visit to Nigeria with a new wife, as his family 'would not hear of him living alone and had insisted on his marrying again' (98). He chooses to raise his sons rather differently to how he was raised at home, eschewing physical discipline. 'My father in Nigeria', he recalls, 'used cane and sometimes belt on us. The mere mention of Papa would make you behave. [...] I started to take [my sons] to the gym to box every Friday, and now they can beat me!' (79–80). In many ways, Enoch's everyday life gives an impression of the daily negotiations between the resources of past and present, Nigeria and the UK, required to build a life in a minoritarian situation. On more than one occasion he refers to Chester as 'An African in the UK' (80) and invites him to see that 'it's hard for black people to succeed here' (84). The Ugwus' narrative is more diasporic than obediently Nigerian, yet Chester's myopic envisioning of Africa means that he will not read their behaviour beyond the confines of a nativist narrative.

Emecheta warns of the dangers of indulging in benign visions of African culture through Enoch's tactical deployment of his Nigerian past for the purposes of control or exploitation, and shows a darker side to the uses of culture as rooted heritage. While Enoch supports Chester, giving him accommodation and employment, he also takes advantage. When Chester senses 'being over-exploited, Mr Ugwu would start quoting from his reservoir of Biblical sayings' (85–6) which he learned as the son of a devout Nigerian Christian. Enoch also playfully gives Chester a third name, Iloefuna, because '[e]very Nigerian has at least three names' (86). The name, which means 'your community will not be extinct' (86) in Igbo, indulges Chester's desire to feel grounded primarily to an African community. Chester is concerned that his adoption severs him from his community, to which Enoch responds: 'Your father's line is not extinct now because he had you, didn't he? It makes no difference that he can't see you, the ancestors know who you are. For God's sake Chester, be an African [...] and stop asking questions' (86). This is an important manoeuvre where Emecheta links together ancestral tradition, subservience and patrilineal survival. Being an African, in these terms, means adhering to the primacy of patriarchal elders and not questioning cultural wisdom – quite a different prospect to the example of Enoch's transplanted, transcultural family. It is worth recalling that Enoch only marries again at the insistence of his Nigerian family who cannot countenance his living unmarried in Liverpool. His new wife, Jo, does all the household chores and calls him 'sah' (98). As *The New Tribe* proceeds through its second part, the distinction is drawn more sharply between, on the one hand, Africa, patriarchy and a damaging subservience to the authority of ancestral culture, and, on the other, flexible, improvisional and transcultural forms of affiliative relations which are definitively assigned as adoptive and linked quite distinctly to women. On this point, the characters of Jimoh and Esther assume an important narrative presence.

Chester encounters Jimoh, a Nigerian asylum seeker, at a leisure centre where he has been working and shares with him his childhood fantasy of being descended from an African king. Jimoh is keen to support Chester's quest to discover heredity in Africa by suggesting a way in which he might travel cheaply to Nigeria, but it soon appears that this is a ploy to exploit him. Jimoh suggests that Chester works on a Nigerian-bound ship and swaps passports with him so that he can enter the country and be welcomed by Jimoh's family, who will help him find his ancestral home. Foolishly, Chester agrees, and comes to encounter at first hand the Africa of his dreams. Once in Nigeria, his initial 'sense of homecoming' (115) quickly gives way to unease. Accompanied by Jimoh's brother, Karimu, he visits a number of possible chiefly palaces in search of his roots. The first seems to look very much like the compound in his dream, but Chester is quickly frustrated by the intransigence of the gateman who will not grant the visitors access to the king, and he takes it upon himself to enter the Oba's throne room:

> On the floor were animal skins, some of which appeared to be leopard, others possibly monkey. There were also snake skins on the walls, along with animal heads and wooden masks. The blind eye holes and gaping mouths of the latter made them look fearsome and grotesque. It was cool inside the room, but there was an overpowering smell which Chester didn't recognise, almost as if something was dead and decomposing. In the corner of the room, Chester now noticed something that looked like a sunken bath filled with brown water, in front of a platform with a high bed covered in animal skins. (128–9)

In Nigeria (as in Pool's Eritrea), a willed encounter with nativity becomes instead a tryst with death. The animal skins and masks, with their empty eyes and vacant mouths, emphasize the paucity not plenitude of vitality, while the stench of putrescence and ugly brown bathwater underline the room as a place of slaughter rather than salvation. It is a site of bodily breakdown rather than natal recovery which demystifies the 'natural' world. Chester's presence underlines his status as an 'outsider' (130) and endangers his life: in encroaching upon the throne room he breaks a major taboo and enrages the locals. He is rescued from harm by the king's son who informs him that the king has 'gone to England for medical treatment' (130). Ironically, at a perceived site of Afrocentric rootedness Chester encounters an example of migratory routing that parallels his own transcultural transplantation overseas.

When Chester and Karimu are granted an audience with the Oba of Chamala, the Oba invites them into his concrete house replete with air-conditioning and bizarre luxury upholstery, speaks with an American accent and demands an array of gifts that must be given as offerings to the gods. Soon after leaving, they almost suffer an armed robbery on the highway at the hands of Oba who has followed them and who dies when his Range Rover collides with a tree. Chester's experiences of death in his hereditary land threaten his very survival, and he ends his visit to Nigeria 'in bed in the Lagos hospital, recovering from severe dehydration and malaria' (144). In *The New Tribe* the sterile pursuit of patrilineal heredity brings the endangerment rather than delivery of being.

Chester is repatriated by Esther, a black British woman whom he met when seeking employment at the leisure centre in Liverpool. From their first encounters, Esther is deeply suspicious of Chester's investment in Africa and invites him to regard the reality of his existence as a black Briton rather than an exiled African: 'We don't belong in Africa, we're British. Black British, maybe, but this is our home now [...] all that roots stuff is so dated. Look how black people have changed the face of British culture. Don't you want to be a part of that?' (113). Esther tries, initially in vain, to orient Chester away from fetishizing his alleged filiation with the old tribes of Africa and towards the 'new tribe' of black Britons, with whom arguably he has much more in common. If membership of the old tribes of Africa depends on tracing heredity and biogenetic filiation back to a male kingly source, then Esther's invitation to join a new tribe turns on resemblances of a different nature, primarily experiential and voiced through a political advocacy of race which denies common ancestral origin. Chester's and Esther's similarity as black Britons is a product of historical circumstance rather than racial heredity or biogenetic resemblance, as suggested by the rhyming of their first names that emphasizes the textual nature of their proximity. In collecting Chester from hospital in Lagos and delivering him back the UK, Esther effects Chester's transition from the anxieties of displaced racial selfhood to the possibilities of adoptive being as part of a multidirectional familial unit in which his indebtedness to his migrant Nigerian-born birth-mother, white adoptive family and black British companions is presented as profoundly productive. This narrative turn also wittily reverses and rewrites the tracing which Chester has embarked. Esther repatriates Chester as a consequence of her meeting Julia (the Arlingtons' adopted daughter) when attempting to find him, and it is she who provides the money to secure his passage back to the UK. Chester's survival, then, ironically depends upon *one adoptee tracing another* – Esther remarks to Julia 'So you managed to trace your brother' (142) when they first meet – and *not* upon the transcultural adoptee experiencing a stabilizing reunion with racial heritage. His recovery is also distinctly indebted to the agency of women and not the exploitation of men.

This new familial unit is clinched in the novel's final chapter, which determinedly displaces race as a prime marker of being, taking Chester beyond a sense of belonging either to a mystical African past or a discrete community of black Britons. He is reunited with Julia as a first step to rebuilding his relationship with his family but learns that his father, Arthur, has passed away and has left him a considerable financial legacy. The impoverishing consequences of pursuing fantasies of racial heredity are laid bare: in chasing around Africa in search of fantastical origins, Chester has lost once and for all his father, whose commitment to and support of Chester has not wavered and will continue after his death in the form of a material legacy. Julia also tells him that his birth-mother has been trying to trace him and wishes to get in touch, and that 'it wasn't your father who was the "wandering Nigerian", it was your mother. She came over from Nigeria as a child and grew up in Northampton' (151). She also reveals the identity of Chester's birth-father, significantly who is African American. The withholding of this information until the novel's end definitely dissolves any uncomplicated sense of Chester as African and disarticulates the conflation of race with culture. Chester's birth-parents may be black, but their itinerant lives make them a loosely affiliated unit, sharing confluent experiences of transculturation rather than ready resemblance. For these reasons, it is difficult to agree with Clement Abiaziem Okafor's view that *The New Tribe* 'comes down on the side of Africa as the homeland of the black diaspora and the authentic source of its invigoration' (128). This argument does not prize the perpetually semi-detached relation with Africa claimed across the novel's transcultural figures: the Ugwus, Esther and ultimately Chester himself. Okafor falls into essentially the same trap as Ginny, which Emecheta is keen to critique, in believing that 'cultural heritage' (117) is a tidy matter of biogenetic imperative rather than the unstable outcome of experiential engagement. To be sure, Chester may wish to have something to do with Africa as part of the constellation of cultural resources that act as compelling co-ordinates for adoptive being, but the notion of Africa as homeland is one which the novel determinedly argues against and which Chester learns through bitter experience is not available.

With the news that Chester's birth-parents have been in recent contact – the birth-father has only recently discovered the fact of Chester's existence – it might be thought that the biogenetic family will soon be reconstituted. But Emecheta resists this romance of family reunion in emphasizing Chester's emotional and material bonding with the Arlingtons, primarily through his meeting with Julia that preoccupies the novel's conclusion. At the end of Emecheta's narrative of an adoptee tracing, then, the key reunion we witness is that between adoptive siblings, not of biogenetic relations (although the birth-family is not absented from the scene). The precious value of this adoptive reunion – Chester punningly calls his sister 'Jules' throughout the novel, let us recall – characterizes the novel's climax. Esther is included in the chapter too, with just a hint of a possible romance on the cards between them. Her (and the novel's) closing words confront Chester with the realization that his pining for Africa was a narrative product fashioned by the well-intentioned Ginny.

Here, then, are the myriad life lines of material attachment which confront Chester, both adoptive and consanguineous. Their singular plural turn empowers adoptive being fashioned from emotional and cultural resources of commensurate substance: a history of African transculturation, the claims of his adoptive family, the affiliations with those such as Esther or Enoch who in their different ways can show him 'the other face of black Britain' (114) as epitomized by the Notting Hill Carnival which Esther attends, where Britain's 'new tribe' refresh and broker creative cultural possibilities through their agency and energies. Chester adoptively epitomizes this 'new tribe': improvisational and sociable, attached to more than one race or heritage, foregoing fictions of racial origin for the challenging materialization of transcultural futures.

Thinking of Chester just prior to his departure to Lagos, Esther asks herself why 'did he find it so painful to accept the fact that he was raised by white adoptive parents?' (115). Emecheta is keen to offer an answer to the matter of genealogical bewilderment in her novelistic imagining of transcultural adoption. The transcultural adoptee's pain is produced by those who stimulate confections of racial collectivity. Emecheta is keen to attend to the damaging consequences of ultimately well-meaning liberal parenting which does not wish to be arrogantly colour-blind. But Chester's fictional fortunes sharply call into question those who assume a mystical connection between race and culture and believe that a black child raised by white parents is severed from the sustenance of racial roots or birthright. Ultimately, *The New Tribe* supports Phil Cohen's albeit rather angular view that it is 'as destructive to force children to learn about their roots as it is to ignore the fact that they have another history and culture from which their adoptive parents are by definition excluded' (71). While one might wish to take issue with the assumption that adoptive parents 'by definition' have no truck with the cultural mores of their child's birth-parents, Cohen's words help us understand the difficult and at times dangerous negotiation between discovering and disregarding 'heritage' which search and reunion quests engender – and which Chester only just survives.

Unlike Hannah Pool, Buchi Emecheta is not an adoptee and has no first-hand experience of tracing birth-parents. This may be one reason why her trace narrative is more optimistically turned to an adoptive future and less concerned with signalling and working through the disorienting affective landscape of search and reunion. This is not to criticize Emecheta for shortcomings – indeed, experience can constrain vision as much as empower it. In turning lastly to the non-fiction of Catherine E. McKinley, we engage with a writer who, like Pool, suffered an extremely painful and disequilibrating process of tracing birth-parents, but who also, recalling Emecheta, has been determined to forge a transfigurative envisioning of adoptive futurity that makes something from the conflicts which have confronted her. If *The New Tribe* approaches the threshold of futurity rather than imagine or enact the new narrative forms required to engender and express such possibilities, McKinley's work takes a step beyond. As such, her remarkable body of work concerning transcultural adoption invites patient critical exploration.

McKinley is a mixed-race adoptee born in 1967 and raised by a white family in the Massachusetts town of Attleboro. In her trace memoir *The Book of Sarahs: A Family in Parts* (2002), McKinley describes the predicament of living as a minoritized adoptee in a predominantly white environment and the impact of race as she grows into adulthood in the United States. Her identitarian crisis as a mixed-race person in a white community and family leads McKinley to decide in her early twenties to search for her birth-parents as a way of bringing resolution to her failing sense of identity, one which does not neatly fit within the prevailing narratives of self. *The Book of Sarahs* records the agonizing twists and turns of her trace which turns up surprising and painful discoveries. At one level, McKinley's trace fails to deliver the stability of normative selfhood for which she quests. At the book's end, while living in Ghana, her daily life at one level remains subject to the definitions of others. Yet again, she muses, 'I sit down in someone else's paradigms and try to figure myself out' (287). Her life as a transcultural adoptee has ever been defined by the persistence of those paradigms which fail in their task to bring her into being. As in Pool's memoir, McKinley's experience of tracing generates more not less unsteadiness and amplifies rather than resolves her keenly felt sense of radical dislocation. But at another level, *The Book of Sarahs* suggests how we might imagine otherwise transpersonal relations across biogenetic and adoptive lines. Pool's quest left her isolated and alone, uncertain of how to figure a future for being after the trace, but McKinley's narrative pushes beyond to constellate more generatively a form of adoptive being in situ, one that might intercalate the transcultural localities of her families' genealogies. In 'try[ing] to figure', McKinley happens upon the necessity of reconfiguring being. This requires new rhetorical resources that might admit and rearrange myriad lines of attachment. These resources are figured via two cultural forms: the photographic series and the woven garment. Each phenomenon – one textual, the other textile – admits a richer opportunity for adoptive being to find expressive form, one that leaves behind the assumptions and narrative lineaments of the conventional trace narrative in which origins and lineage are fundamental.

For much of *The Book of Sarahs*, McKinley's reconfigurative vision is circumscribed by the predominant narrative arc of tracing blood-lines and only emerges fleetingly towards the end as McKinley works towards relinquishing normative modes. In this regard, the form of her memoir for the most adheres to consanguineous chronicity and calendrical time. Yet the possibilities it engenders inform her next book, *Indigo: In Search of the Colour that Seduced the World* (2011), a mixture of travel writing, history and memoir. In what follows, I will bring these two texts together to clinch my reading of how McKinley's quest for biocentric origins and biogenetic genealogy shifts from the preoccupations of the biogenetic trace to the creative threshold of transcultural traces. Her writing empowers adoptees to reconfigure anew the torn texts of parental pasts and reweave relations between genealogy, genetics and genesis.

McKinley's trace engages a great deal of emotional distress and is by no means a glibly celebratory or even fully realized achievement. It causes profound upset and sometimes self-harm, as McKinley brings fully to crisis the search and reunion narrative as one of idealized healing or elated self-discovery. Recalling the memoir's subtitle, *A Family in Parts*, let us note McKinley's sense of being adopted as living 'in parts', devoid of a sense of completeness. Emotionally, she is frequently 'in pieces' as she struggles first with her adoptive family's views of her radical embrace of blackness and later with the bureaucracy of accessing information on her birth-parents, as well as her birth-parents' mendacious behaviour. Nonetheless, if McKinley lays bare the distress of being adopted and exposes her readers to the depths of pain that mark many transcultural adoptees' everyday experiences, her work also serves to release adopted life from the unceasing condition of grieving for the loss of origins and others, including the person they themselves might have been had they not been surrendered. 'I am at the end of mourning' (289), McKinley significantly declares, as *The Book of Sarahs* concludes. Her memoir takes us into new beginnings, to be sure, but its focus remains on the *struggle* to claim existence amidst the prevailing, enduring discourses of the old, where one is persistently being called to 'sit down in someone else's paradigms'.

The Book of Sarahs vividly exposes McKinley's isolating experience of dislocation that underwrites the meanings she attaches to the process of tracing biogenetic parents and the expectations which this stimulates. Its opening chapter, 'Afro-Saxon', conjures a range of environments within which she moves as a young person, none of which seem able readily to admit her to their frame. On a family holiday to Scotland in 1978, aged eleven, McKinley struggles to convince the staff of a local boutique, intrigued by her brown skin-colour, that her 'family is Scotch-Irish' (5) in origin. Such adoptive lines of connection are put under pressure by the curiosity of others so that McKinley's sense of lineage is directed elsewhere. Race offers one opportunity to forge ancestral lines. On the same holiday she is transfixed by the sight of African students in an Edinburgh bar, replete with plaid scarves, not least because her suburban childhood has not previously exposed her to African-descended people. 'I had come all the way from Attleboro, Massachusetts', she remarks, 'to get a good look at Black people' (4). The experience prompts reflections on her struggles at school to situate herself within an increasingly bewildering array of identitarian markers:

> There was the funny confusion I was experiencing of being talked about as 'Afro-American' and 'Black' and 'colored' and 'Negro' all at the same time and knowing those things had something to do with Africa, but what exactly? And when I was able to settle that confusion, someone was there to ask another question about being 'adopted', or (different from my brother) being adopted 'transracially', and having Black and white 'biological parents', and being 'mixed race', and that other list of things all at the same time. I felt tortured by my strange status and by my isolation and distance from so many things. (6–7)

Added to the equally untidy hyphenated sign of 'Afro-Saxon', this torturous list exposes both the predominance and constraints of the prevailing signs of identity which cannot facilitate the narrative means to express the transcultural adoptee. Concomitantly, McKinley's childhood is corrupted by 'a deep sense of shame' (21) as well as her conspicuous anger, each generated in response to the enquiring gaze of others to whom she would appear anomalous.

To compensate, at boarding school McKinley invents a fantasy African American birth-mother, Mattie, in order to convince her fellow students of her secure credentials as African American. She takes a surreptitious photograph of an unknown black woman in a park in Providence which she frames and displays on her dresser as if it were an intimate snapshot of her mother. She maintains this subterfuge while in college to help smooth her relations with other black students and enable her membership of the black students' community: 'I joined them in trading battle cuts as we policed a strong Black line of social identity' (30). The conflation of identity's 'strong Black line' with McKinley's long-standing photographic lie is important in establishing exactly *what* McKinley wants from her subsequent trace of blood-lines. It will be an attempt to demystify her 'strange status' once and for all and settle (into) a resolved rhetoric of selfhood where transpersonal relations might be securely struck through race, one where lines of descent are not forged through lies and deceit. These relations may remain entangled and hyphenated, yet tracing promises to make them distinct and finite, co-ordinated and plottable rather than chaotic and enigmatic. It is intended as an attempt to heal the emotional turmoil of her young life – the '*sickness*' (37) of herself, as she experiences it – and banish the fraudulence she perceives at the heart of her identity and behaviour.

But as *The Book of Sarahs* exposes with coruscating emotional consequences, the notion of the consanguineous line is itself a kind of lie. By its end, it is impossible to take solace in the promise of blood-lines to offer clearer resolution, origins and orientation. McKinley confronts repeatedly the perpetual cancellation of allegedly firm lines of racial and cultural lineage as she searches them out. There emerges instead a different way of thinking about establishing being that turns on the agential imperative of adoptees to make something from their transitive inheritances, to build from the traces left by others whose situations seem as unsteady as her own. This involves readmitting the adoptive family, noticeably absent as the memoir proceeds, to the scene of being, and just in time. One picture, a singular racial fantasy, will not work as the anchor-point of self-orientation.

'It seemed that there was no place that my different worlds met' (74), McKinley recalls, prior to tracing her biogenetic relations. But it is quickly noticeable in her memoir that tracing does not consolidate the self or tidy up her 'funny confusion' but extends the proliferation of ways of situating oneself. The lineaments of blood-lines promise not just emotional relief from the 'the effects of a severely fragmented self' (75) that contribute to her youthful depression, but also suggest a narrative structure that might offer a virtual, vital space to clinch firm links between her birth-parents' past and her displaced present so that her transcultural existence is no longer a conundrum. If tracing is an attempt to bring together self and family, to be a tidy sum of parts that would remedy 'my sense of loss' (85), McKinley's account exposes its impossibility.

First of all, as she begins her research there comes the news that her African American ancestry is not discovered on her mother's side at all, as her birth-mother, Estie, was Jewish. This prompts the revision of McKinley's previous sense of lines of connection to black culture proceeding along the maternal line. The fantasy of Mattie has no possible referent in the world. Next, McKinley discovers that her prior name was Sarah Khan. 'I hated that name', she records: 'It seemed so odd and disconnected – from me, from this woman who had birthed me. Rather than adding flesh to her, and to me, everything seemed to flatten again into the abstract' (86). When she eventually speaks to Estie for the first time by telephone, she immediately learns that Estie has a nine-year-old daughter, also called Sarah Khan, the news of which causes McKinley's stomach to fold 'like it does when you clear a sharp, blind turn' (127). Later, and much to McKinley's distress, it emerges that Estie had given birth to a *third* daughter whom she too had named Sarah Khan – something Estie does not mention to McKinley who finds out by chance. For a short spell it seems like this third daughter was McKinley's twin, but it is eventually established that she preceded McKinley by a few years. Now called Sabine Busby, McKinley traces this sibling to a house in Brooklyn. The proliferation of Sarahs turns McKinley's trace from a quest for origin and orientation into a tryst with proliferation and exposes more questions than answers: '*Estie and Al Green had a baby named Sarah Khan.* Twice? Three times? Four? Did Estie have children with another man, someone she married? Were there truly never twins?' (244–5). Following the blood-line does not steady the self but exposes it to vertiginous, non-individuating replication. McKinley was once Sarah Khan, but so was Sabine Busby, and so is nine-year-old Sarah. Furthermore, it seems that McKinley's birth, unlike Sabine's, was not well known amongst Estie's *confidents*, who may have presumed that, once McKinley had begun to get in touch with people, they were dealing with the first surrendered child and not the second (in other words, with Sabine not Catherine).

This situation cancels the opportunity of McKinley's trace to form a steady narrative arc. It remains impossible to assemble, forever in parts: 'My story, which was so precious to me, was not my story. All of those little pieces of history that [Estie had] given me in her string of letters and notes, when we talked, no longer belonged to me. They belonged to Sarah Khan. Now it felt as though the whole of my fragile new identity, my sense of self within this newly understood history, had been snatched from my hands' (228–9). The facts of her birth-mother's behaviour threaten to displace McKinley from the locus of her own narrative, as Sabine's and the young Sarah's genesis also lay claim to the position of 'Sarah Khan'. Catherine McKinley cannot be Sarah Khan because Sarah Khan keeps coming apart: it is an unrealizable self, distributed across at least three people. Tracing delivers not a steadying sense of singularity but a disconcerting experience of duplication and later triplication – the original encountered as replicant – which does little to consolidate, assign and solidify being. The memoir's title, then, refers to both the discovery of these various Sarahs and the plurality which cannot be evacuated from the disposition of 'Sarah Khan' as the signature as the original self of Catherine McKinley. This incipient self is always already pluralized, pulled between competing claims and people as surely as was the young Catherine McKinley who could not link the different worlds she perceived within herself. The discovery of 'Sarah Khan' repeats the 'funny confusion' of McKinley's childhood rather than resolves it.

Repetition is rife in *The Book of Sarahs*. Each time McKinley thinks she is taking a step closer to defining the particulars of her transcultural provenance and progressing along steady lines of enquiry and ancestry, her discoveries are revealed to be fraudulent. Lines of enquiry lead to lies and mendacity. Every new ancestral narrative in which she places her faith is eventually crossed out or revealed to be a dead end. It appears at first that her birth-father, Al Green, offers the ancestral connection to the 'strong Black line' of African American life. During her first phone-call with Estie, she learns that he was once known as Alfredo Verdene and is from Cape Verde, a cluster of islands off the west coast of Africa with distinctive Portuguese cultural influences and oriented historically as much to South America as to the United States. This significant and surprising reorientation of McKinley's black ancestry triggers her curiosity in Cape Verdean culture and its creole distinctiveness that makes it proximate to but not the same as sub-Saharan African cultures. She begins regularly to frequent a local Brooklyn boutique, Creola, run by Cape Verdeans and to re-plot her ancestral co-ordinates accordingly. Indulgence breeds relief, and it seems for a while that confusion has departed: 'Being Jewish and Cape Verdean gave you a lot more to hang your hat on than just being Black and white in life' (161). Yet, McKinley's lack of creole language skills and her ignorance of the islands' history inevitably maintain her transcultural displacement. She confesses to engaging with her new-found friends always as a 'stranger, sitting inside of someone else's Black world that I was supposed to be a part of, hoping that in time I'd learn the vernacular of their lives and bring to it what I was beginning to think of as my own expanding trans-bi Creolité' (162). This chimerical sense of being fails fully to function, and so little changes. McKinley finds herself anxiously dwelling amidst other people's paradigms once again.

But on eventually meeting Al Green she discovers that his Cape Verdean credentials are actually without foundation. He boasts instead of very different concatenation of transcultural connections that turn towards and away from sub-Saharan Africa:

> 'We have a wonderful heritage, a rich heritage – Choctaw Indian on both sides of my family. My mother's mother was pure-D African from Guinea. Then there's Negro slaves, of course. Your great-great-grandfather was an abolitionist – he helped free about 103 slaves. Of course we have some white folks in there somewhere – something for a writer to write about! *I've been trying to get this story written* – you're a writer, you say? Well!' (205 – emphasis added)

These words effectively cancel McKinley's previous geneticist attempt to deliver transcultural and transpersonal orientation and finitude by tracing blood-lines. Taught lines of attachment are quickly blurred. Has Al forgotten his Cape Verdean ancestry or was it never true? He thinks his name is Italian but cannot be sure, although, as McKinley notes, the names of some of his children sound Portuguese. Later he tells McKinley about his fame in West Africa, his becoming a chief in Sierra Leone and other increasingly far-fetched vignettes of his past. Who, and what, can be trusted? As Al Green would have it, McKinley seems to have a claim on many of the predominant cultures, races and histories of the United States: African, Native American, white, the abolitionist and the slave, as well as Judaism on her mother's side. Rather than reading this richness as the salve to confusion, it prompts self-cancellation not self-consolidation for McKinley. 'Cancel the Portuguese lessons', she thinks. 'Give up on the grant writing for research in Cape Verde. Hide yourself from your father' (205). She learns, too, that Al has fathered several children to the extent that he cannot count them all, and some of them – 'stray shots' (206) – he doesn't count at all. Repeatedly, McKinley finds duplication at the source of origin. She too is a viable 'stray shot': one of several and not one of a kind, with her biogenetic lines of attachment set astray not tidily consolidated.

McKinley's trace of blood relations delivers prolix and untidy entanglements not readily plotted lines, and multiplies her potential cultural inventories rather than resolves the vagueness of thinking of herself as an abstract combination of glib notions of black and white. Strong lines of connection always run out. Estie's history of mental health problems and ongoing emotional fragility contribute to the unsteadiness of her relationship with McKinley and the unreliability of her memory. Al's endearingly mischievous personality, characterized by far-fetched anecdotes and rhetorical bluster, makes him an unreliable source of original knowledge. McKinley's birth-parents are attenuators rather than progenitors of being. At one point, McKinley confesses to feeling buried beneath her discoveries and confined by the consciousness of herself as the biogenetic embodiment of Estie, so that 'I would be standing in the shower and I would feel an urge to hurt myself – I wanted to dash my head against the edge of the tub and kill that part of me that was her – the now pudgy, depressed Jewish woman who had been so immobilized by the past' (199). This challenging depiction of self-harm underscores the transcultural adoptee's trace as an annihilation of self, emotionally and physically. The return of the birth-parent brings more fraudulence, not deliverance from it. At the point of contact with one's biogenetic sources there is no ready origin, only competing claims, proliferating cultural locations, nested histories, multiplying selves, mendacious narratives – books and books of possible 'Sarahs', full of blurred lines, none of them true.

Al's cheerfully voiced problem emphasized above – 'I've been trying to get this story written' – becomes the ultimate challenge of McKinley's tale. How does one write the book of Sarahs if the aesthetics of substantiating one's existence, of finding the right lines to narrate one's being in the world, are not readily available? What lines can be written if '[m]y story [...] was not my story' (228)? McKinley's transcultural adoptive being cannot be made manifest through the orderly lineaments of narrative that seek to trace clear lines of biocentric connection from the birth-parents' past into the adoptees' present and future. As Marina Fedosik argues in her reading of McKinley's memoir, 'newfound genealogical knowledge expose[s] adult adoptees to the limits of their belonging at both sites [biogenetic and adoptive]' (214). 'I wanted to come clean', McKinley writes, 'and put everyone on the same page, with the full story' (*Sarahs* 142). But assembling her manifold, proliferating transcultural connections together in the same place requires a particular rhetorical reconfiguration. While McKinley's memoir narrates the act of tracing with obedient chronology in order to emphasize the many false starts, revisions and repetitions which undercut lineage as considered consolidating and productively transitive, it approaches in its final pages an alternative and productive way of reassembling the life lines of her biogenetic and adoptive attachments 'on the same page'. This figurative manoeuvre rests on the active intercalation of the biogenetic and adoptive pasts which the memoir accrues. Within *The Book of Sarahs* we can discern alternative and fledgling 'Books of Sarahs' carried gestatively within the unhappy and emotionally troubled main text.

To get the measure of these, let us dwell upon *The Book of Sarahs*'s final pages, where possibilities for familial assembly present themselves. The first concerns Sabine's plan to bring together the sundered birth-family in New York City – Estie, Al, Sabine, Catherine, young Sarah and possibly others – as part of a television show that will make a media spectacle from filial reunion. Everyone will appear, if not on the same page, then on the same stage, for the entertainment of others, and for the first time. It is a first chance for both Sabine and McKinley to meet Al, who lives in Las Vegas, since discovering his existence. The programme's producer, Lisa, thinks that their tale has a significant human interest angle not least because of the ways it articulates the rapport between Jewish and African American communities: 'We think this is such a wonderful example of Black and Jewish cooperation. And the *Sarahs*! That is a story!' (256–7). But it is not the kind of story that captures the realities of McKinley's adoptive experience, nor one she wants to tell. In refusing to accede to Lisa's request, McKinley disqualifies once and for all the idealized goal of trace narratives (beloved especially by the media) by cancelling a happy confection of family reunion. If the goal of tracing is to reconstitute families through reuniting its members, then the biogenetic family remains deliberately 'in parts' throughout *The Book of Sarahs*. It does not come together in the television studio, or in Estie's or Al's homes, or in Sabine's or Catherine's Brooklyn abodes. It is a major decision on McKinley's part, and it risks a remarkable degree of emotional anguish and the voiding of self.

That said, this decision presents an opportunity for McKinley to bring together otherwise the parts of her life beyond the lineaments of search and reunion narratives. Although her decision not to meet her biogenetic relations for the benefit of TV is extraordinarily painful, it is also a step towards reconstellating relations across consanguineous and adoptive ancestries. In addition to the impulse to self-harm cited previously, in the section titled 'Aftershock' McKinley admits to feelings of contamination in consanguineous terms that breach the boundary between body and mind: '*Contaminated fantasies, imagination. Contaminated bloodlines, culture. Contaminated by ill parents*' (265). She descends into an isolating process of grieving in which she confronts her loss both of her biogenetic heredity and the aesthetic means to phrase that loss:

> I had been born into loss. People were lost to me. My personal and racial history, my link to communities of people who so much defined my experience in the world, were blotted out. No matter who stepped in, no matter what they gave to me, there was still always this fact of someone missing, this fact that there had been no language for, no structure, no recognition of that immense grief. (263)

The emphasis on the textual amidst emotion is notable here: blotting, language, structure. When placed next to the italicized quotation regarding the bodily contamination of the imagination, we might note how McKinley positions the welfare of her being as the responsibility of her mind to think creatively amidst the pain, to decontaminate her being from the overdetermining geneticism that she finds so corrosively self-destructive. She searches for a way out of emotional fragility by mobilizing representation to challenge the stifling dominion of biogenetics and the body that she now feels, so that her body is rescued from the consanguineous contamination of blood relations and delivered up to transfigurative forms of textualization.

It is here that photographs and garments, texts and textiles – modes of depicting and clothing the body – take on a vitalizing significance in *The Book of Sarahs*. As part of her therapeutic reconfiguring of being, McKinley begins to take a Polaroid photograph of herself each night and displays their collage by her bedside. She begins to talk to the photographic tableau, so that these plural textual traces of her singular bodily being in the world produce another text. This text is the words she utters in response to encountering herself simultaneously as both intimate and stranger, 'I' and 'not I', therapist and patient:

> 'This is who you are. This is what you've accomplished. You are good in these ways. You struggle in these ways. This is your future and all the things that are possibilities.' And what kept me going were those images and my feeling that I wanted to love the person in them. (266)

This radical retextualization, one which bears rather than blots out being, is far from schizoid but marks instead the multidirectionality of the transcultural adoptive self that both stabilizes ('This is who you are') and is open to the vicissitudes of vacillation ('all the things that are possibilities'). There are no clear lines of descent here but opportunities for new textualized contracts and constellations, at the same time, singular plural, 'on the same page' – a 'being-with' in Nancy's parlance, between the photographs and the photographer, the speaker and the image, the past and the future.

In other words, McKinley works towards confronting a reconfiguring of being which relies upon the intercalation of the textual traces of her biogenetic and adoptive pasts, always serrated and incomplete, made manifest by narrative resequencing that eschews the lie of the linear and the privileging of origins. In her photographic dialogues McKinley splices the synchronic and diachronic in order to broker a different mode of telling. The false lineage implied in her dresser photograph of the fictive Mattie, her fraudulent African American birth-mother, here gives way to another use of photography to sculpt being rather than delineate self.

Photographic traces are increasingly important as *The Book of Sarahs* proceeds to its conclusion. At one climactic moment, McKinley eventually meets her birth-father, Al, in Las Vegas, en route to Ghana where she is to embark on a research project concerning indigo dye. It is a short visit and not entirely comfortable. Prior to leaving, she is in her hotel room wearing a cowboy hat which Al has given her as a present, sitting 'for a long time in the three-way, lighted mirror, tracing Al Green and Estie's faces in my own' (280). The proliferation of the mirror image into three here marks bodily tracing, again, as one of manifold replication rather than stability. The scene is ghosted, too, by the three Sarah Khans whom McKinley has found when searching for self. But the moment recalls, too, the image of McKinley staring at the photographs of herself on her wall, toying with the traces of those other selves. There are other pictures to be taken too. At the airport when McKinley takes her leave, Al passes her a set of foxed business cards and 'his old 1976 Massachusetts driver's license. "That's yours, too" [he said]. I sat with him in silence again, fingering the edges of the cards until it was time to board my plane' (281). These textual traces materialize biogenetic attachment. They point to the journeys taken by birth-parents never to be retraced or fully known, imagined only through the flimsy evidence of other histories and routes. The license includes another photograph for McKinley to use creatively, as part of a wider collage of representations that bear the lives of others partially unknown. As McKinley prepares to board her flight, bodies come together and detach: '[Al] looked hard at my face, and then he hugged me. "Okay, Baby-girl. I'm leaving you now"' (281). The moment recalls McKinley's initial surrender – she is a baby again, and her birth-father is leaving – but is also a moment of uncoordinated continuation, as traces of Al are about to be taken to new places in McKinley's narrative, beyond 1970s Massachusetts and 1990s Nevada. The traces of consanguineous attachment discerned in McKinley's face and in Al's license – bodily and textual – are *promisingly* 'in parts', only ever snapshots of pasts and presences that become elements in a new narration of being which draws upon but is not overdetermined by their coincidence. These are the partial and prolix images for an alternative family album where singular plural being – a new book of Sarahs – might begin to be scripted.

Amongst these tales of search and reunion, McKinley remembers her adoptive family and lodges important memories of filial intimacy. Such intercalation expresses something of the possibilities of, in McKinley's parlance, 'post-search life' (280). As a younger woman, McKinley's consciousness of her racial specificity complexified her relationship with her family and led her at times to shun them or turn against them when they seem unable to understand the fragility of self which she experiences. In writing retrospectively of her trace, she is careful to prize these adoptive relations.

One particularly bittersweet memory concerns her mother attending to her hair as a young girl. It is triggered when McKinley looks 'at old photos of us together' (144), and it encompasses 'all of the tenderness and all of the conflicts of our affection' (144). In washing, combing and styling her hair, as McKinley tells it, her mother brokers an adoptive filiation which circumnavigates pain and possibility. 'It seems like all of my feelings lived in my hair', she recalls: 'My mother became the orchestrator, taking me through a tour of emotions that I could not otherwise express. I had her undivided attention; I was under her care. She was helping me to find a grip somehow. At the end of it all, with my head aching from crying as much as from her comb, she would hold me in her arms with a love that made the whole affair worthwhile' (146). Emotionally, McKinley is coming apart together with her mother, expressing pain in the arms of a parent with whom she will struggle as the rage of being adopted grows. That rage blots out such memories for much of the book. But the recall and reinstallation of these memories retrospectively, amidst the narrative of search and reunion, suggest refashioned relations between McKinley's biogenetic and adoptive attachments. Textually, *The Book of Sarahs* advocates an adoptive coming together through the constellation of such parts, like the singular plural photographs pinned on the wall when McKinley struggles to cope near the book's end: tender memories such as this one with her mother, the textual traces of her birth-parents combined with her partial embodiment of their biogenetic characteristics split in the three-way mirror in a Vegas hotel room. None of these parts will substitute for the whole or provide the resolution and the lines of connection that adoptees often seek. But taken together – spliced, proximate, addressed, intercalated – McKinley has at her disposal the multidirectional means to fashion adoptive being from these biogenetic and textual legacies, where a moving memory of hairstyling may have commensurate significance to the hint of a birth-parent's semblance in a mirrored gesture or frown.

This is the alternative wisdom that *The Book of Sarahs* carries within itself and clinches in the final section, 'Epilogue', through a second rhetorical resource. Now in Ghana researching the history of indigo dying which will form the subject of her next book, McKinley suggests a reconfiguration of relations through textile images. Indigo blue blends together McKinley's present life in Ghana and the clothes she is wearing – a 'tie-dyed print Danskin suit' (285) – with her adoptive family's past. She recalls the colour of her parents' farm clothes and that of her grandmother's 'mohair coat' (285) which she wore to work in an elevator company in Long Island City. But indigo is also the colour of 'the bed-spread Estie and I share' (285), and when she plays with the cloth of her Danskin suit, she feels 'a bit of Al Green's artist life in me' (285). We recall, too, that McKinley shares with Estie a love of indigo, 'the blue so deep a sedative' (176). The reference to cloth also routes *The Book of Sarahs* back to its opening scene in the Edinburgh bar where the young McKinley's mind was sent racing by the sight of the African students' clothes, 'so lovely to me, reweaving the dull, familiar textures of that world, of home [in the US], where the only sight of Africa was an occasional face floating behind the windshield of a passing car' (4). In the proliferating associations struck through textile traces, McKinley offers the dyed textile as an alternative mode of textualizing new family ties – a rhetorical reweaving – which take us past the setting at odds of the biogenetic and adoptive.

Indeed, the figurative richness of tie-dyed cloth is revealed when McKinley tells a Ghanaian friend about her difficult life-story:

> After a while she said, 'Catherine, don't be sad. This is our star.' And she told me a story about herself. 'You see that you like indigo. It is our cloth of mourning, and it is the one we use to welcome birth. Tie your cloth to my cloth ("join me") and forget.' She knotted the edge of our wrappers together, and we sat quietly together until it was time to retreat into our rooms, hoping the ovenlike holding of the day's heat had eased. (288)

The tied-together wrappers suggest a new mode of coming together, of joining lives contingently and purposefully in a fashion which acknowledges pain and possibility beyond the lineaments of linearity. In tune with the cultural provenance of indigo, this is a moment in which the teleological markers of birth and death are reconstellated and made proximate to each other, and where McKinley's fortunes are woven into the lives of others. It requires the situating of one story amongst many, all tied up, but without ready closure or completion.

To this end, McKinley's post-search quest to trace the histories and passages of West Africa's ancient indigo-dying technologies stands as an example of enacted adoptive being in the consciousness it brokers. 'I spend my days traveling', she writes, 'exploring the mysteries, the cosmology of the dye pot that, because I am outside of language and uninitiated I can never wholly learn' (286). This is a new kind of tracing aware of its own spectrality, taking place in the full knowledge that there is no end to the journey: 'Each blue cloth, with its complex pigment, its unique feel, and smell, and design, has the depth of narrative I want to enter with my own knowledge. I spend my days seeped in blue, decoding, searching again' (286). The tracing of indigo's routes will produce unguessed, unfinished encounters, where texts and textiles come together – the 'depth of narrative of the cloth', McKinley's 'uninitiated' knowledge – without a clear end or terminus. If being adopted required the adoptee to regard complete selfhood as delivered only by a successful search and reunion, then adoptive being invites one to live searchingly and dynamically amidst multidirectional transcultural provenances.

As a young girl, McKinley had wanted the reassurance of joining the 'strong Black line' and looked for the opportunity when she travelled to Africa for the first time in 1992. But she returns to Africa after her biogenetic tracing searching not for black but for blue. This shift of colour marks the passage she has taken from 'being adopted' to 'adoptive being' – one that often left her emotionally 'black and blue' – that shapes future possibilities from a risky engagement with the past. Here emerge the painful possibilities of finding new relations by tying together anew the past and present, an act of mourning and rebirth all at once.

The Book of Sarahs ends appropriately with a final photographic series that reconfigures McKinley's relations with her adoptive and biogenetic families, so that no triadic position can exhaust the possibilities of being which their confluence engenders. By her bedside she keeps a recent photograph of the McKinley family that immediately reminds her of an early photograph, not on display, in which the eight-year-old McKinley stands next to her brother William whose arm is wrapped around her. In the recent picture, William repeats the gesture – the 'old affectation is still there' (288) – but is joined now by his Filipina wife and their daughters, as well as McKinley's parents, in an image of repetition and renewal. McKinley's looking at the photograph unlocks its conjoining of the past, present and future in a singular plural image. Other photographs share McKinley's domestic space: 'I've lined up photographs of my other families, bearing the faces of these different tribes, all estranged from each other, with little reason to connect. I am in the center of each photo. When I look at myself there, I feel membership in all; in none' (288–9). This duplication of being 'in the center' recalls the proliferation of

Sarahs discovered at the origin of McKinley's trace, but this disconcerting experience has been reconceived as transfigurative. McKinley cannot be fully there in any of these pictured families. Only in their intercalation can the creative substance of adoptive being begin to find expression. Living amidst cross-familial relations, tying and untying knots of connections across the multidirectional landscape of cultural heredity, will not be easy. McKinley confesses to having troubled contact with Estie and Al since moving to Ghana, while her loving paean to the McKinleys on the memoir's last page also records how she feels her bond with them 'as vexing and as intractable as our distances' (289). There is no happy ending to be had in this search and reunion tale, only the unfinished transfigurative possibilities of living searchingly.

McKinley subsequently wrote further about her research in West Africa in her book *Indigo*. This memoir is notable for its transitive, shape-shifting narrative form that shuttles adoptively between memoir, history, political critique and travel writing. In terms of its structure, it is more readily 'adoptive' in its intercalation of relations, anecdotes and journeys. It also undemonstratively represents the particulars of McKinley's adoptive being especially as regards the familial relations she weaves together from her parents' pasts and her itinerant present. Let me conclude by noting some of its most interesting elements.

Indigo records that in Accra, and quite by chance, McKinley has joined a Yoruba family featuring Eurama and her husband Mr Gilchreist. Eurama becomes something of an adoptive mother-figure for McKinley who is soon deeply involved in the family's day-to-day life, especially when Mr Gilchreist dies. Before McKinley leaves Ghana, she befriends a young girl, Kwale, from an impoverished family, who attaches to her. Eurama declares one morning that she is taking Kwale into her family almost as the adoptive daughter of McKinley, and brooks no discussion on the matter: '[…] "You are a mother now. This child is going to sleep in this house from now on. She's your darling; everyone knows you care for her. I'll feed her and you can find a school for her and manage her school fees. Even when you leave for New York you can send twenty dollars a month"' (168–9). Back in the United States, McKinley provides for Kwale as instructed. Soon McKinley gives birth to her first child, prompting Eurama to travel from Accra and stay for three months, 'doing the work of a grandmother' (223). Meanwhile, this moment of birth is narrated alongside the story of McKinley's adoptive grandmother's death – a woman with whom McKinley had shared a vexed relationship, partly due to the former's often unsympathetic view of her granddaughter's interest in Africa. When McKinley's mother calls her to ask if she knows who might want her deceased grandmother's bed, she is amused to discover that the bed belonged first to her grandmother's friend Helena, whose son, a former Head of Unilever Global, worked for a firm which helped destabilize indigo production in Africa. McKinley sees the chance to weave new textual connections which reconfigure her parental pasts: 'My grandmother, who had never understood my pull toward Africa or believed that its history was at all tied to our own, had died on a bed that Unilever had bought. [...] How near our lives are to Africa; how strong and intertwined the threads' (229). These are not the secure threads of ancestral connection but the adoptive entanglements of affinitive chance. These McKinley comes to prize and uses generously to admit her grandmother to her own narration of her being in the world, despite her resistance when alive.

McKinley's trace narratives take us through and far beyond the geneticist expectations which adoptees are schooled to accept. Her work offers one answer to the predicament experienced by Hannah Pool – of what a post-search life might be – without ever extracting the emotionally bruising aspects of reaching for adoptive being or idealizing the unresolved demands which this entails. McKinley reconfigures and intercalates her multidirectional transcultural heredities and, by the end of her two books, occupies a place in each triadic position but escapes each too. She is the adopted daughter of the McKinleys, the creation of Estie and Al's relationship, a mother of two children and a virtual adoptive parent of a young Ghanaian girl. None of these positionings is primary nor painless. If the blue of indigo signifies both mourning and birth in Yoruba and other West African cultures, it retains its North American sense of creativity amidst sorrow as encapsulated musically by the blues. 'I live now in blue', concludes McKinley, 'with my children, in a life fashioned between New York and West Africa, learning, as Eurama insisted, to really "taste life", through devotion to others, through the beauty of acts of sacrifice' (231). Here we might espy, finally for now, the transfigurative agency promised by adoptive being. After much labour, McKinley's writing transforms that 'no place [where] my different worlds met' (*Sarahs* 74) into a site of intercalation where the adoptive ('as Eurama insisted') is tied to the biogenetic ('with my children') in an attempt not to fetishize origins but to source the future with recourse to the past's complex and painful life lines.

So long as being adopted is presented as a crisis of identity and a state of harm, genealogically bewildered and incomplete, the smooth lines of connection promised by search and reunion narratives will ever beckon and frustrate those seeking normative answers to the question of being. The transcultural adoption texts we have considered in this chapter bring to crisis the normative narrative designs of personhood by calling into question the biocentric conceptions of race and natal culture to fasten transcultural adoptees to steadfast identitarian anchor-points. Rather than uncover taught lines of connection, in their different ways Pool, Emecheta and McKinley encounter entangled, unsteady and proliferating attachments, the pursuit of which materializes the transversal travails and historical routes that may empower one to fashion singular plural being from the intercalated traces of biogenetic and adoptive heredities. This is no mean feat nor a task to be quickly idealized. Pool's memoir demonstrates the difficulty in confronting the hollow promises of search and reunion quests and the precarious and solitary position where transcultural adoptees can end up. Emecheta's novel locates empathetically the production of genealogical bewilderment in the practices of liberal colour-blind parenting and propels her central character beyond tracing's line of sight and towards a new tribe of diasporic dwelling where Nigerian, British and transatlantic pasts might be intercalated to forge new singular plural futurity. That futurity is imagined from the dark place where McKinley withdraws, brought to crisis by her search and reunion, through the figurative and representational resources of photographs and (as in Mei-Ling Hopgood's *Lucky Girl*) textiles. In pushing to breaking point the narrative arc of tracing consanguineous relations, each of these works approaches the threshold of formal innovation rather than enact it from the start in their literary design (although *Indigo* is certainly shaped in terms of the entanglement and intercalations of manifold genres, locations and lives). Such necessary formal innovation will be witnessed more readily in the following chapter, especially in Jackie Kay's work. There, as in this chapter, the incomplete puzzle of being adopted is relinquished in favour of prizing, as Lemn Sissay puts it in *Something Dark*, the 'different truth' (347) which adoptive being illuminates.

4

Bearings: Barbara Kingsolver,
Caryl Phillips, Jackie Kay

For birth-mothers, adoptees and their parents, transcultural adoption can sometimes be very hard to bear. In addition, those beyond the triad who imagine transcultural adoption have often presented the predicament of being adopted in terms of vulnerability and hurt. In Hanif Kureishi's novel of late 1980s' pop-cultural creativity and multicultural breakdown, *The Black Album* (1995), a sense of the painful marginalization of young Muslims in London's racist and austere environs is presented through the British Asian character of Chad, formerly known as Trevor Buss, who was adopted by white British parents. The novel's central character, Shahid Hasan, learns from his lecturer and lover Deedee Osgood that Chad's adoptive mother was racist and insisted that he had to fit in amongst 'ordinary English people who were secure, who effortlessly belonged' (89). As a teenager, Chad turned instead towards his South Asian 'heritage' and sought cultural connections with Pakistan initially by learning Urdu, '[b]ut when he tried asking for the salt in Southall everyone fell about at his accent' (89). Deedee describes Chad's life as liminal and lost: 'In England white people looked at him as if he were going to steal their car or their handbag, particularly as he dressed like a ragamuffin. But in Pakistan they looked at him even more strangely. Why should he be able to fit into a Third World theocracy?' (89). As a young man whose 'soul got lost in translation' (89), Chad finds the pain of diasporic dwelling accentuated by his transcultural adopted life. 'I don't know what it is to feel like a normal citizen' (90), he confesses to Deedee, and speaks of lacking a secure sense of national rootedness. Lacking the usual bearings of identity and belonging, Chad eventually turns to a local militant Muslim group which is increasingly active and incendiary in the wake of the *fatwa* issued against Salman Rushdie in relation to his novel *The Satanic Verses* (1988). Here at least, Chad is welcome in a fraternal environment where his personhood is valued rather than reviled and where he no longer has to bear the weight of others' prejudice. Kureishi's message is sharply drawn: if those who are marginalized by illiberal discourses of race, nation or culture remain insistently rejected, one should not be surprised by their susceptibility to the militant politics of those keen to induct them into a deepening atavistic conflict.

This vignette from Kureishi's novel reminds us, as have other texts previously discussed, of the harms that emerge when transcultural adoptees attempt to fix the compass-points of their personhood in terms of the predominant bearings of self: race, nation, birth-place, 'birth culture', consanguinity, biogenetics, heritage, resemblance, distinctive sameness. To bear one's being otherwise, in a different relationship to identity's prefabricated design, may be a matter of psychosocial necessity and not simply a philosophical nicety. David L. Eng regards the transnational adoptive family as 'one crucial site to reengage the politics of race, gender, nation, and capital' (136) in which '[r]estoring collective history to the process of a transnational adoptee's social psychic development is crucial to the survival of the new global family' (137). As Eng sees it, transnational adoption is not a solipsistic matter for the pathologized adoptee but a common concern which reaches into the central political contests of our age. It shapes powerful examples of the new psychic structures and forms of family-making required for an ethical future that dismantles 'the liberal model of private and public, as well as the ideals of the white heteronormative nuclear family, as the standard against which all social orderings must be measured' (137). In turning in this final chapter to consider representations of transcultural adoption as formulating new bearings of adoptive being, we must sustain cognition of the utopian politics that drive the attempts at transfiguration I shall critique, rather than approach them as idealized or transcendent reckonings with personhood that evade the sociability and materiality of being-with. Throughout *Life Lines* I have remained mindful, to borrow Eng's terms, of transcultural adoption's embedding in 'larger public histories' (94) and have taken a critical approach to those texts which play loosely with these material particulars. But we have seen, too, as in the example of Toni Morrison's work, how an inventive rendition of adoption history may be required to imagine ways out of constraining habits of living. In this final chapter, I wish to consider the speculative propensity of transcultural adoption writing to offer transfigurative knowledge that is as ethically pointed as it is aesthetically daring.

Most scholarly engagements with adoption that originate in the arts and humanities invite us to think about how representations of adoptive family-making can be generative rather than compliant. Mark C. Jerng's exploration of transracial adoption in the United States uses the wisdom of adoption writing to empower 'a way of reimagining the vocabularies of race and belonging' (xxxiii). Cynthia Callahan finds in transracial adoption texts opportunities for reconfiguring existing power hierarchies 'that significantly challenge the social order' (3). Marianne Novy fittingly argues that '[g]iven the power of belief in heredity, twenty-first-century culture desperately needs some belief in bonds that cross "bloodlines"' (23). Her reading of adoption texts excavates a literary history of exploring the ups and downs of transversal as opposed to consanguineous filial attachments. Margaret Homans concludes her rich study of representations of adoption by valuing 'the creativity that can be prompted by adoption's challenges' (292) and underwriting the contributions of those, adopted and non-adopted alike, 'who have written their way through and beyond those struggles to make something very new' (293). Each of these scholars weighs the substantiality of adoption creativity very much in relation to the conflicts, societies and struggles where transcultural adoptions have taken place. To think of transcultural adoption as promising critical transformation is not to ignore the imposed harms of being adopted. We must face the conditions and constraints which Kureishi intimates through the figure of Chad, last spotted in *The Black Album* burning homes and beating others, lost in the identitarian pain which his political ardour fails fully to salve. But at the same time, in critically pursuing transcultural adoption writing's attempts not to be circumscribed by or encased within these conditions, we might become open to the possibilities which creative writers determinedly inaugurate. As we shall see in this chapter, not all such endeavours necessarily succeed or are free of risk. But the ambition they contain is rarely without the capacity steadfastly to challenge the received state of affairs. While being adopted has been made into a condition hard to bear for some, transcultural adoption texts bravely chart new bearings of personhood that I have sought to capture in this book in terms of adoptive being.

The present chapter draws upon the issues explored in the previous three as it works towards a rounded expression of adoptive being. Matters of secrecy are germane to my discussion below of Barbara Kingsolver's early novels and Jackie Kay's memoir, while the entanglements between public histories and private family-making preoccupy Caryl Phillips's fiction in particular. All three writers engage with moments and matters of tracing birth-relatives, most overtly in Jackie Kay's trace narrative which captures wonderfully in its form the intercalations and redrawn lines that phrase adoptive being. Each of the four texts I discuss here are deliberately, delightfully ambitious while also firmly imbricated in a range of disquieting histories of dispossession and disenfranchisement, so that their visions of adoptive being – by no means unproblematic, as we shall see – carry within them scars and severances which are at the very least dutifully acknowledged, if not, as in the case of Kingsolver's work, always readily articulated or fully understood.

Indeed, Kingsolver's work is a good place from which to proceed due to its mixed fortunes. Her fictional account of the transcultural adoption of a Native American child by a white American mother has impacted both on the trajectory of her writing and her critical reception amongst Native writers and scholars and also the adoption studies community, to the extent that her work has been declared deeply problematic. I have no wish to rehabilitate Kingsolver's reputation or defend her curtailed transcultural literacy. That said, in my reading of *The Bean Trees* and (1988) and its sequel *Pigs in Heaven* (1993), I am keen to get closer to the daringly transfigurative envisioning of adoptive being which Kingsolver risks.

As Margaret Homans has observed, Kingsolver's debut novels are 'among the most frequently studied fictional representations of transracial adoption' (131). Several critics have raised questions about Kingsolver's representation of the adoption of Cherokee-born Turtle by a white American woman, Taylor Greer, usually because of Kingsolver's ignorance of the unhappy history of Native transcultural adoptions in the United States or her clichéd rendering of Cherokee life. In my readings of these two much-discussed texts in adoption literary studies, I want to gauge Kingsolver's refusal to counterpoint the consanguineous with the behavioural in order innovatively to propose that in *The Bean Trees* there emerges a new ecology of human relations that are post-anthropocentric and organically sanctioned – an environmentalist mode of adoptive being, if you will. While this mode does not reappear in *Pigs in Heaven*, that novel, too, searches for opportunities to align adoptive and biogenetic attachments as part of a wider envisioning, albeit faulty, of transcultural reconstruction.

In *The Bean Trees*, Kingsolver mobilizes adoption to help construct new transpersonal relations alternative to heteronormative and consanguineous versions of family. At its commencement, Taylor Greer seems fated to a life in Pittman Country, Kentucky, amidst austerity and patriarchal authority. By its conclusion, having escaped Pittman by driving westwards, Taylor has set up home in Tucson, Arizona, with her adopted Native American three-year-old child. Turtle was born to a Native American birth-mother, whose sister passes the child to Taylor when she stops at an uninviting service station on Cherokee lands in Oklahoma during her initial car journey from Kentucky. Taylor and Turtle live with Lou Ann, mother to the infant Dwayne Ray, and are supported by two elderly female neighbours, Edna and Virgie Mae. Taylor works at a local garage run by Mattie, a kindly neighbour who is also involved in helping so-called illegal immigrants on the run from persecution in Latin America. These include Esperanza and Estevan, two Guatemalan refugees who lodge above her garage. This micro community, then, shapes an alternative version of the United States where the authority of race, whiteness and patriarchy are no longer ascendant. Taylor travels from one version of America in which women remain materially and emotionally impoverished, subservient to the actions of irresponsible men, to a new envisioning of social life forged through female community and mindful of an ethical, affective and political responsibility for others not usually considered kin.

That said, *The Bean Trees* falls foul of a damaging ignorance of the contexts of Native adoption upon which its plot rests, and does not enquire into the conditions which have shaped a troubling history of transcultural adoption for Native peoples and produced Native children as adoptable. In Cynthia Callahan's summary, several readers have objected to Kingsolver's failure to consider Turtle 'in terms of her cultural identity, using her instead as a vehicle for addressing her white adoptive mother's development' (105). When Taylor is unexpectedly given Turtle by the unnamed Native woman in Oklahoma, the child seems traumatized into inactivity and silence. It is soon intimated that she has been sexually abused due to the 'bruises and worse' that mark her: 'The Indian child was a girl. A girl, poor thing. That fact had already burdened

her short life with a kind of misery I could not imagine' (23). Taylor names
her Turtle on account of the ferocity of her grip that embodies the emotional
anxiety created by the loss of attachment. These details frame Turtle's adoption
squarely in terms of rescue. At one point, Taylor remembers watching television
footage of an airplane crash in which a helicopter is seen dropping a rope to
rescue a surviving stewardess who clings to it 'like Turtle' (75). This framing of
transcultural adoption as rescue does little to dislodge a negative rendering of
Native life as the locale of emotional impoverishment and a threat to well-being.
Neither is Turtle's adoption contextualized in relation to the long and painful
history of the removal of Native American children to the care of white families
that has played a significant role in the disempowering of Native peoples.

As Laura Briggs describes it, involuntary emplacement 'has defined life in
Native communities for most of the twentieth century' (59), encompassing, for
example, the creation of off-reservation boarding schools for Native children
since the late nineteenth century and the activities of state welfare workers
determined to remove Native children from their unmarried mothers or
from non-nuclear parenting arrangements. Such tactics constituted colonial
attempts at '[d]e-tribalising Native children' (67) and prompted a long and
hard-fought campaign by Native peoples that culminated in Congress passing
the Indian Child Welfare Act (ICWA) of 1978. The act placed the matter of
Native child welfare within the jurisdiction of the tribal courts (if children lived
on a reservation) and upheld the principle that Native children should remain
within their families and communities. *The Bean Trees* seems unconcerned
with these historical and juridical contexts and pursues its journey towards
a transformed transcultural vision of filial reconstitution by effectively
bypassing them. Indeed, Turtle's formal adoption at the novel's end in an
Oklahoma courtroom, which already rests on an act of subterfuge involving
Esperanza and Estevan who stand in as birth-parents, is in defiance of US law
as it does not involve a Native court. To remember Callahan's words, many of
the novel's first readers were angered by its ignorance of the ICWA and by its
instrumentalization of a Cherokee child who was not imagined 'in terms of
her cultural identity, [but used] instead as a vehicle for addressing her white
adoptive mother's development' (105). *The Bean Trees* is less transcultural than
neocolonial when viewed from this position, as it appears to uphold rather
than challenge the appropriation and figurative exploitation of Native peoples.

Kingsolver seeks to correct her oversights in the novel's sequel, *Pigs in Heaven*, in which, as we shall see, a more considered transcultural envisioning of adoption's possibilities is pursued through the attempt to clinch a multidirectional model of adoptive being. But rather than writing off wholesale *The Bean Trees* as terminally flawed, we might pause to identify and evaluate its ingenious attempt to fashion adoptive being in concert with environmentalist concerns. Its representation of transcultural adoption proposes reconditioned forms of attachment which take their cue from ecological and environmental precedent. At its most radical, *The Bean Trees* daringly presents adoption as a matter of biological normality rather than cultured or affiliative rearrangement. The novel turns to transcultural adoption to help search for what we might term a new 'ecology of being', feminist in intent, the concerns of which are political, philosophical and eco-critical. To be sure, Kingsolver's highly problematic use of transcultural adoption's possibilities to these ends is ultimately damaged by its complicity with the very neocolonial conditions which perpetuate the oppression of Native peoples. And as we shall see, its radical design as a transcultural adoption narrative is contradicted by its biocentric imagining of blood relations, despite its otherwise determined attempt to derealize the exclusivity of consanguineous models of attachment. But as an attempt to render adoptive being transculturally it is no less fascinating for its flaws, and not least because its example enables us to gauge comparatively the more sophisticated bearings of adoptive being struck by Caryl Phillips and Jackie Kay.

To get the measure of the novel's innovative intent, let us dwell on its representation of biological and organic matters. Taylor's journey westwards is motivated by her rejection of normative female life amidst blood and birth. At home she has endured an austere upbringing with her hard-working mother and done her best to avoid getting 'hogtied to a future as a tobacco farmer's wife. Mama always said barefoot and pregnant was not my style' (3). This representation of pregnancy as a means of entrapment and denial of futurity de-idealizes biocentric modes of nurturing from the novel's start. Taylor works in Pittman as a laboratory assistant at the local hospital where she spends five monotonous years analysing biological data. 'I learned to look in a microscope at red blood cells, platelets they are called', she remembers, 'and to count them in the little squares. It was the kind of thing I'm positive could make you go blind if you kept it up' (6). Things take a sinister turn when, just a week into the job, Taylor sees a young mother and school acquaintance, Jolene, admitted to hospital with a gunshot wound due to a domestic incident in which her husband, Newt, is shot dead by his father. She resembles 'the part of the movie you don't want to watch. There was a wet tongue of blood from her right shoulder all the way down her bosom, and all the color was pulled out of her lips and face, her big face like a piece of something cut out of white dough' (7). Jolene is an image of constrained, bloodied and wounded womanhood. She tells Taylor that 'my daddy'd been calling me a slut practically since I was thirteen [...]. Newt was just who it happened to be. You know the way it is' (9). After the incident Taylor returns to her tasks, watching blood platelets through a microscope, 'counting the same ones over and over all afternoon' (9). The preponderance of images of blood connected to violence, repetition, boredom and constraint joins with the rendering of pregnancy as a mechanism of patriarchal confinement. This makes Taylor's flight from Pittman an attempt to escape a distinctly biologized and gendered predicament of human being (it is interesting that, when settled in Tucson, she declines to earn money by giving blood, despite being financially desperate). In Pittman, blood and pregnancy are the signs of recursive female subservience, a form of violated life rendered dramatic in the incident of Jolene's bloodied body sapped of vitality or in Taylor's microscopic encounter with blood platelets that threaten her vision.

As Taylor travels West in her decrepit Volkswagen bug, the novel searches for an alternative vision of female existence located not in the consanguineous but in the adoptive. Within a few pages of leaving Kentucky, Taylor narrates her stopping by chance at an uninviting service station in the middle of Cherokee territory in Oklahoma, outside which she is asked by a nervous Native woman to take the child she is holding who is, she claims, her 'dead sister's' (18). The informal adoption of Turtle makes Taylor's journey become one towards motherhood rather than away from it, while also suggesting that Taylor's mothering of Turtle is part of a problematic twofold rescue, of both adoptive mother and adoptee, because it sets Taylor on a path to a new life. Callahan accurately summarizes the novel in terms of adoptive mutuality: '[Taylor] is delivered into greater social consciousness by choosing to adopt. Kingsolver injects into the novel a conceptualization of adoption as an act of mutual rescue [...] characteristic of early twentieth-century [American] orphan stories in which sheltering an orphan also offers adoptive parents a better life' (112). Taylor's flight from her Pittman past is central to the novel's progressive envisioning of womanhood, in which nurturing is something other than the subservience apparently fated by the biological parameters of blood and birth. Through adoptive relations, Kingsolver begins to open alternative ways of figuring transpersonal relations where the adoptive and the biogenetic need not be counterpointed. Crucially, *both* are forms of human attachment which can be understood as organic. As is mooted through the representation of Turtle in particular, the adoptive is not a substitute for biogenetic relations but an organic, not improvised, alternative.

The language of Turtle's characterization forges a particular relationship between her and other forms of organic matter. She is rhetorically situated in relation to animals, vegetables, blooms and plants, and brings into view several planes of organic provenance as shaping a different way of thinking about human coexistence. The amphibious resonances of her name suggest a body which can transition between environments and is part of a wider representation of Turtle as more zoological than anthropoid. When Taylor bathes her for the first time she sees her new daughter 'splashing like a toad frog' (23). As Turtle learns to speak she amusingly misnames people and things always in terms of fauna and vegetables. Edna and Virgie Mae become 'Poppy and Parsnip. [Turtle] knew the names of more vegetables than many a greengrocer' (114). Turtle endlessly scans magazines in search of pictures of vegetables and is entranced by the plants which Mattie grows by her garage and the night-blooming cereus in the elderly women's garden. In one crucial episode, Taylor takes Turtle to a local doctor's surgery for an X-ray. The examination soberly reveals that Turtle's bones have been fractured due to abuse and that her age is closer to three years than two. Dr Pelinowsky tells Taylor that '[s]ometimes in an environment of physical or emotional deprivation a child will simply stop growing, although certain internal maturation does continue. It's a condition we call failure to thrive' (123). As Taylor remarks, Turtle is indeed thriving in her post-adoption environment in Tucson. But who, or indeed what, is thriving? As Taylor looks at the unhappy evidence of fractures captured by the X-ray, her vision sees beyond the limits of Turtle's human body:

> [The doctor] put up some more of the x-rays in the window, saying things like 'spiral fibular fracture here' and 'excellent healing' and 'some contraindications

for psychomotor development'. I couldn't really listen. I looked through the bones to the garden on the other side. There was a cactus with bushy arms and a coat of yellow spines as thick as fur. A bird had built her nest in it. In and out she flew among the horrible spiny branches, never once hesitating. You just couldn't imagine how she'd made a home in there. (124)

This act of seeing beckons a new vision of the human where the translucent image of Turtle's once-broken bones merges with the sight of plants and animal life: the human-like cactus with its arms and coat, the itinerant bird making a home in a precarious dwelling. If Turtle, like Taylor, could not thrive in her previous environment, then this compelling moment pictures human life in a different environment by resituating being in relation to non-human matter. Just as the X-ray affords a view of the body's workings otherwise concealed, Taylor's description of it puts on display another sense of the human body, not complete in itself but part of a wider ecology of organic life. Turtle comes to represent an alternative way of imagining human relations which goes beyond the anthropocentric towards a wider ecological context.

Consequently, the novel turns to the environment for a different envisaging of human existence that is offered as the organic grounds for a refashioned adoptive community which takes its cue from nature. Late in *The Bean Trees*, after the Oklahoma court has been fooled into believing that Turtle has been willingly surrendered by her birth-parents and the court has contracted her adoption, Taylor and Turtle share an empowering act of reading as they leaf through the *Horticultural Encyclopedia* at Oklahoma City Main Library. Turtle becomes excited by a picture of wisteria. Taylor reads to her that wisteria is a legume, a form of bean, and is not native to the United States. It is able to thrive in poor soil due to rhizobia, 'microscopic bugs that live underground in little knots on the roots' and 'suck nitrogen gas right out of the soil and turn it into fertilizer for the plant' (227). Although the rhizobia are 'separate creatures [...] they always live with the legumes' (227). Kingsolver underlines this organic precedent for adoptive relations when she has Taylor explain that the Tucson micro community is organized in the same way: 'It's just the same as with people' (227), she says. 'The wisteria vines on their own would just barely get by, is how I explained it to Turtle, but put them together with rhizobia and they make miracles' (228). We might remember, too, that Kingsolver has Taylor drive a decrepit Volkswagen 'bug' (10) in anticipation of the miraculous things which bugs engender, namely in this case the delivery of a child into her care as she sits in the driver's seat while parked by the Oklahoma service station.

Additionally, the mention of wisteria refers us back to an earlier moment in the novel when Turtle utters her first word, 'Bean' (97), while Taylor is involved in planting some beans in Mattie's yard. In her excitement, Taylor explains to Turtle the different kinds of beans they have: '[…] these are playing-with beans. There's eating beans at home. And the rest of these in here are putting-in-the-ground beans' (98). But it is actually Turtle who is trying to tell something to Taylor. These are not the usual beans, according to Turtle, but a 'Humbean' (97) – a point she makes twice during the episode. The word is an infant's attempt to say something new, of course, but also an important pun on 'human being'. In other words, Turtle's ability to envision organic plant life as no different from human existence beckons the wider ecological transformation for which the novel quests and which Taylor realizes at its end in her explanation of wisteria. The novel's title contains a pun on bean/being that anticipates its recasting of human relations in leguminous terms, struck organically between 'separate creatures'. The adoptive is presented *as* organic and not as purely affiliative or as a form of substitution that mimics the allegedly natural.

In these terms, the realm and role of transpersonal nurturing is rescued from the austere conditions from which Taylor fled in the first place, where motherhood sentences women to the dramatic as well as slow violence of normative patriarchal servitude. Nurturing is resituated in a new ecology of being where human life is arranged not according to the protocol of blood-lines but from the rhizobic attachments of others that provide sustaining life lines. So it is not entirely the case that, in Callahan's reading, 'a family [is] created not by biology but through nurturing and willing affiliation' (112). As *The Bean Trees* would have it, biology and nurturing should no longer be counterpointed. The affiliative attachments that obtain in Taylor and Turtle's relationship have organic, ecological precedent, to the extent that adoption is reconceived as a facet of post-anthropocentric organic reality. Turtle's fierce physical clinging to Taylor is both materially produced (the result of trauma) and organically sanctioned. Just as the rhizobia live in the wisteria's roots 'in little knots' (227), Turtle clings to the knotted braid in Taylor's hair 'like a lifeline' (73). Hence, *The Bean Trees* mobilizes a narrative of transcultural adoption to engender no less than a new way of being: a 'Humbean', in Turtle's parlance. Turtle is its prototype.

We might understand, then, why Kingsolver makes Turtle's adoption a specifically transcultural matter, and also why this fact irreversibly fractures the novel's otherwise laudable intentions. The polycultural provenance of the Tucson micro community is important in keeping to the fore the novel's emphasis on family as a rhizobic environment which welcomes the separate not the same, cheerfully exogenous and open to cross-cultural communion. Paradoxically, however, the novel must insist on Turtle's hereditary cultural provenance as a Native child at the same time as showing that this fact does not inhibit her being raised by a non-Native mother. In order to resolve this paradox, Kingsolver falls back on the very image of attachment which is elsewhere presented as a part of a rhetoric of constraint: that is, blood. The absence in the novel of any cognizance of Native adoption history requires Kingsolver to mystify Native family connections via a familiar consanguineous vocabulary and damagingly do away with a more rigorous enquiry into the materiality of Native life and the problematic role which transcultural adoption has played. To aid her quest to refuse thinking of the adoptive and the organic as ontologically separate, Kingsolver puts in a place a spurious possible biogenetic confluence between Taylor and Turtle by making the former also have Cherokee consanguineous ancestry. As Taylor journeys through Oklahoma prior to encountering Turtle she remembers her mother's grandfather, a 'full-blooded Cherokee [...]. Mama would say, "If we run out of luck we can always go live on the Cherokee Nation." She and I had enough blood to qualify. According to Mama, if you're one-eighth or more they let you in' (13). Importantly, Taylor never lays claim to her Cherokee heredity as legitimating her claiming of Turtle as her daughter. But her embodied connection to Native peoples enables Kingsolver to have things both ways (and in a fashion which parallels Andrea Levy's similar manoeuvre in *Small Island*) by making Taylor have consanguineous links with Turtle, so that their attachment is organic both biogenetically and rhizobically. The specifics of Cherokee culture are replaced by a mythic contract of consanguinity, with blood standing in biocentrically for the unconsidered materiality of Cherokee life which lies beyond the horizon of the novel's transformative vision. So when Taylor gives Turtle her adoption certificate on the novel's last page, telling her that it means 'you'll always know who you are' (232), these words phrase an impossibility. Given the absence of Cherokee materiality or cosmology, there is no way that Turtle, or Taylor, or indeed Kingsolver, can possibly know exactly what 'being' might mean in Cherokee terms.

For these reasons, Kingsolver's daring attempt to shape a new ecology of personhood in *The Bean Trees* stops short of a transfigurative mode of enabling adoptive being, as it does not make available the concrete particulars of blood-lines that might be productively intercalated. Despite its squeamishness over blood as a sign as female servitude, the novel cannot shake off a biocentric rendering of cultural genealogy as mystically transported along Cherokee ancestry. Mystified rather than material notions of consanguineous kinship troublingly remain to the end, so that the novel's tale of transcultural adoption remains complicit within neocolonial confines. Despite its euphoric environmentalist, post-anthropocentric ending – where the new Tucson micro community is hymned in Turtle's 'vegetable-soup song' with 'people mixed in with the beans and potatoes: Dwayne Ray, Mattie, Esperanza, Lou Ann and all the rest' (232) – *The Bean Trees* never leaves behind, as it had promised, a vision-damaging tryst with blood.

In its sequel, *Pigs in Heaven*, Kingsolver seeks to redress the bypassing of the Cherokee Nation and align the fortunes of Taylor and Turtle with Cherokee cultural and judicial claims over Turtle's genealogical heredity. The innovative ecological redrafting of human attachments is superseded by a seemingly more sensitive and informed engagement with transcultural affairs. When Turtle, now six years old, helps save the life of a man who falls into the Hoover Dam and appears on television as a consequence, she is spotted by a young Native lawyer, Annawake Fourkiller, who becomes intrigued by the story of Turtle's adoption. Annawake discovers that the adoption has been conducted improperly and contravenes the 1978 ICWA, and so she visits Taylor in Tucson to raise the matter with her. Terrified that she is about to lose Turtle, Taylor drives west once again, ending up eventually in Seattle struggling to make ends meet. Meanwhile, her mother Alice, who has left her husband and is increasingly concerned about her daughter's and granddaughter's well-being, travels to the small town of Heaven, part of the Cherokee Nation in Oklahoma, to visit her cousin, Sugar, and see if she can find a way of keeping Taylor and Turtle together. Eventually she strikes up a relationship with Cash Stillwater and persuades Taylor to bring Turtle to Heaven and meet with Annawake. The novel closes with the revelation that Cash is Turtle's biogenetic grandfather, with Alice and Cash deciding to marry and with a tribal court deciding that Taylor can have custody of Turtle but that she must ensure that Turtle spends at least three months each year on the reservation with her Cherokee relations.

Annawake's characterization brings to the novel a sense of the history and the hurt of Native adoptions. Known since childhood as especially intelligent, Annawake's work on behalf of the Cherokee Nation is driven in part by experiencing the damage done to Native peoples at close quarters. When her mother was hospitalized through alcoholism, her family was broken up by social workers who separated Annawake from her twin brother, Gabriel, by placing him in a white family. Gabriel's life as a transcultural adoptee exposed him to persistent discrimination and led to his descent into criminality and incarceration. Kingsolver also sketches the life of Turtle's biogenetic grandfather, Cash, who was sent to boarding school, 'a prison for children' (257) where speaking Cherokee was banned and where '[y]ou forgot about your family' (257). While Annawake's pursuit of Taylor is not devoid of compassion, it is fuelled by a righteousness borne from the injustices she has both learned of and lived through, to the extent that her quest to recover Turtle for the tribe is derived from her desire to compensate for the seizing of Gabriel in childhood, to act in a way she could not as a young girl.

Clearly, Annawake's knowledge of Native adoptions is Kingsolver's attempt to correct the oversight of the previous novel. Annawake knows the particulars of the ICWA and several chilling statistics. When she meets Taylor for the first time, she offers her a history lesson of tribal breakup: 'I'm talking about as recently as the seventies, when you and I were in high school. A third of all our kids were still being taken from their families and adopted into white homes. One out of *three*' (75). Importantly, Kingsolver underlines the principles which motivate Annawake's attempt to invalidate Turtle's adoption as based on historical experience and legal propriety rather than motivated solely by consanguineous notions of Cherokee kinship. The view that Turtle needs to be raised conscious of her Cherokee legacy is framed in terms of cultural politics and presented to protest the practice of colour-blind adoptive parenting. As Annawake writes to Taylor's boyfriend, Jax, she is concerned that as Turtle grows she will encounter a prejudicial world with little sense of how to survive: 'What these kids find is that they have no sense of themselves as Native Americans, but live in a society that won't let them go on being white, either. Not past childhood' (148). Annawake's advocacy ensures that the representation of Cherokee life is given impeccable political credentials. But Kingsolver requires more from her novel than a narrative of Native injustice. As in her previous novel, there is a wider tale to be told about the possibility of reconstituted human relations enabled by transcultural adoption. Whereas *The Bean Trees* sought to combine human and environmental matters, *Pigs in Heaven* attempts to mix blood and water.

Pigs in Heaven is very keen to reconstitute blood-lines in terms other than exclusionary purity or mystical attachment. The status of one's parentage – whether one is a 'full-blooded' Cherokee or not – seems of limited significance in the novel. When Annawake learns that Alice and Taylor possess Cherokee biogenetic descent, she describes the significance of blood-lines in the Nation as not conforming to the racisms of modernity: 'We're not into racial purity [...] It's a funny thing about us eastern tribes, we've been mixed blood from way back, even a lot of our holy people and our historical leaders. Like John Ross. He was half-blood. It's no stigma at all' (278). Blood is often mobilized as a reason to include rather than exclude. Annawake's boss, Franklin Turnbo, has a white father and is something of a 'born-again Indian' (64) whose decision to live and work for Cherokee interests has given his life a clear purpose. When Annawake tells him of her memories of the perch in Tenkiller Lake that kept her focused when she was in law school – specifically the sense that in the lake there was always a 'world of free breakfast, waiting to help get you into another day' (67) – Franklin understands. The narrator interjects that, consequently, '[w]hether or not he knew it, he was always Cherokee' (67), underlining the novel's wider presentation of Cherokee selfhood as forged experientially and, here, intriguingly through a memory of water.

Pigs in Heaven proposes an understanding of biogenetic relations as cheerfully impure and ever-proliferating by rhetorically mixing blood with water, a situation signalled by Turtle's biogenetic descent from a Cherokee grandfather with a distinctly aquatic surname: Cash Stillwater. If consanguinity signifies one plane of Cherokee human attachment, it does not do so solely or exclusively. It is combined with the images of aquatic life, such as the perch-filled Tenkiller Lake or indeed Turtle's post-adoption name. When Annawake describes her understanding of Cherokee family to Alice, she senses it as 'a notion as fluid as *river*' (227) – a key image, as Marianne Novy notes, of tribal communality (*Reading* 203). During her stay in Heaven, Alice is taken to an idyllic creek with 'cool, turquoise blue water' (*Pigs in Heaven* 221) where she sees children playing in the water and behaving with unimpeachable manners: 'Alice can't get over what she is seeing: adolescent boys being polite' (222). At this liquid heart of Heaven, Kingsolver keeps proximate images of water and the theme of adoption. In a remark which recalls Turtle's naming, Sugar tells Alice that they recently caught 'a snapping turtle in the mud. Leon poked a stick at it and it bit it and wouldn't turn loose' (222). When Alice asks Sugar if one of the boys, Stand, is her grandson, Sugar's response points to the normative practice of informal adoption in Cherokee daily life: '[Stand] is Quatie's, but she already had six or seven when he was born, so Junior adopted him. You know how people do. Share the kids around' (223). Cherokee culture appears in general as readily entangling the adoptive and consanguineous, expressed in these images of incidences by water as much as imagined through the mystical lineaments of blood-lines. 'Being Cherokee is more a less a mind-set' (275), says Sugar, when telling Alice of the mixed-race condition of the contemporary nation: 'We're all so watered down here, anyway' (275). Let us remember, too, that Annawake is made aware of Turtle's existence not through discovering a firm blood relation but because of her actions by water, namely helping rescue Lucky Buster from the Hoover Dam. When Taylor decides to relinquish her lonely life on the run, her decision is strategically linked to images of liquidity. As she stands by the Seattle locks watching the salmon trying to swim upstream against the tide to their place of birth, she sees an image of the futility of her flight, 'working yourself for all you're worth to get ahead, and still going backwards' (251). And when Turtle's lactose intolerance comes to light a few pages later (she suffers from stomach cramps due to drinking milk), Taylor decides to travel to the Cherokee Nation: a journey that, like the salmon's, constitutes a going backwards and also a journey forwards and beyond, into a future as much as into the past.

This rendering of blood-lines as part of a wider liquid notion of Cherokee life – a 'solution' in the scientific sense, mixed from more than one source – plays a major role in Kingsolver's appropriation of Native culture for adoptive purposes. As Annawake seeks to track down Turtle, the white American characters learn about Cherokee mythology as well as enforced adoptions through various moments of transcultural translation where languages and cultural inventories mix. In her first encounter with Taylor, Annawake explains that her surname refers to her great-great-grandfather carving four notches in his rifle barrel, one for each of his children, but that 'the white guys took it to mean he'd shot four men' (73). She also tells Jax, as they stare at the sky during her second visit to the Greers' home, that the Pleiades or Seven Sisters star formation is known to the Cherokee as the *anitsutsa* or *disihgwa*, 'The Six Pigs in Heaven'. According to myth, six misbehaving boys were transformed into pigs by the spirits as they ran around tribal grounds and floated skywards, to become fixed amidst the stars. These matters of myth and mistranslation not only keep prevalent the issue of filial Cherokee life in the novel, but also present its key concern: the potential lack of contact between American and Cherokee Nation values. Jax chides Annawake for not possessing the ability to see both sides in her pursuit of Turtle: 'There is no point of intersection in this dialogue' (89). But in bringing together Native and white peoples due to her position as a transcultural adoptee, Turtle provides exactly this opportunity for amphibious transcultural contact and co-operation, where the cultural inventories of distinct communities are taken, like Turtle at the novel's climax, into joint custody.

As we have seen, Cherokee culture has been presented as 'watered' as well as consanguineous, functioning adoptively as a normative mode. The challenge which *Pigs in Heaven* presents to white or settler-descended peoples is precisely this: can they, too, enter adoptively into co-operative transcultural relations with minoritized peoples, in order to mix a solution for America's political inequalities. Turtle is shaped as a symbol of this hopeful possibility. Situated across Cherokee and white attachments, she both encapsulates and makes possible the kinds of translative activity, drawing upon a polycultural range of ways of being, that her adoption unpredictably triggered. Turtle is not so much returned to her Cherokee tribal 'birthright' but instead delivers an alternative way of being singular plural that is transactional and transcultural, and which involves the novel's myriad characters accepting that they must have something to do with each other. At its most utopian, then, *Pigs in Heaven* offers not just a way into the materiality of Native adoptions and the disenfranchisement they evidence, but a way out of that history too, so that the Cherokee and white

Americans no longer engage through the insidious practices of administered adoption but the transformative possibilities of transcultural adoptive being.

The translative admixture of Native and settler-descended cultural inventories dreamed up by the novel can be detected in its tendency to look skywards to the heavens. Drawing upon Native cultural inventories of aviation, *Pigs in Heaven* is festooned with descriptions of birds – from the 'seven or eight shrieking birds' (119) in Mr Crittenden's office to the birds that invade Taylor's apricot tree which she tries to scare away by playing at loud volume Jax's music. Taylor even has a brief friendship in Seattle with an air-traffic controller, Steven Kant, whose job it is to co-ordinate flight. Kingsolver also presents her characters in aerial terms. When Annawake writes to Jax of her reasons for claiming Turtle for the Cherokee, she describes herself as a 'bird of prey' (149): a hawk who has lost one of her wings, namely her twin brother Gabriel. She first sees Taylor climbing a tree, installing the speakers which she hopes will scare birds. When Alice attends the stomp dance late in the novel she is invited to sit on the 'Bird Clan benches' (266) due to her biogenetic maternal line. Birds thematize flight, freedom of movement and migration, and beckon notions of collective existence in the mobile habitat of the flock. In folding human and aerial forms of existence into each other like this, Kingsolver maintains something of her re-ecologizing of human life (the 'Humbean' of *The Bean Trees*) while anchoring it adoptively to Native cultural symbolization. The gathering of the novel's characters in Heaven's tribal court at the novel's end synchronizes its material and utopian concerns. Heaven is at once a jurisdiction where the ICWA is obeyed, but is also somewhere more ethereal, a figurative space of projection where transcultural relations cheerily flock together.

Does *Pigs in Heaven* ever fully escape the biocentrism of *The Bean Trees*, where blood-lines mystified more complex cultural attachments? The representation of blood and water might suggest so, with consanguineous attachment seemingly scaled down as a key arbiter of legitimate human attachment and identity. Yet the fact that Turtle's lactose intolerance ultimately triggers Taylor's decision to take her to the Cherokee Nation sits a little awkwardly, with matters of biological provenance winning out over Taylor's valiant attempt to nurture her child without recourse to the primacy of biogenetics. More problematic is the rendering of Cherokee life which, for all of Kingsolver's newfound knowledge of the history of the ICWA and enforced adoptions, never fully escapes instrumentalization as an essentially benign cultural dispensation. Marianne Novy moots the possibility that the novel may be looking to propose an image of the United States as one 'of joint partnership with other cultures, not admission of them on the basis of their childlike status' (*Reading* 209), where assimilation is replaced by a meaningful polycultural engagement. But Kingsolver's limiting representation of the Cherokee Nation effectively puts paid to this. The text never expends much energy confronting head-on the incidence of Turtle's abuse nor the wider realities and obscenities created through the oppression and minoritization of Native peoples. Rather, it wants to believe in a preconception of Native culture that Alice sees at the stomp dance: 'simply people having a good time in each other's company, because they want to' (269). Margaret Homans rightly admonishes the novel for its penchant for 'idealized examples of nurturant extended family' (134) and argues forcefully that its ultimate goal is to legitimate Taylor, more than Turtle, as a member of the Cherokee Nation to the extent that Turtle comes to stand for 'Taylor's belated origin' (135). And as Kristina Fagan argues, by presenting a harmonious transcultural confection at the novel's conclusion, 'Kingsolver avoids the task of imagining how Native peoples and settlers can learn to live together as large communities' (260). To my mind, *Pigs in Heaven*'s saccharine representation of Native life as benignly collective and welcomingly communal restrains the radicalism of the novel's presentation of adoptive being, because it cannot think beyond its effectively neocolonial exoticization of Cherokee culture, despite Kingsolver's dutiful efforts to point to the depressed economic circumstances of the Nation and its ongoing subservience to the economy of tourism. The material viscosity of Native culture is notably watered down in Kingsolver's rendition of convivial stomp dances and hog fries. So while Kingsolver's novels set their bearings to head for new ecologies of personhood or for transformative modes of adoptive being, their capacity to deliver each is pulled back by the ongoing agency of either biocentric mystification or the romanticization of a still-oppressed people.

As Kingsolver's work demonstrates, an enthusiasm for transcultural affinity should not be mistaken for the achievement of its possibilities. In turning next to the fiction of Caryl Phillips, we encounter a writer whose often sombre and bleak depictions of the psychic and material cost of prejudice challenge the premature celebration of its hoped-for demise. While *Pigs in Heaven* shapes a vision of changed relations through a tale of tribal repatriation, Phillips's novel *Crossing the River* (1993) offers no such hope of restoring sundered relations. In the words of Joan Miller Powell, the novel expresses Phillips's recurrent 'troping of orphanage and familial dysfunctionality as key markers of displacement' that can be discerned in a number of his works that thematize 'filial disruption and paternal betrayal, orphanhood, and states of psychic abandonment, as well as interracial relationships that expand the notion of kin' (88). The waterways in *Crossing the River* which separate family members from each other – the Atlantic Ocean, the Missouri River, the Mediterranean Sea – enable routes of passage while simultaneously cancelling the possibility of return. 'There are no paths in water' muses the unnamed African father figure whose voice sounds in the novel's prologue and epilogue: 'No signposts. There is no return' (1–2).

In its portrayal of the fortunes of a range of characters caught up in the legacies of Atlantic slavery and the Middle Passage across Africa, Europe and the Americas, *Crossing the River* underscores the grim realities of abandonment, exploitation and suffering that blighted the lives of the African-descended diaspora during slavery and since abolition. It also resolutely opposes a distinctly Afrocentric politics or racialized vision of oppression and resistance. Typically for Phillips, the novel is as much interested in the ways in which white European-descended figures have been caught up in slavery's designs, sometimes to the detriment of their emotional health, even while they benefited from slavery's fiscal and social dividends. Phillips guards against creating, in Derek Walcott's phrase, a 'literature of recrimination and despair' (37) with determined forthrightness. In the place of a separatist Afrocentric politics of racialized solidarity, he proffers a wished-for post-racial vision of ethical engagement through a reimagining of history that emphasizes the potential fecundity of transcultural crossing, connection and contact.

The 'expanded' notions of kin which Millar Powell finds in *Crossing the River* point to an instructive and highly tentative reformulation of family in the novel as source of possibility as well as pain. In Abigail Ward's reading, Phillips refuses to reconstitute filiative notions of genealogical attachment beloved of modernity's modes of identitarian categorization (nation as family, racial kinship) and instead negotiates a progressive envisioning of post-racial collectivity by the novel's close: '[t]he disruption of the stable family unit, one could argue, is one of the legacies of slavery although [...] in this novel it is replaced with affiliative "families"' (49). Ward's reading is conceptually resourced by Edward Said's discussion of filiative and affiliative relations in his essay 'Secular Criticism' (1983) and turns on her perceptive reading of the novel's key climactic moment set in 1963 when a white birth-mother meets the mixed-race son she surrendered eighteen years previously. In my reading I want to push these ideas a little further and think of this crucial and complex scene as both filial and affiliative, consanguineous as well as contingent: an emotionally charged and entangled moment of biogenetic reunion which is commensurately an encounter between strangers. From Phillips's decision not to set the biogenetic and adoptive at odds, a muted if hopeful politics of possibility is borne from a little-known but grim facet of British and American adoption history.

Families are never romanticized in Phillips's fiction. They are often sites of violation whose sundering marks the prejudicial provenance of historical and social influence, as well as the difficult decision-making of its participants. In opening *Crossing the River* with the voice of an African father figure who sells his children into slavery when his crops fail – the 'desperate foolishness' (1) which triggers the diasporic travels of his ancestors – Phillips exposes the intervention of public affairs in private matters while also admitting the complicity of Africans in the slave trade. He closes the novel with the same father figure listening from the distant shore of Africa to the subsequent centuries' stories of diasporic survival. The father's voice gathers 'the many-tongued chorus of the common memory' (235) of all those sundered by slavery, and significantly lists among his diasporan children the figure of Joyce, a white working-class woman whose life preoccupies much of the novel's fourth section, 'Somewhere in England': 'But my Joyce, and my other children, their voices hurt but determined, they will survive the hardships of the far bank' (235). This inclusion of Joyce is strategically provocative. In an interview with Stephen Clingman, Phillips recalls an incident at a book signing: 'a black woman – and I think it is important that she was black – came up to me, publicly, and was, clearly, very angry with me for including Joyce in the book [...]; and she was particularly upset that Joyce was included as part of the family at the end of the book' (111–12). Joyce's status as diasporic family member challenges, in Phillips's words, the 'racially narrow reading' which he felt this black reader had imposed not just on his book but on his character's imagined life, and was decidedly a 'risk' (112) in the novel's design. As Bénédicte Ledent has spotted, in the prologue the African narrator emerges figuratively as an adoptive father figure as much as a biogenetic one by claiming the white British Joyce 'as his own daughter' (114). In developing from the novel's singularly narrated prologue to its pluralizing epilogue, the diasporic family at the heart of the novel comes to include a newcomer who breaches consanguineous attachments but is claimed in the language of kin. This manoeuvre indexes Phillips's general attempt to expose the violating legacies of slavery while seeking a response to them which sensitively requisitions the matter of adoption as a possible transfigurative resource.

The African father figure is not the only character who entangles biogenetic and adoptive relations. The white birth-mother, Joyce, has no African ancestry but contingently comes to have something to do with the consanguineous heredity of the father figure's children by bearing and surrendering a mixed-race child, Greer, conceived with an African American soldier. Joyce is situated between and beyond the Saidian distinction of the filial and affiliative. Her characterization pushes the novel towards a complex rather than counter-intuitive approach to sundered relations. If affiliative relations were all that mattered, then why does Greer search for his birth-mother? His trace would have no meaning in a radically affiliative framework. Instead, Phillips opens fresh directions for thinking through political as well as transpersonal attachments that bear us past the romance or recriminations of race and of biocentric bodily reunion, looking instead for what futurity might be salvaged from the violation of intimate relations.

In *Crossing the River* families are often careless, constraining and indeed abusive, with the language of kin sometimes mobilized as a guise for exploitative forms of human contact. In the novel's first section, 'The Pagan Coast', a seemingly benevolent nineteenth-century American philanthropist, Edward Williams, joins the work of the American Colonization Society in 'repatriating' Christianized slaves. But it soon appears that those in his care, and who have been encouraged to call Edward 'father', struggled to adapt in Africa. Furthermore, it is hinted that Edward's interest in his slaves has a distinctly sexual element which severely complexifies Edward's image as a benign father figure. Edward's journey to Liberia to find one such former 'child', Nash, is futile and ends with Edward's sense of his own abandonment as he stands outside Nash's empty hut. In the second section, 'West', a destitute slave, Martha, spends her last days seeking out the whereabouts of her daughter, Eliza Mae, who has been sold at a slave auction, only to die heartbroken with her quest unfulfilled. Her final hours, spent in the care of a stranger who finds her freezing to death in the street, evidence a spark of compassion beyond consanguineous kinship, while recognizing the unredeemed obscenity of Martha's maternal violation. The third section, 'Crossing the River', depicts Captain Hamilton, a seafaring slave-trader, whose letters to his beloved reveal his emotional complexity as he struggles both to understand and to grieve for his late father, also a slave-trader, while all the time he records in his journal his commercial transactions regarding slaves with chilling detachment. In portraying the intricacies of Hamilton's emotional life and his filial struggles, Phillips courageously humanizes Hamilton in order to disconcert his swift dismissal as evil or inhumane. Condemnation or excuse, recrimination or despair are unproductive and potentially ahistorical responses to family-making and family-breaking, especially if they keep in place residual notions of race and kin which are proffered as explanatory mechanisms for discrete or predictable human behaviours. For these reasons, *Crossing the River* does not countenance the consanguineous family as either a recoverable refuge from moral corruption or as immune to the agency of history's severing violence.

The novel's fourth and longest section, 'Somewhere in England', is set predominantly between 1936 and 1945. It concerns a white working-class Northern English woman, Joyce, and her relationship with an African American GI, Travis, who is stationed in her Yorkshire village while Joyce's husband, Len, is imprisoned for dealing on the black market. After divorcing Len and risking the villagers' disapproval, Joyce and Travis conceive a child and marry in 1945 while Travis is on compassionate leave. Their son, Greer, is born just prior to VE Day. But Travis is killed in action in Italy, and Joyce is compelled by a 'lady with the blue coat and maroon scarf' to surrender Greer to the care of the county council as she insists that life will be better for all concerned: 'If you're lucky, it might be legally adopted into a well-to-do family. Some are, you know' (223). The chapter climaxes with Greer's tracing of Joyce in 1963, and their brief encounter at her home.

As we shall see, the narration of this key moment, the only time in the novel when a nominal parent is reunited with their child, is of fundamental significance to Phillips's quest to plot adoptive being's possible bearings. While attending to a specific historical conjuncture which produced transcultural adoptees, Phillips is at his most figurative in reframing a tale of surrender, search and reunion as the productive means to articulate transcultural diasporic transformation that impacts beyond the adoption triad and possesses political pedigree as well as ethical propriety. To open these possibilities, 'Somewhere in England' resequences temporality so that Joyce's narrative criss-crosses calendrical time and unfolds out of synch. The chapter is composed of a series of narrative vignettes of various length, all narrated by Joyce, each of which bears a date, most frequently a year. This formal patterning enables Phillips to release information about Joyce at certain well-timed moments. The relating of her abortion in 1937 happens about two-thirds of the way through her narrative which until this point has predominantly dealt with Joyce's life during wartime as Len's wife and a shop-assistant. Phillips's resequencing of calendrical time underscores his attempts to free his narrative from the illusions of genealogical orderliness beloved of modernity's casting of race and nation. It also enables him to call particular attention to the significance of Joyce's initial surprised response in 1963 on seeing Greer appear outside her home as an adult. Phillips places this moment of surprise at the end of the chapter, *after* the characters' subsequent brief and difficult conversation that concludes with Greer leaving Joyce's house.

The historical provenance which Phillips tells through Joyce's resequenced tale is a particularly sorry chapter in the history of surrender and adoption, infrequently remembered today. The arrival in the UK of American troops after the United States entered the Second World War engendered new occasions for transcultural human intimacies. Most white Britons, especially those living outside cities and of working-class backgrounds, had never met African Americans. For their part, the GIs made contact with a constituency of white people who, while not at all immune from racial prejudice, did not necessarily or automatically share exactly the same perceptions of African Americans at large in the United States. Sabine Lee estimates that between 1942 and 1945, approximately 130,000 African American troops were stationed in the Britain 'within a segregated military' (161). Almost immediately questions were raised within military and government circles on both sides of the Atlantic as to the alleged deleterious impact of their intimate encounters. Graham Smith has recorded that the official queasiness with transracial relations led to a 'whispering campaign' which promoted an image of black men as carriers of venereal disease, and of the white women who met with them as sexually licentious and of loose morals. In Lee's words, 'It is important to stress that the comparative acceptance of interracial mixing was limited to contacts in public, and that it did not extend to the private sphere, let alone to intimate relations. Such contacts between African-American GIs and white British women were condemned no less vehemently by the British than the Americans' (162). Yet romantic and sexual relations were soon forthcoming, a possible consequence of the loneliness both of the men and women concerned: the former found themselves sequestered in a strange country with little to do as they waited for military deployment on the European mainland, while the latter's partners were often overseas on military service. The increased mobility of women during wartime, living and working away from home, was also a factor in enabling opportunities to meet new people.

The result of the US military presence, according to Lee, was the birth of 22,000 children to American and British parents, 'of whom around 1,700 were of African-American descent' (163). The fortunes of these mixed-race children, known as brown babies, were sombre. The US military frowned upon marriages between the GIs and their British partners. Even those granted permission to wed could not effectively do so due to the laws in approximately twenty states which prohibited cross-racial marriages, making it impossible for some British brides to emigrate. Isolated in the UK, socially stigmatized for their cross-racial liaisons and single motherhood, many women were encouraged or compelled by circumstance to surrender their children for adoption, as Lee summarizes: 'instead of supporting young mothers of GI-children to bring up their children in a nuclear or extended family, a blanket solution of placing the children in care in preparation for adoption into mixed-race or black families at a later stage was favoured' (180). The United States had no desire to receive these children after the war. Although a couple of media campaigns in the late 1940s were successful in stimulating interest in these children amongst would-be American adopters, the prevailing response from US officialdom was not at all welcoming. Smith cites Mississippi Congressman John E. Rankin's opposition to 'bringing to this country a lot of illegitimate half-breed Negro children [...] the offspring of the scum of the British Isles' (211).

In 'Somewhere in England', Phillips's attention to the history of these so-called brown babies is focalized through the figure of Joyce rather than Greer. This enables him to contend with two forms of prejudice: racial discrimination and the demonization of the figure of the birth-mother. The decision to imagine history in terms of Joyce's life rather than Greer's engenders the rehabilitation of a much-maligned figure. If the prevailing view of the white lovers of black GIs was grim, holding them to be immoral women of dubious social standing – a form of denigration which would be visited upon their mixed-race offspring as products of morally and socially degenerate women – then Phillips's representation of Joyce confronts these assumptions. In his characterization of her, Phillips releases the figure of the wartime birth-mother from the discursive dismissal of the time, which contributed to the compulsion to surrender mixed-race children for adoption.

Joyce's relationship with Travis is contextualized by the predominantly loveless relations that have characterized her life and which contribute to the affinity she may feel for someone who appears displaced and isolated. Her father was killed in the First World War and she was raised by her mother, a devout Christian who displayed a diminishing interest in her daughter's life. Joyce recalls that she was compelled to leave school before she could achieve her school certificate, and that her mother beat her 'because she said I read too much. [...] Everything was seen as some kind of betrayal of her. I was always a disappointment' (190). Joyce's mother is unsympathetic to her daughter's first broken heart (concerning Herbert, an actor) and offers little support when Joyce has an abortion in 1937, other than inducting her into the church. When Joyce's brief encounter with Christianity comes to naught, her mother deserts her: 'And then she left me. My abandonment of Christ was the last straw. I'd chosen to leave He who had made her life possible. This was, for her, the unkindest cut of all' (194). Her mother greets the news of Joyce's betrothal to Len with indifference and attends her daughter's wedding with studied reluctance. Joyce learns at close quarters that filial kinship is no guarantee of support, care or loving relations. These have to be sourced elsewhere.

In this context, Phillips fashions Joyce as a deeply moral being, imperfectly human and sceptical of normative behaviour. She refuses to accommodate the weaknesses and exploitative chauvinism of Len and his associates, and she eschews the village's hostility to the GIs' arrival. She is far from seeming degenerate, sexually licentious and socially delinquent, so often the image of birth-mothers and partners of GIs. While a great deal of her behaviour might beckon applause, she is by no means devoid of problematic behaviour. Her marriage to Len is one of convenience on both sides as it enables her to leave the unhappy home of her mother. Her surrendering of Greer, while compelled by the county council, is mystified by her phrase '[a]nd so we were sensible, my son and I' (228) in acquiescing to the will of the anonymous 'lady with the blue coat' (228). Ledent notes that here Joyce 'also contributes to the camouflage of Britain's racial others by not keeping her son with her' (121). As in much of Phillips's fiction, 'Somewhere in England' avoids quick moral or political reckonings in seeking to challenge the clichés and mystifications of historical happenings and attend to the particular material and discursive circumstances that direct but never entirely dictate hard decisions.

Crucially, Joyce is something of an outsider. Her marriage to Len in 1939 brought her out of town and to a small parochial village. Her status as a newcomer from elsewhere, in but not of the village, sensitizes her to the predicaments of other newcomers, especially the GIs, whose arrival she witnesses in June 1942:

Then men began to tumble from the trucks. They stretched and looked around. Then, one by one, they began to saunter down the drive. They looked sad, like little lost boys. Some of the villagers couldn't contain themselves. They began to whisper to each other, and they pointed. I suppose we were all shocked, for we had nothing to prepare us for this. [...] I wanted to warn them, but in no time they were gone. [...] Once the men had vanished, eyes turned upon me. I was now the object of curiosity. The uninvited outsider. There was nobody with whom I might whisper. I stared back at their accusing eyes and then stepped back into the shop. (129)

The GIs' appearance as 'little lost boys' points to the strangeness of England for these newcomers who have 'crossed the river' to fight a war far from home in a segregated military, subject to the shocked whispers of their hosts. As herself an 'uninvited outsider', Joyce's subsequent relationship with Travis will not be between a black foreigner and a white native, but forged between two different kinds of outsider figures who ultimately refuse to conform to prejudicial racial and gendered protocols. Joyce's unexplained impulse to 'warn' the GIs is instructive in this regard, and a way of signalling the undercurrent of violence and intolerance which defines, rather than is exceptional to, provincial English village life. When set against the endogamous intolerance of the villagers, the exogamous relations between those like Joyce and Travis assume a particular political as well as emotional charge.

The moral vacuity that characterizes English provincial life is measured by how the villagers treat children. When Len first regards the arrival of evacuees in the village, another micro constituency of lost figures having to make a life away from home, 'the girls and scrawny boys close to tears' (144), his antipathy is chilling: 'I looked across at Len, who firmly shook his head. Not even one of them, he said. They can bloody well go back to where they come from. We're not in the charity business' (144). Len's use of a phrase that became popular amongst opponents of migration in the post-war years establishes an antipathy to newcomers as generic of English life rather than specific to a discrete historical moment, while also asserts racial antipathy as part of a general English queasiness with foreignness, as Joyce comes to experience in the village at close quarters. In another example, Joyce's friend Sandra is shot by her husband who has returned from military service to discover that his wife is pregnant by Len's friend Terry. The husband is arrested by the police; meanwhile, Terry and Len enjoy a drink in the pub, with Terry 'sipping a pint like nothing was the matter' (170). All three men seem indifferent to the fate of Tommy, the couple's son. It falls to Joyce to muse '[a]nd what about Tommy? I supposed they'd find a good home for him' (170), although news of the child's fate is never forthcoming. 'Somewhere in England' is full of abandoned or adoptable children – Joyce, the evacuees, the 'little lost boys', Tommy, Greer. Their fictional manifestation serves to index the prejudicial disposition of English life at the time and since.

Phillips's representation of the toxic intolerance of endogamous communities and the violations which are both visited on and stem from consanguineous family-making importantly frame the reunion between Joyce and Greer in 1963. The chapter's critical rendering of intimate filial relations effectively cancels the notion that biogenetic reunion discharges pain or resolves problems, so that these characters' coming together is not mistaken as a happy return. Phillips instead writes of the awkwardness and perilous emotional character of such encounters. Having entered Joyce's home, Greer stays only for a short time as it soon becomes clear that her husband, Alan, and their children do not know of Greer's existence. Their conversation becomes punctuated with silences which at least are free of 'accusation' (223). Joyce longs for him to leave as much as she longs for him to stay, and it is uncertain if their encounter will be repeated. Greer does not call Joyce his mother, while Joyce has little to offer him other than the scraps of her memories, having 'destroyed everything. Letters, pictures, everything. When I met Alan. It seemed the right thing to do, but I was stupid. He spoke again. I'd better go now, he said' (224). Joyce's position is particularly unsteady as she has remained complicit in the secreting of Greer's existence since his surrendering. The scene seems to replay that initial severance rather than offer a redemptive vision of reconnection. Greer's last words in the scene are of departure, while Joyce sits before him experiencing again her maternal feelings towards her son as well as her long-buried love for Travis. There is clearly no return when consanguineous relations are reunited.

Why does Phillips place his account of Joyce and Greer's initial contact *after* we are told of their muted conversation and Greer's departure from Joyce's home? In narrating things out of sequence, what is fashioned by Phillips's highlighting of the moment of incipient contact? The chapter's final passage gives a richly descriptive account of Joyce's first vision of Greer as an adult:

> I was in the kitchen, wringing out clothes in the sink. I happened to glance up. I saw him, standing at the front gate. I knew that it was him. I knew that one day he would come looking. That he would find me. I could hear myself breathing. But apart from this, I was calm. I surprised myself. [...] He stepped by me, dipping a shoulder as he did so in order that we didn't have to touch. I closed in the door but for a moment I didn't turn around. I was ashamed. I wasn't ready. Standing there in a plain dress, with my lank hair, and my bare legs, and my slippers looking like the left-over scraps from somebody's fluffy rug. Forty-five years old, and I knew I looked awful, but there wasn't any time to fret over appearances. Not now. I took a deep breath and turned to face him. I almost said make yourself at home, but I didn't. At least I avoided that. Sit down. Please, sit down. (231–2)

This unscheduled moment of contact is a surprise that compels us to face the irreparable realities of adoption's emotional and political terrain. Phillips cancels any sense of this encounter as a homecoming or as bringing heightened emotional fulfilment, as Joyce's unsteady breathing and feelings of shame testify. Bodies do not come together: Greer avoids touching Joyce, while Joyce hesitates before facing him. Her sensitive refusal to indulge Greer with a fiction of home and homecoming keeps apart the filial, familial and homely. Phillips chooses not to indulge normative notions of resolving consanguineous kinship at this vital moment. Instead, he directs our attention to the contingent task of shaping future-facing relations from the sundered kinships of old. Or in other words, at this climactic point of the novel, Joyce is tasked with rethinking the sundered blood-lines of the past as the generative life lines of the future. Even though the reunion remains unfulfilling, especially for Greer, Phillips wishes to extract from this fleeting moment of contact the bearings for a different set of possibilities regarding how previously sundered relations might alternatively attach.

Consider the reunion's key details. Joyce is clearly surprised, but willing to face a troubled past, ready to open a conversation despite her anxious condition and prepared not to indulge in a fiction of home. It is a private moment with public resonances: it describes a wider condition which all must face in trying to think forwards and through the entanglements and severances which have harmed human relations previously. Whether she likes it or not, Joyce has to leave behind the security of her new life and step outside its comforts and confines, risking new relations with the past. Phillips positions her more in an adoptive rather than consanguineous relation to the grown-up Greer, preparing to build a relationship with someone who is not a member of her family and who has no automatic right to call her house his home. Those who consider themselves blood-related cannot take blood-lines as any guarantee of attachment or integrity, but must work at building and maintaining relations which depend upon material activities not mystical bonds.

But neither can the realities, vocabularies and emotional impact of filiation and kinship be quickly dismissed. Phillips does not counterpoint the biogenetic and the adoptive but seeks to elide a clear distinction between each, so that it is difficult to make any steady distinction between those considered kin and those deemed of another kind. This elision produces a state of affairs which might be summarized as such: we are all related to strangers and cannot presume to rely on our own. The consanguineous and contingent become entangled as commensurate life lines, compounding a multidirectional set of circumstances that demand a response. Joyce and Greer's reunion bears the trace of blood- and adoptive relations that, as the bulk of *Crossing the River* proves, are ever unpredictable. (The stranger who offered Eliza Mae her hand possessed an ethical disposition far in excess of Joyce's heartless mother.) The public as well as private tenor of the scene is indicated by the political language of brotherhood that Joyce uses. As Ward notes, the request that Greer 'sit down' with Joyce 'ventriloquises' (60) the words of Martin Luther King, significantly cited a few pages later by the African father figure in the novel's singular plural epilogue: 'one day on the red hills of Georgia, the sons of former slaves and the sons of former slave-owners will be able to sit down together at the table of brotherhood' (*Crossing the River* 237). Laura Briggs cites King's speech as part of the 'antihereditarian racial justice politics of the 1960s and 1970s' (106). The anticipatory echo of this politics in 1963 amplifies the creative implications of Joyce's surprised encounter with Greer and grants it political pedigree. The political futurity which Phillips moots requires us to relinquish those familiar bearings of belonging that uphold endogamous and biocentric discourses of race, native and stranger. Instead, he moots just for a moment a more precarious and antihereditarian position which brokers ethical engagement across all lines of attachment, where nothing can be dismissed as foreign or considered legitimately at home.

This disposition of adoptive being which Phillips considers is clinched, ultimately, by Joyce, who becomes a simultaneously consanguineous *and* adoptive figure. She occupies all positions within the triad: as Greer's birth-mother, as the African father figure's adopted child and as a stranger who faces Greer with the resonant invitation to sit down. In crossing between these triadic points, Joyce dissolves ontological distinctions between adopted relations and consanguineous kin, anticipating the choral voice of the epilogue's father figure whose many-tongued chorus sounds the depths of diasporic being-with. Amidst its sobering and sombre engagement with the many legacies of slavery, racism and prejudice, *Crossing the River* finds in history a means of shaping figuratively new bearings of adoptive being that extend far beyond the immediate contexts of surrender and adoption. These are offered to all as the beginnings of new kinds of human relations that detach from the normative kinships of race and nation. In the novel's final pages, Phillips excavates these possibilities from the sobering historical consequences which attenuated the lives of the likes of Joyce, Travis and Greer. They may be taken into the unfinished business of the diasporic critique of modernity's consanguineous categorizations that still would have us believe that each of us should be ever moored to a single, rather than singular plural, condition.

My reading of the final text to preoccupy us, Jackie Kay's *Red Dust Road* (2010), calls up many of the ideas we have explored in *Life Lines*. Kay's memoir of her life as a mixed-race adoptee and her search for biogenetic relatives is ethically grounded in a commitment to openness as opposed to secrecy, and also challenges those who might regard the transcultural family as ill-equipped to formulate the political and emotional resources to combat racism. It tracks the challenges of being adopted as it formulates with exhilaration the possibilities of adoptive being, while facing the hard truths uncovered by search and reunion as part of a wider task of reconditioning personhood. The book's form captures its inventive and seriously playful attempt to capture adoptive being aesthetically in a similar fashion to Phillips's 'Somewhere in England', partly by resequencing narrative in order to release from consanguineous chronicity the creative possibilities of adoptive personhood. As such, the book continues her career-long refusal, in Matthew Pateman's words, 'to simplify either herself or her self's relation to history' (65). This aim begins as far back as her debut poetry collection, *The Adoption Papers* (1991), that included the eponymous long poetic sequence which, certainly in the UK, did much to bring into literature the post-war phenomenon of transcultural adoption. But whereas 'The Adoption Papers' was published prior to Kay's tracing, *Red Dust Road* is written in the light of experiencing the upheavals and surprises of search and reunion. More successfully than any other such text currently available, I would hazard, Kay's memoir works creatively with the narrative conventions and emotional expectations of tracing birth-relatives to fashion a new kind of text, discursively pluralized, in which adoptive being finds expression.

Red Dust Road uses search and reunion to think personhood differently. 'Tracing', Kay writes, 'suddenly asks someone who has had one life to have two; and you can't have two lives, you can only have one' (276). Kay's comment speaks to the shadow cast over adopted lives by the imagined person they might have been had they not been surrendered, and the disconcerting doubling of self which this may bring. This doubled self, substantial and spectral at the same time, is rejected in favour of a singular plural personhood. Central to the book's achievement is Kay's cheerful insistence that adoptive life should not be imagined as forever split or fractured, but that the adoptee's singular person can circumscribe the multidirectional possibilities born from their past as a mode of clinching a productive futurity. As she warns, tracing is a serious business: 'It turns your life upside down. It is something that should not be done lightly. You wouldn't imagine such an innocent activity, tracing, sketching over something that had already keen sketched over before, could be so life-changing' (48). While *Red Dust Road* does not portray tracing as a trifling activity, the vertiginous possibilities of having one's world destabilized lie behind the book's attempt to give voice to the progressive possibilities of 'sketching over'. The narrative's tonal levity is not 'done lightly' but central to its representation of tracing as progressively enriching, one that can bring together the hitherto displaced attachments of the triad into newly non-normative relations that do not deny the persistence of pain and the significance of biogenetic heredity.

Kay's memoir bears many traces. It records her attempts to trace her biogenetic relations that take her to Abuja and Ukpor in Nigeria where her birth-father, Jonathan, lives, and to Milton Keynes in England via Nairn in Scotland to meet her birth-mother, Elizabeth. Near the book's close she also manages to contact and meet her biogenetic sibling Sidney just prior to leaving Nigeria. Of equal importance is Kay's tracing of her adoptive past that includes memories of growing up in the 1960s and 1970s as the daughter of John and Helen (or Ellen, as her husband calls her), a white Glaswegian couple and one-time migrants to New Zealand's South Island who were active in the Communist Party, and who adopted Kay and her brother, Maxwell, as infants. *Red Dust Road* is equally concerned with sketching over key points in her transcultural family's fortunes as she grew up in Glasgow's Bishopbriggs. In addition, Kay also includes a series of narrative vignettes, titled with a date ('1971', '1977', '1988', etc.), which relate significant experiences in her coming of age: her grim experiences of racism, her youthful exploration of her lesbianism, her pregnancy and more besides. These short narrative segments are intercalated with the other narrative events and textual materials (letters, emails) and are printed in a different font. This design recalls the form of 'The Adoption Papers', although in *Red Dust Road* the lines of connection between the triadic positions of birth-parent, adoptee and adoptive parent are more fluid and supple, and the positions themselves are less siloed and disjunctive.

Kay's attempt to articulate the emotional consequences of being adopted draws upon some instructive figurative language:

> My mum all those years ago sensed a child who had been adopted was also a child who could feel terribly hurt. And no matter how much she loved me, no matter how much my dad loved me, there is still a windy place right at the core of my heart. The windy place is like Wuthering Heights, out on the open moors, rugged and wild and free and lonely. The wind rages and batters at the trees. I struggle against the windy place. I sometimes even forget it. But there it is. I am partly defeated by it. You think adoption is a story which has an end. But the point about it is that it has no end. I keep changing its ending. […] There's this ghostly something. I am only alone in the way that everybody is alone. And yet it seems that the bundle of child that is wrapped up in the ghostly shawl of adoption does have another layer of aloneness wrapped up in there. (45–6)

Kay's articulation of adoption in terms of spectrality is a resonant figure for the existential predicament of adoptees. It captures a pervasive sense of hollowness in the reference to the 'windy place' of personhood. Like ghosts, the wind is both tangible yet not fully discernable, sensed rather than seen, a felt presence which is not embodied in three dimensions. The challenge made by the wind to the trees in this Brontë-esque landscape, assaulted by its veracity, subtly captures the painful uprooting which adoption effects. If trees are the metaphor par excellence for stable family roots and grounding connections across generations, the adoptee's windswept hollowness threatens such normative arboreal certainty. As *Red Dust Road* drives towards its conclusions, as we shall see, Kay offers a way of imagining adoptive being by rewriting the image of the family tree in terms of transitive attachment and imaginative branching where the deflated hollowness of living alone no longer takes root.

In its depiction of tracing birth-relatives, *Red Dust Road* is unconventional. In contrast to Mei-Ling Hopgood's *Lucky Girl* and Catherine McKinley's *The Book of Sarahs*, Kay begins her memoir with a moment of reunion with a birth-parent rather than positioning this occasion near the centre or as climax of her text: 'Jonathan is suddenly there in the hotel corridor' (*Red Dust Road* 1). The ensuing meeting is awkward and uncomfortable. Jonathan, a lay preacher, insists on inviting Kay to pray with him in her hotel room – a matter which takes over two hours – and he seems discomfited by meeting the daughter he conceived with Elizabeth after they met in 1961 at a dance hall in Aberdeen. He speaks about Kay in religious terms as evidence of the sins he committed while a younger man yet to receive God, and makes it clear that he wishes not to meet her again (unless she converts to Christianity) now that he has acknowledged her presence: 'I used to go clubbing and such, and drink wine and meet women and now I am a preacher. You are my before; this is my after. You are my sin, now I lead this life' (10). Throughout the meeting, the impact upon Kay of Jonathan's abdication of responsibility is discernible. She ponders that, in her birth-father's eyes, 'I'm a secret, a forty-year-old secret, and must remain one unless I accept the Lord' (10). The realization that she is regarded as the embodiment of another's sin fills her with 'fresh horror' (6) and she remains uneasy throughout, gulping glasses of wine to help her deal with the gamut of emotions triggered by her father's scriptural 'assault' (5).

While Kay makes sure not to narrate their meeting as one of tender reunion, she also avoids presenting it as a moment mainly of existential upset, crisis and distress (as we witnessed in Hannah Pool's sobering account). This is due to the at-times comical manner of the narration which, often through Kay's choice of figurative strategies, turns the unsettling into an approachable form of the bizarre. The gravitas of the reunion is placed under the command of the narration's defusing levity. The serious business of Jonathan's praying is described as a 'whirling and twirling and shouting to God Almighty. More clapping and foot-tapping and spinning and reciting. A whole big wad of the Bible rolls out of his mouth like ectoplasm' (7). As Jonathan wheels, Kay's imagination turns him into a figure more comical than sinister. He 'needs believers', she muses, 'like some people need cocaine. He needs the fresh hit, the new blood of a beginner believer. I start to see him as kind of a holy vampire, dressed in white, ready to take me in, to help me receive Christ. There's not even a wee wafer or anything in the room' (8). The presentation of Jonathan as vampiric offers a comically startling way of figuring blood relations. After two hours of praying Kay admits to feeling 'exhausted. All the blood has drained out of my face. I can feel how pale I must look. My father has drunk my blood' (9). At this reunion, the blood-lines between biogenetic father and daughter are presented as unwholesome. The antic presentation of Jonathan as comic vampire suggests his relationship with Kay as oddly predatory rather than snugly paternal. Kay makes blood connections into the cliché stuff of horror films, and in so doing she displaces the primacy of blood relations from becoming established in terms of the mystical, benign or healing. Here, in the plush hotel room, blood appears siphoned not shared.

Kay's envisioning of Jonathan as a 'holy vampire' cushions the unhappy, emotionally deleterious effects of his words and actions. But also, and crucially, it maintains her sense of connection to and compassion for her birth-father. Kay refuses to let him fully become the monster he might otherwise seem. Her representation both chides and cherishes. In playing the reunion scene for laughs, Kay seeks to accommodate Jonathan beyond the stark polarities of homecoming or displacement, welcome or rejection. It is a narrative approach that refuses mystifying consanguinity without giving up on Jonathan's significance or the material particulars of his life story as a Scottish-educated, Nigerian academic and preacher, with which Kay is inevitably imbricated. Despite Jonathan's troubling behaviour at their reunion (on learning of Kay's lesbianism he promptly asks a series of personal questions about her sex life), Kay never loses full patience with her birth-father's behaviour and faces the challenge of admitting his presence into her present and future. As she subsequently travels more widely in Nigeria, she reflects appreciatively upon the long, difficult and risky journey which Jonathan must have taken to visit the hotel. Kay's readiness to value the journeys of others, we shall note further soon, is a central element in her quest to strike adoptive being by orienting her own transcultural travels in relation to others.

Kay's comically discomfiting reunion with Jonathan concludes with her relating the whole encounter by telephone to her mother in Bishopbriggs. Hence she routes the opening chapter as proceeding from birth-parent to adoptive parent, and forges an attachment for herself between both families. The 'incredibly clear line' (11) which connects Kay with Helen and the news of Jonathan keeps open the lines which Helen has always wanted to materialize for her daughter. Since Kay's early childhood, Helen has compelled her to think about her birth-parents and the lives they might be leading. In Bishopbriggs Kay had always known that she has something to do with the environments of her birth-parents, Nigerian and British, and that these links were not necessarily in conflict with adoption's family-making. *Red Dust Road* locates

Kay's family always in relation to these life lines, even when they were not fully known.

Encouraged by Helen, as a young girl Kay built an important fantasy relationship with Africa which stood in for the material history which attached her to Nigeria but which was not mistaken as authentic. Kay admits to imagining her birth-father as a 'Sidney Poitier or Nelson Mandela or Martin Luther King or Cassius Clay – the only real images of black men I have at my disposal' (37) and makes up a picture of his home as 'flat land […] the earth was dark and rich. There was a red-dust road. I couldn't really get much further than that' (42). Almost like Ginny from Buchi Emecheta's *The New Tribe*, Helen wonders if Kay's birth-father was an African chief with land to bequeath to his surrendered daughter, and if she is 'an African princess' (*Red Dust Road* 41). But in contrast to Emecheta's fictional adoptive mother, Helen posits these visions irreverently, as part of an opportunity to play with a range of fanciful and possible pasts rather than resolve racial belonging. Helen's musing on her daughter's birth-relations compels Kay to imagine a range of (un)likely scenarios rather than advocating just one. She legitimates a promiscuous approach to narrative, inviting her daughter to make herself up time and again through cultural creativity. Later, Kay uses these very tactics of playing imaginatively with tales of African descent in building important imaginative links with postcolonial and diasporic literature, as a way of building a being-with that possesses significant emotional and political substance. Kay explores the writing of Frantz Fanon, Audre Lord, Alice Walker, Toni Morrison and Ralph Ellison – 'reading them changed my life' (41), she records. Consequently, when she confronts racism as a young woman, she possesses important resources that empower resistance that have been struck adoptively and are indebted to Helen's parenting. In an interview with Maya Jaggi, Kay has spoken of the necessity of exploring black cultural expression as a way of building vital relations: 'I think that it is very important when you are black and you grow up in an environment that isn't, to find people that you can relate to imaginatively if you like. So I did have a number of different fantasy relationships with various black people from around the world, you know, Nelson Mandela, Angela Davis, Bessie Smith or Louis Armstrong or Ella Fitzgerald' (51). In *Red Dust Road*, these fantasy relationships offset the temptations of a narrower model of Afrocentrism and make possible an important, transformative mode of vitality for the youthful

Kay where the significance of black people as cultural icons overrides any alleged union they may share due to race.

The empowering agency of this transcultural adoptive assembly of diasporic relations is evidenced in Kay's encounters with racism. After being threatened while a student at Stirling University, Kay organizes a public meeting at which she cites the work of James Baldwin and Angela Davis, and which results in the university taking action to support her. As a child she avidly watches the television adaptation of Alex Haley's *Roots* (1976) and learns something about the function of humour as 'a kind of defence against racism; you can get me down, but you won't get my soul' (186). She prizes the value of reading Wole Soyinka's poem 'Telephone Conversation' as a fourteen-year-old as opening up a vital line of affinity: 'The Soyinka poem suddenly appeared in my classroom and showed me some solidarity. It was a fantastic feeling' (*Red Dust Road* 195). These multidirectional resources are learned as a compound culture of African-related political resistance that helps her face facts. In a racist environment, as she argues, Kay cannot readily ignore that she has something to do with Africa. 'It is important to think about it', she writes, 'especially when you are a black person yourself and still have to struggle to remove the assumptions and stereotypes that nibble at your own brain' (40). The example of Kay's anti-racist political consciousness, encouraged by adoptive parenting, severely challenges the view that only black parents are best equipped to prepare black children for survival in a racist environment. For Derek Kirton, 'while there are some white families with the potential to meet these needs successfully, these are likely to be highly unusual in their life experiences, networks and personal qualities' (99). This line of argument would think of adoptive families such as the Kays in terms of exceptionality. Contrariwise, it is the delightful *ordinariness* of domestic life which is often stressed in *Red Dust Road*: entertaining squabbles between siblings, family holidays, illnesses and accidents, memories of old family cars, shopping for clothes in Drymen. The clear link between the particular ordinariness of the Kays' domesticity and Kay's radical model of transcultural political agency, nurtured at home and supported by her family, challenges the problematic assumptions of racial exceptionality which underwrite the advocacy of same-race family-making.

In its focus on the serious business of striking narrative connections, *Red Dust Road* positions storytelling as a generative act in the context of transcultural adoptive personhood. While the image of the 'windy place' of hollowness and loneliness captures the spectral selfhood of being adopted where one may not feel real, storytelling presents for Kay an opportunity to materialize substantive personhood by sketching one's multidirectional life lines. She acknowledges adoptive life as one lived without full facts where the self may arise 'like the story of some stranger, or even the story of a fictional character. It's hard to make it real. [...] The whole business of being adopted seems on the one level to be a fantastic fiction' (134). The material facticity of adoptive being is struck through the 'hard' work of perpetual storytelling. Kay's remark on tracing Jonathan – 'I keep telling people the story to tell myself that it is real' (134) – might well be taken as one of the signature lessons of the book as a whole. Narrative is generative not palliative in *Red Dust Road*. 'It is what the imagination feasts off', reflects Kay, 'the bone, not the meat, the bits that are left behind. The less you are given the more you can make up' (43). Acknowledging that Helen often told stories about adoption, perhaps as a compensation for the circumstance of her children's surrendering, Kay finds in narrative the capacity to recondition attachments across the adoption triad. Helen's imagined account of Kay's birth-mother's life in a mother and baby home 'was a heartbreaking story and it was mine. In a way my mum and I loved it, the story of me. It was a big bond, the story' (44). Narrative conjecture bonds Kay to her birth-mother as much as to Helen so that Kay is not compelled to prioritize certain bonds over others. This is the serious work of storytelling for adoptive being: it can circumnavigate the real and the imagined, the natal and the adoptive, without classifying or dividing these bonds across the received nodal points of personhood. Kay by no means idealizes or romanticizes the capabilities of storytelling at such moments. The imagined life of Kay's pregnant birth-mother 'having to mop floors and clean toilets on her own' (44) is unequivocally 'heartbreaking'. But as Kay points out, her imagination also negotiates love and compassion from heartbreak. She finds in the productive agency of storytelling a way of crafting being from the painful possibilities of adoption's material fictionality.

Red Dust Road intercalates imagined tales of possible birth-parents, tricky moments of search and reunion and the stories (and storytelling rituals) of transcultural family-making. The tales Kay tells of her Scottish childhood frequently involve the synchronization of two kinds of passages: the holidays by car which the family took throughout Scotland and the passages from songs which they would sing together to pass the time as they travelled. Songs and stories enable participation in family-making. 'The soundtrack to our holidays was my dad singing; and my mum joining in', Kay remembers. 'We have sung our way all over Scotland' (117). In later life, the family return to these journeys when sharing their memories, so that their capacity to bond through songs, stories and journeys is perpetually rehearsed:

> Now we sit around the table and play the holidays back: family holidays go quicker into the past than anything else; but also, peculiarly, stay in the land of the permanent present, quickly assessed with their fund of memorabilia and materials. Remember that caravan in Avielochan where the hens were so confident they came right into the kitchen and pecked at scraps of bacon, and I got my first period? So you did! You came running up to me and asked if you could tell your brother the special news. What age were you, eleven? Who was the friend you had with you again? (118)

The family experience a shared moment of tracing the past akin to Kay's description of it cited previously: the 'sketching over something that had already been sketched over' (48) which emphasizes tracing as a textual act, a moment of narrative-making based on shared experience. The layering of memory is proffered as a form of affective bonding that rivals anything to be discovered in the reassurances of biogenetic resemblance. The embedding of the past in terms of the present secures a sense of 'permanence' here, but it is deliberately and delightfully incomplete. The missing pieces that make Helen's recall imperfect – how old *were* you? who *was* that friend? – keep buoyant a sense of selfhood as a perpetual questioning and indeed questing, devoid of secure origin or terminus, marked by the irrecoverable absences that, like the wind, invisibly animate the sense that something tangible is always beyond vision. It is on the tarmac roads of Scotland as much as on the red-dust roads of Nigeria where Kay discovers a cherished, mobile mode of bonding and being.

It is interesting to note that in *Bessie Smith* (1997), Kay's impressionistic account of her favourite singer's life and work, Kay records that Smith spent most of her career travelling and effectively 'grew up on the road' (31). In a similar fashion, *Red Dust Road* presents imaginative creativity as coincident with transportation. The transcultural disposition of Kay's family has been produced by multidirectional journeys: of Kay's parents in New Zealand, the family's motoring holidays, her mother's travels across Europe by train en route to a World Youth Congress meeting in Russia in 1958, Kay's motorcycle accident which played an important role in her wanting to become a writer. The twinning of travelling with tale-telling is Kay's means of establishing the life lines – lines of voyage, lines from a song – that are as fertile to family-making as the blood-lines of normative attachment. Each time she hears of her mother's story of journeying to Russia, remarks Kay, 'I think of it as a story that leads to my brother and me; in an imaginary way, the train stopped at us. We could have been picked up en route. We could have been from anywhere in the world' (33–4). Significantly, when Jonathan invites her to choose an Igbo name from two of his suggestions, she chooses Ijeoma, meaning 'good journey': '"Ijeomoa", I say out loud, thinking about good journeys, from Manchester to Abuja, from Enugu to Aberdeen' (107). In Kay's imagination her recent flight from the UK to Nigeria repeats Jonathan's trip to Aberdeen as a student where he met Elizabeth. Both are key passages in a textualization of adoptive being as the product of ongoing and unending journeys, along with Kay's family holidays, her mother's trip to Russia and many more.

Kay discovers imperfect lines of narrative connection within consanguineous relations as well as adoptive ones and presents their common commensurability. Her birth-parents' memories of her nativity are also subject to the ambiguating passage of time. Elizabeth's recall and recounting of Kay's early life is clouded by the beginnings of her dementia, something which Kay narrates in some of the book's most poignant and sensitive moments. When probing her birth-parents' past, Kay confronts not confirmation of her early life but uncertainty. Jonathan 'can barely remember anything about Elizabeth, not even what she looked like' (97). He challenges Elizabeth's recollection that the couple had spent two weeks together after Elizabeth returned to Aberdeen once she had surrendered Kay for adoption: 'No, no, no. The university would never have allowed me to share my digs for so long. Two days. Two days more like' (97). An especially significant index of the unsteadiness of memory concerns a 'wee knitted yellow cardigan […] knitted by your birth mother' (27) which Helen received not long after Kay's adoption, although she confesses to remembering this detail imperfectly when she recalls the incident many years later. During one of Kay's meetings with her birth-mother, Elizabeth mentions sending the infant Kay, via the adoption agency, a knitted gift, 'a lovely little outfit, a pink and white cardigan, and little boots' (74). It may be that, due to her condition, Elizabeth is confused, or it could be the case that either she or Helen is mis-remembering the original colour of the gift. Either way, the truth of the issue cannot be settled. Kay's encounter with her birth-parents' memories brings more possibilities, not less. Tracing reveals more potential versions and accounts that one might make from the passages, journeys and memories which are unearthed, while the promise of secure origins as well as a metanarrative unadulterated by the unreliability of recall remains firmly beyond the horizon. The past always returns in traces – vague sketches, half-remembered anecdotes fading due to the passage of time or illness – that are firm but fragmentary, persistent yet partial: like dust.

Kay takes care to articulate the mixed emotions provoked during the meetings with Elizabeth in Milton Keynes that range across awkwardness, compassion, frustration, care and love. One of the most affecting moments in their encounters occurs during Kay's first visit to Elizabeth's home (they had previously met only in hotels or public places) when she notices that the house is speckled with pink Post-It notes that prompt Elizabeth's failing memory: '*Check cooker. Milk. Phone Aisha. Church Homework. Jackie*' (77). Kay notices on the side-board one that reads '*Don't forget Jackie*' (86). These aides-memoire offer an insight into the difficult task of living for those suffering from dementia and enable readers to catch a sense of Elizabeth's challenging life as an elderly woman. But there is a secondary level of significance available here too: the necessity for adoptees to engage with their birth-parents' memories of their nativity *as memories*, devoid of the concrete certainties of fact which tracing so often desires, subject to the emotional, medical and material circumstances that uproot their reliability. Adoptive being involves accommodating these sketchy memories – the contradictions they might bring, their gaps and inaccuracies – as part of a series of stories that circumscribe the adoption triad, in which no one account can stand as a reliable, verifiable origin.

As the structure of *Red Dust Road* enacts, the transcultural adoptee, adoptive parents and birth-parents are brought together within a common complex narrative, each wedded to the compulsion not to forget that which can only be imperfectly remembered. Significantly, Elizabeth's most direct declaration of maternal feeling for Kay is delivered in writing:

When I get home, I find a little pink heart-shaped Post-It note, stuck inside the zipped part of my purse, which reads, *Jackie, Elizabeth loves you* which moves me to tears because I don't know if she's reminding herself or me, and because her little habit of hiding secret notes has surprised me with this sudden gift. (89–90)

This affecting moment foregrounds the textual element of bonding for biogenetic relations. Consanguineous kinship does not secure or guarantee these connections which have to be perpetually prompted, shared and communicated in situ. Kay carefully shows how even these cherished declarations of maternal love retain an unsteadiness which tracing can never banish. To whom is this note truly addressed? And what does it *really* mean?

The interweaving of consanguineous and adoptive passages is captured resonantly when Kay decides to travel to Ukpor to find Jonathan's ancestral village. She goes by car, a difficult and long journey that her friends advise against. On approaching Ukpor, Kay spies a red-dust road 'exactly like the one in my imagination' (213) when she was younger, and so she stops and stands on it barefoot:

It's as if my footprints were already on the road before I even got there. I walk into them, my waiting footprints. [...] It also feels a million miles away from Glasgow, from my lovely Fintry Hills, but, surprisingly, it also feels like home. I feel shy with the landscape too, like I might be meeting a new blood relation. I almost feel like talking to it whispering sweet nothings into its listening ear. The road welcomes me; it is benevolent, warm, friendly, accepting and for now it feels enough, the red, red of it, the vivid green against it, the long and winding red-dust road. (213)

Kay's elated encounter with landscape offers her a moment of nativist attachment that contrasts with the cool reception she later receives from the Ukpor villagers who tease her as 'Oyibo' (216), a white person. Here she discovers affinity in the road, in a mode of passage rather than a moment of filial arrival. The claim to Nigeria in terms of feelings of home combines with her consciousness of Glasgow, which materializes as a means of comparison, and with her British acculturation: the reference at the quotation's end is to The Beatles' 1970 song 'The Long and Winding Road', itself inspired by a road journey in Scotland. The mention of 'meeting a new blood relation' invites us to regard the road's red colour as figuring the red arteries of blood, so that the passage is posed in terms of lost biogenetic ancestry, the paternal figure and hereditary home. But the quotation's geographical bearings also direct us towards Stirling's Fintry Hills and the Scottish songlines that Kay so treasures. In depicting the weighty importance of feeling rooted to a route, of seeming related to a means of passage, Kay weaves the multidirectional lines of attachment that confront as well as empower her capacity to make herself up. The possibilities of the imagination and narrative are tethered to these temporal and transcultural journeys, although they are not contained or restricted by them. Adoptive being requires the intercalation of different times and places, imagined and concrete lives, biogenetic and willed ancestors (Elizabeth, Jonathan, James Baldwin, Audre Lord) as part of the creative propensity to fashion futurity by facing materialized and multidirectional claims.

It is part of the value and honesty of *Red Dust Road* that Kay records her feelings of wonder in meeting one of her biogenetic siblings on her father's side, Sidney, just before leaving Nigeria (and at the end of another frantic journey, en route to the airport): 'I feel a strange almost ecstatic sensation of recognition. It is nearly primitive. I could happily sniff his ears and lick his forehead. It has completely ambushed me; I wasn't expecting it at all' (272). Kay does not hold up these feelings as a moment of ancestral homecoming or of gaining a more solid sense of self that compensates for the 'windy place' rendered by her adoption. Rather, our attention is turned to the 'ambush' of these feelings, the experience of another surprise that tracing has exposed her to, similar to the shock of finding Elizabeth's pink Post-It note in her purse. The emotions unleashed by the 'ambush' of recognition need to be accommodated as part of the perpetual surprise of the transcultural adoptee's ongoing journey, intercalated with everything else, not amplified as the teleological goal of tracing heredity nor deleted as having no significance at all. Kay's adoption story keeps changing its ending, turning up unforeseen things. The unexpected consequences of being surprised or 'ambushed' maintain the formal mobility of the narrative throughout the book that is ever en route.

Red Dust Road concludes by giving figurative expression to the post-paradoxical possibilities of adoptive being with a vignette set in 2009. In the book's closing paragraphs, Kay subtly reformulates the well-known image of filial connection, the family tree, through the metaphorical transformation of the tree into a figure for circumlocational and intercalated life lines. The vignette concerns a return visit Kay makes to the woods at Quarry Bank Mill near Manchester Airport in England, in search of a tree with a secret hollow in which she wishes to place a pound coin as an offering. The trip immediately recalls a similar visit in 2003, when Kay slipped a coin into a beech tree's hollow, likened to a 'dark womb, the tree's tiny cradle' (166). The connection made between this beech tree and nativity points towards the arboreal rhetoric of family in terms of trees and branches (one coincidentally strengthened by Jonathan's professional career as an ethnobotanist with expertise in plant taxonomy and domestic trees). The description of the beech tree also recalls Kay's Brontë-esque representation of being adopted as hollowed at the core. When Kay returns to the woods in 2009, she does not visit the same tree. This time she chooses an oak tree coloured by autumnal foliage which stands amidst others soon to lose their leaves. Such diurnal shedding beckons loss and decline into the frame. Standing before the tree having surrendered her coin, Kay thinks of the *Moringa oleifera* tree pods given to her by her Uncle Nwora in Nigeria which she intends to plant in her garden in Manchester. But again, an image of ancestral rooting combines quickly with a memory of adoption. Kay will plant the tree to celebrate meeting Sidney just as Helen 'planted the cherry blossom to celebrate adopting my brother Maxwell' (289). The consanguineous and the adoptive are made commensurate through the rewritten metaphor of trees:

> I try and imagine my own moringa growing in the front garden of my terraced house in Manchester, far away from its home. I wonder if the pods will ever take root. I picture my healthy, tall moringa in ten years' time. Will I still be living here then? I imagine a magical moringa, years and years away from now; its roots have happily absorbed and transported water and minerals from the dark, moist soil to the rest of the splendid tree. (289)

The moringa is articulated as an image of both rootedness and flux, dwelling and departure, soil and transport. In Matthew Pateman's reading, it indicates 'a material future made immaterial in present conjecture' (80). Transplanted, the moringa offers an image of transcultural survival and a measure of dwelling, putting down roots. But Kay immediately confounds its sedentary associations of permanence in questioning the length of her dwelling in England's North West, and by the end of the passage the tree has become a means of transport. As well as an image of ancestral survival in a transplanted milieu, the tree has become another opportunity for Kay's imagination to tell tales, to make up possible futures. Roots entangle with the imaginative, botanical and peripatetic routes in this quotation. The energetic meanderings of Kay's physical and creative movements remain earthed in ancestral traces, signified by her unforeseen acquisition of the moringa pods on her Nigerian journey.

In Ukpor, standing nervously outside Jonathan's compound, Kay thinks of Robert Frost's poem 'The Road Not Taken' (1916) which she cites to reflect upon the predicament of adoptive existence. The adoptee has involuntarily switched tracks from one possible life to another, and one is continually conscious of the path not travelled, the spectral life not lived and the difference this has made. In its intercalation of manifold voices, painful memories, multidirectional pasts and possible futures, tough tales of tracing and sentimental songs of childhood, *Red Dust Road* realizes a way of gathering the myriad elements of Kay's transcultural adoptive personhood that cannot be phrased within prefabricated narrative arcs but requires instead the energy and agency of imaginative creativity to fashion from them adoptive being. 'It occurs to me', she writes, 'that all anyone adopted really needs is a good imagination: more than genes or blood, it offers the possibility of redemption' (149). Through the transformative agency of 'sketching over', Kay leaves behind the split selfhood of being adopted, ever conscious of the road not travelled. In pursuit of the life lines of multidirectional attachment, all roads are taken, in the end.

Kay's generative rendition of transcultural adoption, making something of her circumstances in situ, is not ideal. Nor should it be. Her search and reunion have delivered new experiences of severance and emotional upheaval. Jonathan wants little to do with her after their strange meeting at the hotel, while Elizabeth's failing health curtails the chance Kay might otherwise have had to build new relations. As in *Crossing the River*, tracing the pasts of others does not engender return or the resolution of identity. The lines of connection can be threadbare, with missing strands and frayed edges, so that being-with is always incomplete and on the move, aware of that which cannot necessarily be known. Kureishi's characterization of Chad – as with Mei-Ling Hopgood's and Hannah Pool's accounts of their consanguineous attachments – situates transcultural adoption proximate to the losses of translation. In the texts we have explored in this chapter, the attempts to strike adoptive being still bear the harms of loss and the silences of those who cannot or will not be heard. Barbara Kingsolver's inventive appropriation of transcultural adoption locates the figure of Turtle in an abusive past which she cannot read or articulate. Caryl Phillips's returnee, Greer, exits the novel as quickly and quietly as he came, with little new knowledge of Travis and without having admitted very much of his own youth and adolescence to Joyce. In making transcultural adoption bear responsibility for brokering new ways of imagining how to deal with the multidirectional lines of attachment that materialized adoptability, the writers we have considered in this chapter neither deny nor forget the painful disposition of being adopted. But in choosing not to encase transcultural adoption within this experiential horizon, they seek hopefully to open up ways of thinking and acting adoptively by bearing new rhetorics of transpersonal relations that orient us all towards alternative and empowering forms of human possibility.

Coda: Victoria Station, 1969/2015

A montage of snapshots, inspired by Catherine McKinley, modestly my own. I am sitting in the breakfast room in the basement of a pleasant hotel in Salerno, near Italy's Amalfi Coast. The hotel was for many centuries a convent; beneath the glass floor of the lounge, ancient Roman excavations are illuminated. Cut into the far wall that separates the room from the bar is a hatch in which there sits an elegant vase on an ornamental turntable. I am informed that in the original building this was probably the hatch where surrendered babies were passed to the care of the nuns. From the spoon in my right hand a helping of yogurt spills back into the open pot beneath it as I stare at the hatch, innocuous and chic in the hotel's plush surroundings. I am squirming in my wooden chair during my first week at high school, feeling strange in my unfamiliar grey uniform and red and black tie. My Social Sciences teacher recognizes my surname when taking the register and confidently declares that I look just like my sister who finished her schooling the previous summer. I wonder about my teacher's wisdom for the next five years. I am queuing to register for an adoption studies conference at Scripps College, Claremont, California, when two delegates mistake me for the adoptee novelist Dan Chaon. I find the irony amusingly apt, as does Dan whom I have the pleasure of meeting later that evening. I am eighteen years old and sitting in my first undergraduate seminar at the University of Leeds next to a student whom I happen to discover is also an adoptee from the North West of England. I am startled by the coincidence and we become friends for life, sharing an office as graduate students, achieving our doctorates at the same time and establishing our careers along parallel lines. I am reading on a warm subway train in Boston, Massachusetts, when I am distracted by a small child squirming on the seat opposite. When I look up at the man I assume is the child's father, I experience the violent vertiginous trip of a sudden missed heartbeat, because I seem to be looking in a mirror as I stare at this man. I am stood before a glass case in Tokyo's Yasukuni Museum containing a *hanayome ningyo* or 'bride doll', one of thousands dedicated to the souls of deceased soldiers or pilots by their mothers at the controversial Yasukuni Shrine. In this symbol of severance, of relations attenuated or often unbegun, I stumble upon a figure that unwittingly articulates the ghosting of my adoption. I cannot look away. I am holding a feeding card which bears an unfamiliar surname and describes neatly both when and what 'baby John' should eat. My Mum tells me that she thinks the handwriting is my birth-mother's although we can't be sure, but she made sure she kept it for me all these years just in case. I scrutinize the lines, searching for quirks of personality and style. I am gazing at Dalí's *Figura asomada a la ventana* (1925) at the Museo Nacional Reina Sofia in Madrid. It depicts a woman with her back turned to me, face hidden, contemplating the ocean through an open window. I am sitting in the elevated offices of Leeds City Council above the supermarket, where I shopped as a student and from where I can see a view of the city that I have come to think of in terms of home. The kindly social worker passes me a form on which, for the first time, I encounter my birth-mother's name. I am dining with my parents at a small bistro and enjoying a typically lively conversation when a friendly woman at the next table asks me whereabouts in Scotland I am from.

As these intercalated fragments intimate, for me adoption is perpetually surprising and nothing out of the ordinary. I have found that everyday life continues to bring unexpected evidence of the chance encounters which those inward of the adoption triad understand all-too-readily as definitive and not exceptional to transpersonal relations. Living amidst the unforeseen and contingent may be less a grieving of self than a gifting of being. For every missed beat and hidden semblance, there have been cords of coincidence and unguessed contacts. The emotional weather is sometimes more wuthering than becalmed, and I do not like surprises. But amidst these fortunes I play my hand.

All of this is nothing special. The historical and human traces of adoption reside at the heart of the everyday: in architecture, art, friendships, public life; at work, or at breakfast or dinner; on the subway or at school. As I have argued in this book, such particulars speak of disenfranchisement, disempowerment, intercultural conflict and the maintenance of privileged norms of biocentric identification. But they also enable critical leverage which, if put to good use, can begin to fashion future possibility from past woes without forgetting or giving up on those for whom adoption was not a choice. Adoption is created but not constrained by the material conditions of its possibility. It can be productively articulated to think both across and through the multidirectional lines of attachment which interlace the polycultural and plural historical provenances of those inward of adoption triads, each time singular. It contains the capacity, too, to invite the non-adopted to entertain the extent to which their own personhood, readily legitimated by normative narrative arcs and assumptions, is the product of passages – of the journeys taken by, or with, intimate others, and the narratives created to remember the experiences of family-making that happen in real time. As Marianne Novy has argued, adoptive families are different to biogenetic ones, but the wisdom they enable is not restricted exclusively to them. It could be the case that 'adoptees have a better chance to see that parenthood is actually more about love than about biology' or that 'all parents have to deal with their children's difference from them' (*Reading* 27). Adoption's insights might be of interest to anyone, not least because – as we have seen – the labour of family-making in adoptive contexts is not radically different from in other kinds of families, even if the family units which result are perceived to be out of the ordinary. Adoptability may be engendered by unfortunate circumstances which one hopes will not be repeated in the future, but its insights, struck in situ, mean that adoption sometimes has something to offer beyond the scars and harms that mark our or other people's pain.

Transcultural adoptees often carry a distinctive degree of consciousness regarding the racial, national, cultural and social norms of personhood and identification, as their often conspicuous presence within, but not fully of, their daily environments may leave them vulnerable to the designs of others. In *Life Lines*, I have sought not to instrumentalize transcultural families as firm evidence of either colour-blind or polycultural achievement. I have tried to avoid, too, a starry-eyed envisioning of transcultural adoption as a ready metaphor for reconditioned futures that have conveniently slipped their moorings from the ongoing disquiet which marks the emotional life of many. As Jackie Kay discusses in *Red Dust Road*, adoption stories keep changing their ending so that surprises lurk up ahead, like unpredictable weather, ready to bear one off course. Or, as was the case in Catherine McKinley's account of her stay in Ghana, they head towards new transpersonal attachments that take their chances with others.

The ubiquity of adoption is at large in creative texts as well as in history and in social life, embedded at the heart of literature and culture. In July 2014, I visited The Foundling Museum in London's Brunswick Square to see Lemn Sissay's magnificent installation 'Superman Was a Foundling'. Sissay had covered the museum café's white walls with a series of statements about a wealth of fictional characters: 'Jane Eyre was fostered', 'Lisbeth Salander was adopted', 'Luke Skywalker was adopted', 'Scarlett O'Hara was orphaned', 'Tom Sawyer was adopted', 'Harry Potter was fostered', 'Dorothy Gale was adopted' and many more besides. The prevalence of such figures across a range of cultural media indexes the long-standing fascination with and demand for adoption and concomitant stories. Caren Irr has made the point that '[n]o matter how powerful adoption memoirs or fiction – not to mention sentimental orphan stories and rescue fantasies – might be for those inside the adoption triad, by sheer numbers alone their largest audience share must surely be comprised of watchful strangers. Scholars of adoption need to know more about how and why strangers demand adoption stories and what these stories provide them' (394). The preponderance of such narratives across many centuries suggests that the trope of adoption affords writers a place to expose, rehearse or becalm anxieties about the nature and legitimacy of human attachments, the extent to which our emotional and moral character is bred or born, how much might race or 'royal blood' direct our behaviours regardless of environment and other such concerns. Certainly the popularity on television of search and reunion documentaries affords an opportunity for the majority to imagine life beyond consanguineous attachments just for a little while before such relations are tear-jerkingly reunited as if to prove the permanence of blood-lines that protects us from the vicissitudes and hard labour of love. I have always been a little bit frustrated by British television programmes, such as the sensitively made series *Long Lost Family*, which conclude each episode with an elated reunion yet offer scant information about the difficult passages, emotional challenges and indeed often short-lived relationships which reunions commence, as we have witnessed. Further evidence of these can be found across a range of recent adoption memoirs, including that of the series' co-presenter Nicky Campbell who writes fascinatingly about the challenges of his own search and reunion consequences in *Blue-Eyed Son: The Story of an Adoption* (2004). Indeed, contemporary adoption writing has begun to call time on those prodigal narratives of the lost and found that support a view of human sociability as naturally inclined towards blood relations, national communities, racial collectives, noble lineages and the like.

The transcultural adoption texts we have considered in *Life Lines* often refuse to participate in the generic confections of search and reunion tales and challenge their readers to think differently about consanguineous attachments and the matter of kinship. As evidenced by Hannah Pool's *My Fathers' Daughter*, the experiential condition of adopted life is not a temporary hiatus that ceases when sundered attachments are recovered. In Caryl Phillips's terms, reunion does not mean return. Instead, and like Jean-Luc Nancy's sense of each day's particulars, in post-adoption lives something else takes its turn, different from the last or what was lost, which marks an originary opportunity to source reconditioned relations. I have argued that transcultural adoption writing confronts the discursive legitimacy of ideas such as race, national identity and cultural authenticity or purity by exposing their porous borders and precarious design as the product of myth rather than truth. We have seen, too, how blood-lines are not relinquished but instead rethought as material life lines to the imperfectly understood concrete and historical circumstances which demand attention if the secrets of adoption's transcultural inequalities are to be faced.

Just as important, I have also shown how the transcultural family may be an assimilative rather than dissident unit, in harmony with the predominant scripts of family-making even as it would appear to render them suspect. Time and again, as in the work of Sebastian Barry and Mei-Ling Hopgood, writers insist that it is *what we do* with the occasion of transcultural adoption – purposefully, agentially, in situ – which matters most. Adoptive being is forged through the difficult business of reckoning across the multidirectional vectors of myriad family attachments, biogenetic and adoptive, not gifted by the incidence of transcultural adoption per se. As we have seen in the work of E. R. Braithwaite and Barbara Kingsolver, the appropriation of transcultural adoption, however well-meaning and politically motivated, can also complexify or cancel the opportunity to establish transfigurative thought. We have considered as well how difficult it is for some to relinquish the privileging of consanguineous relations even when seeking to represent sympathetically the social inequalities which inflect transcultural adoption, as in Andrea Levy's *Small Island*.

Along the way, we have noticed the speculative propensity of transcultural adoption writing, from Kingsolver's post-anthropocentric 'humbeans' to Hopgood's and McKinley's multidirectional tapestries that tie new knots. Cultural texts may be at their most valuable when they invite us to hypothesize capriciously, just as writers imagine what might be done with and undone by the phenomenon of adopted life. Why, for example, is resemblance considered a matter of vision not sound? Braithwaite's colour-blind critique of racist family-making in *Paid Servant* posits sound as preferable to vision. In Toni Morrison's *Jazz*, the musical endeavours that percolate through the spring air of the 'City' sound the sonic signature of selfhood renewed in terms of adoptive being: improvisational and intimate, sociable and sustaining. What matters more: sound or vision? I do not readily look like my parents, but I do sound like them (prompting, as I mentioned, a friendly stranger to ask where in Scotland I had been raised, even though I have never lived there). The sonic aspects of my being – the sound and accent of my voice – are as embodied as they are aesthetic and depend upon organic and physical capabilities: vocal chords, lungs, tongue, teeth, lips. My parents' historical and cultural lives materialize in my speech and leave vocal traces. My physical propensity for speech embodies the presence of those with whom I have no biogenetic attachment. This is not a paradoxical or unique state of affairs. One thinks of Jackie Kay and her family singing their way all over Scotland. Don't most people, adopted or not, enjoy a version of this? If we speculate on resemblance beyond the consanguineous and biogenetic, what might we think or do differently? Who do you sound like?

As I have hinted previously in *Life Lines*, adoptive being may echo beyond the immediate contexts of transcultural adoption and non-normative family-making more generally. That said, I would not want to present this idea as endlessly portable or the key to all mythologies of personhood, not least because of the danger of disconnecting adoption from its material particulars and contextual domains, transcultural or otherwise. As my analysis of Mike Leigh's *Secrets and Lies* suggested, the ready requisitioning of transcultural adoption for other purposes can quickly become complicit with prevailing discourses of race, even if this was never the intention. To be sure, adoptive being affords us an opportunity to approach a range of contexts and issues with particular concerns in mind, and remain mindful of and vigilant towards the articulation of notions of natal, nativist, national, racial and cultural attachment, either normative or dissident. And it may also empower many of us, adopted or otherwise, to think about the ways in which our intimate attachments with and claims on others are the product of a narrative labour that circumscribes biogenetic heredity as much as adoptive relations: tactile and textile. Adoption writing these days suggests that personhood is wrought from textual and transpersonal fusion and not just biogenetic transfusion, legitimated by shared memories which none can retrieve reliably – a plural imperfect text which takes its turn, each time singular, when we remember to sketch its emotional and affective narrative lines.

Did you remember Maria, living near Victoria Station right by Elizabeth Bridge? She disappeared from view after she signed the relinquishment agreement in December 1969 and may be hard to trace. But of the child more is known. His adoption was formalized in January 1970 in a Beverley court. Soon he had moved with his new family to Stockport where he enjoyed a happy, ordinary childhood. He read English at University and developed a passion for literature, eventually writing a doctoral thesis on postcolonial fiction. As he pursued an academic career, he studied the writing of postcolonial migrants and their descendents in London, and soon developed a keen interest in transcultural adoption stories. Once, on a cold, clear January afternoon, he found himself outside Maria's old address near the train lines wondering if the book he was writing would help him sketch something of himself using the crossed lines of heredity and happenstance he had to hand. Writing these lines. These life lines.

Works Cited

[NB: For general bibliography on adoption, see the special issue of *Adoption and Culture* 4 (2014): 'The Bibliographies Issue: Adoption Studies Research'.]

Ahokas, Pirjo. 'Challenging the Color-Blind American Dream: Transnational Adoption in *A Gesture Life*, *The Love Wife*, and *Digging to America*'. *American Studies in Scandinavia* 45.1–2 (2014): 109–33.

Appiah, Kwame Anthony. *The Ethics of Identity*. Princeton: Princeton University Press, 2005.

Armstrong, Richard. 'The Shock of Otherness: *Secrets and Lies*'. *Screen Education* 38 (2005): 111–14.

Barn, Ravinder. 'Race, Ethnicity and Transracial Adoption' in *The Dynamics of Adoption*. Ed. by Amal Treacher and Ilan Katz. London and Philadelphia: Jessica Kingsley Publishers, 2000: 111–26.

Barry, Sebastian. *A Long Long Way*. London: Faber and Faber, 2005.

Barry, Sebastian. *The Secret Scripture*. London: Faber and Faber, 2008.

Barry, Sebastian. *On Canaan's Side*. London: Faber and Faber, 2011.

Bourne, Stephen. 'Secrets and Lies: Black Histories and British Historical Films' in *British Historical Cinema: The History, Heritage and Costume Film*. Ed. by Claire Monk and Amy Sargeant. London: Routledge, 2002: 47–65.

Braithwaite, E. R. *Paid Servant*. London: Four Square, 1965 [1962].

Braithwaite, E. R. *Reluctant Neighbours*. London: Nel Books, 1978 [1972].

Braithwaite, E. R. *To Sir, With Love*. London: Vintage, 2005 [1959].

Brannigan, Tim. *Where Are You Really From*? Belfast: The Blackstaff Press, 2010.

Briggs, Laura. *Somebody's Children: The Politics of Transracial and Transnational Adoption*. Durham and London: Duke University Press, 2012.

Brodzinsky, David M., Marshall D. Schechter and Robin Marantz Henig. *Being Adopted: The Lifelong Search for Self*. New York: Anchor Books, 1992.

Brontë, Emily. *Wuthering Heights*. Harmondsworth: Penguin, 1965 [1847].

Callahan, Cynthia. *Kin of Another Kind: Transracial Adoption in American Literature*. Ann Arbor: University of Michigan Press, 2011.

Campbell, Nicky. *Blue-Eyed Son. The Story of an Adoption*. London: Macmillan, 2004.

Cardullo, Bert. 'Secrets and Lies'. *The Hudson Review* 50.3 (1997): 477–86.

Carp, E. Wayne. 'A Revolutionary in the Making: Jean Paton and the Early Decades of Sealed Adoption Records, 1949–1977'. *Adoption and Culture* 3 (2012): 33–62.

Carroll, Rachel. '*Small Island*, Small Screen: Adapting Black British Fiction' in *Andrea Levy: Contemporary Critical Perspectives*. Ed. by Jeannette Baxter and David James. London: Bloomsbury, 2014: 65–77.

Chang, Jung. *Wild Swans: Three Daughters of China*. London: HarperCollins, 1991.

Cheng, Vincent J. *Inauthentic: The Anxiety over Culture and Identity*. New Brunswick: Rutgers University Press, 2004.

Clingman, Stephen. 'Other Voices: An Interview with Caryl Phillips' (2002) in *Conversations with Caryl Phillips*. Ed. by Renée T. Schatteman. Jackson: University Press of Mississippi, 2009: 95–117.

Clingman, Stephen. *The Grammar of Identity: Transnational Fiction and the Nature of the Boundary*. Oxford: Oxford University Press, 2009.

Cohen, Phil. 'Yesterday's Words, Tomorrow's World: From the Racialisation of Adoption to the Politics of Difference' in *In the Best Interests of the Child: Culture, Identity and Transracial Adoption*. Ed. by Ivor Gaber and Jane Aldridge. London: Free Association Books, 1994: 43–76.

Conn, Peter. *Adoption: A Brief Social and Cultural History*. New York: Palgrave Macmillan, 2013.

Cooper, Brenda. 'The Rhetoric of a New Essentialism versus Multiple Worlds: Isidore Okpewho's *Call Me By My Rightful Name* and Buchi Emecheta's *The New Tribe* in Conversation'. *Journal of Commonwealth Literature* 42.2 (2007): 19–36.

De Soto, Paris. 'Genealogy Revised in *Secrets and Lies*' in *Imagining Adoption: Essays on Literature and Culture*. Ed. by Marianne Novy. Ann Arbor: University of Michigan Press, 2001: 193–206.

Dorow, Sara K. *Transnational Adoption: A Cultural Economy of Race, Gender, and Kinship*. New York and London: New York University Press, 2006.

Elliott, Sue. *Love Child: A Memoir of Adoption, Reunion, Loss and Love*. London: Vermillion, 2005.

Emecheta, Buchi. *The New Tribe*. Oxford: Heinemann. 2000.

Eng, David L. *The Feeling of Kinship: Queer Liberalism and the Racialization of Intimacy*. Durham and London: Duke University Press, 2010.

Fagan, Kristina. 'Adoption as National Fantasy in Barbara Kingsolver's *Pigs in Heaven* and Margaret Laurence's *The Diviners*' in *Imagining Adoption: Essays on Literature and Culture*. Ed. by Marianne Novy. Ann Arbor: University of Michigan Press, 2001: 251–66.

Farrell, J. G. 'J. G. Farrell Comments' in *Contemporary Novelists*. Ed. by James Vinson. London: St James Press, 1979: 147–8.

Fedosik, Marina. 'Grafted Belongings: Identification in Autobiographical Narratives of African American Transracial Adoptees'. *a/b: Auto/Biography Studies* 27.1 (2012): 211–30.

Fessler, Ann. *The Girls Who Went Away: The Hidden History of Women Who Surrendered Children for Adoption in the Decades Before Roe v Wade*. With a New Afterword. New York and London: Penguin, 2007.

Frears, Stephen, dir. *Philomena*. Pathé, 2013.

Gill, Owen and Barbara Jackson. *Adoption and Race: Black, Asian and Mixed Race Children in White Families*. London: Batsford, 1983.

Gilroy, Paul. 'Foreword' in *In the Best Interests of the Child: Culture, Identity and Transracial Adoption*. Ed. by Ivor Gaber and Jane Aldridge. London: Free Association Books, 1994: ix–xiii.

Goulding, June. *The Light in the Window*. Dublin: Poolbeg, 2004 [1998].

Graham, Colin. *Deconstructing Ireland: Identity, Theory, Culture*. Edinburgh: Edinburgh University Press, 2001.

Grewal, Gurleen. *Circles of Sorrow, Lines of Struggle: The Novels of Toni Morrison*. Baton Rouge: Louisiana State University Press, 1998.

Haley, Alex. *Roots*. New York: Doubleday, 1976.

Homans, Margaret. *The Imprint of Another Life: Adoption Narratives and Human Possibility*. Ann Arbor: University of Michigan Press, 2013.

Homes, A. M. *The Mistress's Daughter*. London: Granta, 2007.

Hopgood, Mei-Ling. *Lucky Girl*. Chapel Hill: Algonquin Books of Chapel Hill, 2009.

Huggan, Graham. 'Virtual Multiculturalism: The Case of Contemporary Britain'. *European Studies* 16 (2001): 67–85.

Irr, Caren. 'Literature and Adoption: Themes, Theses, Questions'. *American Literary History* 26.2 (2014): 385–95.

Jaggi, Maya. 'Jackie Kay in Conversation'. *Wasafiri* 29 (1999): 53–61.

Jerng, Mark C. *Claiming Others: Transracial Adoption and National Belonging*. Minneapolis: University of Minnesota Press, 2010.

Kareh, Diana. *Adoption and the Coloured Child*. London: Epworth Press, 1970.

Kay, Jackie. *The Adoption Papers*. Newcastle upon Tyne: Bloodaxe, 1991.

Kay, Jackie. *Bessie Smith*. Bath: Absolute Press, 1997.

Kay, Jackie. *Trumpet*. London: Picador, 1998.

Kay, Jackie. *Red Dust Road*. London: Picador, 2010.

Kiberd, Declan. *Inventing Ireland: The Literature of the Modern Nation*. London: Vintage 1996 [1995].

King, Bruce. 'Towards the Post-Postcolonial?'. *Journal of Postcolonial Writing* 43.1 (2007): 100–5.

Kingsolver, Barbara. *Pigs in Heaven*. London: Faber and Faber, 1993.

Kingsolver, Barbara. *The Bean Trees*. London: Abacus, 2001 [1988].

Kirton, Derek. '*Race*', *Ethnicity and Adoption*. Buckingham: Open University Press. 2000.

Kureishi, Hanif. *The Black Album*. London: Faber and Faber, 1995.

Ledent, Bénédicte. *Caryl Phillips*. Manchester: Manchester University Press, 2002.

Lee, Chang-rae. *A Gesture Life*. London: Granta, 2001 [1999].

Lee, Sabine. 'A Forgotten Legacy of the Second World War: GI Children in Post-War Britain and Germany'. *Contemporary European History* 20.2 (2011): 157–81.

Leigh, Mike, dir. *Secrets and Lies*. Film Four, 1996.

Leigh, Mike. *Secrets and Lies*. London: Faber and Faber, 1997.

Leighton, Kimberly. 'Addressing the Harms of Not Knowing One's Heredity: Lessons from Genealogical Bewilderment'. *Adoption and Culture* 3 (2012): 63–107.

Levy, Andrea. *Small Island*. London: Review, 2004.

Lifton, Betty Jean. *Lost and Found: The Adoption Experience*. Updated edition with a new afterword. New York: Harper Perennial, 1988.

Lifton, Betty Jean. *Twice Born: Memoirs of an Adopted Daughter*. New York: Other Press. 2006 [1975].

McGregor, Jon. *So Many Ways to Begin*. London: Bloomsbury, 2006.

McKinley, Catherine. *The Book of Sarahs: A Family in Parts*. New York: Counterpoint, 2002.

McKinley, Catherine. *Indigo: In Search of the Colour That Seduced the World*. London: Bloomsbury, 2011.

Miller, Nancy K. 'Getting Transpersonal'. *Prose Studies: History, Theory, Criticism* 31.3 (2009): 166–80.

Miller Powell, Joan. 'Hybrid Inventiveness: Caryl Phillips's Black-Atlantic Subjectivity – *The European Tribe* and *The Atlantic Sound*' in *Caryl Phillips: Writing in the Key of Life*. Ed. by Bénédicte Ledent and Daria Tunca. Amsterdam: Rodopi, 2012: 87–105.

Morrison, Toni. *Tar Baby*. New York: Knopf, 1981.

Morrison, Toni. *Beloved*. London: Chatto and Windus, 1987.

Morrison, Toni. *Jazz*. London: Vintage, 2005 [1992].

Mullan, Peter, dir. *The Magdalene Sisters*. Momentum Pictures, 2002.

Nancy, Jean-Luc. *Being Singular Plural*. Translated by Robert D. Richardson and Anne E. O'Byrne. Stanford: Stanford University Press, 2000.

Novy, Marianne, 'Introduction: Imagining Adoption' in *Imagining Adoption: Essays on Literature and Culture*. Ed. by Marianne Novy. Ann Arbor: University of Michigan Press, 2001: 1–16.

Novy, Marianne. *Reading Adoption: Family and Difference in Fiction and Drama*. Ann Arbor: University of Michigan Press, 2007 [2005].

Okafor, Clement Abiaziem. 'Exile and Identity in Buchi Emecheta's *The New Tribe*'. *African Literature Today* 24 (2004): 115–29.

Oparah, Julia Chinyere, Sun Yungh Shin and Jane Jeong Trenka. 'Introduction' in *Outsiders Within: Writing on Transracial Adoption*. Ed. by Jane Jeong Trenka, Julia Chinyere Oparah and Sun Yung Shin. Cambridge: South End Press, 2006: 1–15.

O'Reilly, Andrea. 'In Search of My Mother's Garden, I Found My Own: Mother-Love, Healing, and Identity in Toni Morrison's *Jazz*'. *African American Review* 30.3 (1996): 367–79.

Pateman, Matthew. 'Adopting Cultures and Embodying Myths in Jackie Kay's *The Adoption Papers* and *Red Dust Road*' in *Roots and Fruits of Scottish Culture: Scottish Identities, History and Contemporary Literature*. Ed. by Ian Brown and Jean Burton. Glasgow: Scottish Literature International, 2014: 65–81.

Perfect, Michael. *Contemporary Fictions of Multiculturalism: Diversity and the Millennial London Novel*. Basingstoke: Palgrave Macmillan, 2014.

Phillips, Caryl. *Crossing the River*. London: Bloomsbury, 1993.

Phillips, Caryl. *The Lost Child*. London: Oneworld, 2015.

Pool, Hannah. *My Fathers' Daughter*. London: Penguin. 2006 [2005].

Pratt, Mary Louise. *Imperial Eyes: Travel Writing and Transculturation*. Second edition. London and New York: Routledge, 2008.

Raynor, Lois. *Adoption of Non-White Children: The Experience of a British Adoption Project*. London: George Allen and Unwin. 1970.

Richards, Barry. 'What is Identity?' in *In the Best Interests of the Child: Culture, Identity and Transracial Adoption*. Ed. by Ivor Gaber and Jane Aldridge. London: Free Association Books, 1994: 77–88.

Roberts, Dorothy. 'Adoption Myths and Racial Realities in the United States' in *Outsiders Within: Writing on Transracial Adoption*. Ed. by Jane Jeong Trenka, Julia Chinyere Oparah and Sun Yung Shin. Cambridge: South End Press, 2006: 49–56.

Rothberg, Michael. *Multidirectional Memory. Remembering the Holocaust in the Age of Decolonization*. Stanford: Standford University Press, 2009.

Rushdie, Salman. *The Satanic Verses*. London: Viking, 1988.

Said, Edward. 'Secular Criticism' in *The World, the Text and the Critic*. Cambridge: Harvard University Press, 1983: 1–30.

Sales, Sally. *Adoption, Family and the Paradox of Origins: A Foucauldian History*. Basingstoke: Palgrave Macmillan, 2012.

Schulze-Engler, Frank. 'Introduction' in *Transcultural English Studies: Theories, Fictions, Realities*. Ed. by Frank Schulze-Engler and Sissy Helf. Amsterdam: Rodopi, 2009: ix–xvi.

Sissay, Lemn. *Something Dark* (2004) in *Hidden Gems: Contemporary Black British Plays*. Ed. by Deirdre Osborne. London: Oberon, 2008: 327–47.

Sixsmith, Martin. *The Lost Child of Philomena Lee*. London: Pan, 2009.

Small, John W. 'The Crisis in Adoption.' *International Journal of Social Psychiatry* 30 (1984): 129–42.

Smith, Graham. *When Jim Crow Met John Bull: Black American Soldiers in World War II Britain*. London: I. B. Tauris & Co., 1987.

Smith, James M. *Ireland's Magdalen Laundries and the Nation's Architecture of Containment*. Manchester: Manchester University Press, 2008 [2007].

Stein, Mark. 'The Location of Transculture' in *Transcultural English Studies: Theories, Fictions, Realities*. Ed. by Frank Schulze-Engler and Sissy Helf. Amsterdam: Rodopi, 2009: 251–66.

Treacher, Amal and Ilan Katz, eds. *The Dynamics of Adoption: Social and Personal Perspectives*. London and Philadelphia: Jessica Kingsley Publishers, 2000.

Trenka, Jane Jeong. *The Language of Blood: A Memoir*. Minnesota: Borealis Books, 2003.

Triseliotis, John, Julia Feast and Fiona Kyle. *The Adoption Triangle Revisited: A Study of Adoption, Search and Reunion Experiences*. London: British Association of Adoption and Fostering, 2005.

Valiulis, Maryann Gialanella. 'Power, Gender, and Identity in the Irish Free State'. *Journal of Women's History* 6.4/7.1 (1995): 117–36.

Verrier, Nancy Newton. *The Primal Wound: Understanding the Adopted Child*. Baltimore: Gateway Press, 1993.

Volkman, Toby Alice. 'Embodying Chinese Culture: Transnational Adoption in North America' in *Cultures of Transnational Adoption*. Ed. by Toby Alice Volkman. Durham and London: Duke University Press, 2005: 81–113.

Volkman, Toby Alice. 'Introduction: New Geographies of Kinship' in *Cultures of Transnational Adoption*. Ed. by Toby Alice Volkman. Durham and London: Duke University Press, 2005: 1–22.

Walcott, Derek. *What the Twilight Says: Essays*. London: Faber and Faber, 1998.

Walter, Bronwen. 'Personal Lives: Narrative Accounts of Irish Women in the Diaspora'. *Irish Studies Review* 13.1 (2013): 1–18.

Ward, Abigail. *Caryl Phillips, David Dabydeen and Fred D'Aguiar: Representations of Slavery*. Manchester and New York: Manchester University Press, 2011.

Welsch, Wolfgang. 'Transculturality: The Puzzling Form of Cultures Today' in *Spaces of Culture: City, Nation, World*. Ed. by Mike Featherstone and Scott Lash. London: Sage, 1999: 194–213.

Whitehead, Tony. *Mike Leigh*. Manchester and New York: Manchester University Press. 2007.

Yngvesson, Barbara. 'Placing the "Gift Child" in Transnational Adoption'. *Law and Society Review* 36.2 (2002): 227–56.

Yngvesson, Barbara. *Belonging in an Adopted World: Race, Identity, and Transnational Adoption*. Chicago and London: University of Chicago Press, 2010.

Index